SOWING THE BODY

Women in Culture and Society
A Series Edited by Catharine R. Stimpson

SOWING THE BODY

Psychoanalysis and Ancient Representations of Women

Page duBois

THE UNIVERSITY OF CHICAGO PRESS · CHICAGO AND LONDON

THE UNIVERSITY OF CHICAGO PRESS, CHICAGO 60637
THE UNIVERSITY OF CHICAGO PRESS, LTD., LONDON

Paperback edition 1991
Printed in the United States of America
97 96 95 94 93 92 91 5 4 3 2

Library of Congress Cataloging-in-Publication Data

DuBois, Page.
Sowing the body : psychoanalysis and ancient representations of women / Page duBois.
p. cm.—(Women in culture and society)
Bibliography: p.
Includes index.
ISBN 0-226-16757-7 (cloth)
ISBN 0-226-16758-5 (paperback)
1. Women—History—To 500. 2. Women in literature. 3. Classical literature. 4. Women in art. 5. Symbolism (Psychology). I. Title. II. Series.
HQ1127.D83 1988
305.4—dc19
87-30212
CIP

♾ The paper used in this publication meets the minimum requirements of the American National Standard for Information Sciences—Permanence of Paper for Printed Library Materials, ANSI Z39.48-1984.

For Bill

CONTENTS

ILLUSTRATIONS

SERIES EDITOR'S FOREWORD

The first sentence of the entry "Greece" in the *Oxford Classical Dictionary* states: "Greece constitutes, in regard to its land-forms, the terminus of the central mountain structure of southern Europe." However, the other entries and sentences in this sober *Dictionary* show how ruggedly and powerfully the cultural-forms of Greece are no terminus, but an initial point of departure for the West in its political, intellectual, and psychological quests.

Of course, on course, Western questors have told and retold the story of such origins. "Greece" has been less a land-form than a landscape that must weather the surveys various cultures make of it. Like Luce Iragaray and other feminist thinkers, Page duBois looks levelly at an influential band of modern surveyors, Freud and Freudian psychoanalysts. Candidly, she admits that they have influenced her, but, irrevocably, she speaks of the errors of their maps.

For Freud uses antiquity as a site in which to dig up "the undisguised raw material of present repressed consciousness." *His* "Greece" is what we moderns were and now fear to be. In brief, Freud has substituted mythic for historical narratives—a picture of a universal, timeless human nature for pictures of human beings changing in and over time. That ahistorical picture represents sexual difference as a tragic difference between fortunate men, who carry the plenitude of the phallus with them, and unfortunate women, who lack that boon and bounty. This binary opposition, in which men are both different from and better than women, can accommodate later inequitable distinctions among classes and races only too efficiently.

Even as *Sowing the Body* homes in on psychoanalysis, it spreads out to integrate the theories of Freud's older cultural brother and rival, Marx. DuBois is consistently sensitive to the links between a culture and its economy. Freud's ideas were congruent with an industrial society. Like a commodity, the phallus takes off with an apparent life of its own. However, the West is now plunging toward a postindustrial society. We must adapt Freud to our much-ballyhooed Age of Information. For Lacan, then, the phallus is less the thing than "the name" of the father.

A skilled, ingenious, brave archaeologist of knowledge, duBois inspects antiquity for herself and for itself, insofar as antiquity can be seen for itself. Her fragmented terrain is that of the pre-Socratics, before we believed that a "single, masculine, rational disciplined self" was "identical with the subject of history." Her pre-Socratic Greeks may be our ancestors, but they are not the mirror images they have been cracked up to be. One great gap between us lies in their vision of sexual difference itself. Seeing analogies between sexual reproduction and the agricultural production on which their livelihoods depended, the pre-Socratics picture the female body, not as castrated, but as full, present, self-sufficient. If women inspire fear, it is not because they are wounded, but because they have the power to wound.

In a series of chapters that re-sew the tapestries of the past, *Sowing the Body* explores five Greek representations of the female body: field, furrow, oven, stone, and tablet. Contested zones, each was malleable enough to meet varying cultural demands and political ends. Yet, as duBois's flashing intelligence moves from the metaphor of "field" to that of "tablet," she illuminates two mutually reinforcing shifts in the vocabulary of social relations. More and more, men colonize women and their powers. They plough the fields they evoke as female. Next, culture becomes more and more alienated from nature. Men now write, only sometimes about nature, on blank tablets they categorize as female.

DuBois's last chapter is about the erasure of the pre-Socratics and the triumph of Plato, the author of the Socratic dialogues that formed Western metaphysics. He authorizes the search for one source of the good, be it god, father, or son/sun. Born near the beginning of the long Peloponnesian War, Plato came to maturity during the defeats of Athenian democracy and, not coincidentally, while women's lives were becoming more constricted. In an audacious act of appropriation, Plato grants to the male philosopher the fertile self-sufficiency that pre-Socratic culture had once associated with the female. The seeds she nurtured are now the words he utters.

Because of the imperatives of Greek culture, education, and literacy, the voices that duBois can hear are mostly those of men; the texts that she can read are mostly those by men. Yet, one speaking and writing woman—Sappho—haunts this book. Indeed, delicately, but daringly, duBois suggests that the homoeroticism of Sappho and her poetry metamorphosized into the homoeroticism of Socrates and his blooming philosophy. For modern women writers, Sappho is the transgressive origin of Western traditions of female creativity. If Sappho subverted Greek culture, her "daughters" have had to subvert the legacy of a "Greece" that would mutilate them. No matter how discreetly, they have had to practice confrontational art.

Sowing the Body is self-aware, confrontational scholarship. Its return to pre-Socratic Greece rejects a nerve-blurring nostalgia for goddesses who roam and hug the earth. It has other motives for reinscribing ancient Greece: to retrieve the pastness of the past; to remind us of the presentness of the present through measuring its distance from the past; to decouple the present from its enchantment with the narrative of psychoanalysis; to read history as a complex series of struggles and changes; to show how points in that series construct subjectivity; to imagine a future in which we free ourselves from a gendered subjectivity; and to warn us against any theory that reifies social diversities as immutable and ranks some now putatively immutable classes as superior, others inferior.

Some theoreticians of sexual difference have been rough-tongued bullies. Others, like Plato's Socrates, have been old seducers and cajoling charmers. Scrutinizing antique words and vases, scrutinizing the scholarship about antiquity, *Sowing the Body* asks us to suspect both bullies and charmers if they have the same end: to dominate and then to announce what domination means.

CATHARINE R. STIMPSON

ACKNOWLEDGMENTS

Many friends sustained me in the writing of this book. More than to any others, I owe thanks to the members of my writing group—Susan Kirkpatrick, Stephanie Jed, Kathryn Shevelow, Lori Chamberlain, Nancy Armstrong, and Julie Hemker—who patiently read myriad drafts, taught me about collective work again and again, and helped me find my way.

I want also to thank my friends at the University of California at Santa Cruz, especially Mary-Kay Gamel, John Lynch, and Harry Berger, Jr., who made my visits there such happy ones.

Don Wayne, for his time and care, deserves special thanks. I am most grateful to Kristin Ross, and to Alain Renoir, William Fitzgerald, Moira Roth, Judy Rosenthal, Carol Becker, and Kate Harper. Dr. Charles Moss and Shirley Lovejoy Hecht also took good care of me when I needed it most.

I owe thanks to the American School in Athens for permission to work in their library, and real gratitude to the American Academy in Rome, where I wrote much of this book. And I want to acknowledge with thanks the warm Roman hospitality of Ron Strom.

The Academic Senate Committee on Research of the University of California at San Diego generously supported my work. I want also to express my gratitude to the J. Paul Getty Museum for allowing me to reproduce works of art from their collection. I should thank Roy Harvey Pearce, who invented the Department of Literature at the University of California at San Diego as a place for interdisciplinary and unorthodox work to flourish. The graduate students in my seminars on Theories of the Body, Feminist Theory, and Psychoanalysis and Feminism helped me greatly in working through the theoretical problems associated with my argument; I want to thank in particular Lucia Folena, Shelley White, Sherry Quart, Anita Levy, Roxanne Klein, Carol Mavor, Wendy Geller, and Julia Simon Ingram.

I am grateful to the several anonymous readers of various drafts of the manuscript; their suggestions for changes and amplification were often illuminating, and I hope this final version reflects my engagement with their readings.

And last and most, I thank Bill Luoma.

INTRODUCTION

> I do not know what meaning classical scholarship may have for our time except in its being "unseasonable"—that is, contrary to our time, and yet with an influence on it for the benefit, it may be hoped, of a future time.
>
> Nietzsche
> *The Use and Abuse of History*

The contemporary practice in many fields of cultural studies of considering only the most recent historical periods threatens to trap us in an extraordinarily narrow definition of culture, leaving us with an impoverished set of possibilities for representing gender difference, or even indifference. In our time, the psychoanalyzed female body is represented as a symbolically castrated male body. Ancient Greek culture is here unseasonable, in Nietzsche's sense,[1] in that it offers us an alternative figuration: the female body as a fertile field, as the earth ready for furrowing. The study of ancient history allows us to see the particularity of our own culture, to be critical of its categories, to imagine otherwise.

Attempting to use ancient history for the benefit of the present and a future, this book engages with current work in several different intellectual fields: classical scholarship, feminist theory, and psychoanalysis. It has emerged from my interest in these disparate bodies of work and represents a particular intersection of the debates in these fields. Having chosen to engage in ongoing controversies rather than to explain and arbitrate the issues, I must warn readers unfamiliar with these fields that I make no claim to represent the history and current state of these fields to those who have not yet approached them; I will not explain feminism to classicists, nor antiquity to feminists. There are excellent introductory books within each of these categories, and books which represent intersections of these interests different from my own.[2] This book is neither definitive nor encyclopedic; it is rather an argument about a possible reading of the relations of certain disciplines and of the representations of the female body in psychoanalytic work and in ancient Greek literature, ritual, and artistic "texts." In keeping with this objective, I reject the sort of comprehensive framework that goes back to Plato, a framework that subordinates the female and the body to the metaphysical project of the philosophical subject.

In making my argument, I attempt to avoid certain hallowed philosophical reflexes. To illustrate my own view that even new attempts to rethink relations among disciplinary categories rely on unexamined distinctions inherited from our tradition, I point to one of the most exciting new books in the field of classical studies, Michel Foucault's book *L'Usage des plaisirs*.[3] Although it is an important contribution to the history of sexuality and of the subject, breaking radically with the traditional concerns of classical scholarship, Foucault's work on ancient sexuality remains within the terms of the philosophical tradition from which I want to distance myself. It ignores the prehistory of the disciplining of the subject, the *askêsis* Foucault's work describes, and the *reasons* for its development. Although his own principles, described in an earlier stage of his work in *L'archéologie du savoir,* suggest that the *objects* and *forms* of discourses are interested and mark significant breaks in the constitution of knowledge, Foucault does not take account of what precedes Platonic philosophy—the pre-Socratics, Greek tragedy, Herodotus, Aristophanes, the daily life of the democratic *polis* or city-state—and thus cannot see how the creation of a discourse of discipline marks a rupture in human history. For example, Plato himself is not "the Greeks"; he changes the course of ideology, intervening in it in a new way both to reaffirm old patterns of dominance and to establish through new rationalization certain objects of knowledge, certain forms of power. Assuming Plato's description of the philosophic man—the point where my discussion ends—Foucault fails to ask a crucial question: Why was it considered necessary for the philosophic man of Greek antiquity to "master" himself, to cultivate superiority as a philosophical practice? Foucault, who so often has turned our conceptual world upside down, here remains fixed inside the universe as defined by Plato, a world where the single, masculine, rational, disciplined self is identical with the subject of history. He takes for granted, and thus "authorizes," exactly what needs to be explained: the philosophical establishment of the autonomous male subject, *l'homme de désir* as master and superior. Foucault's work is a superior example of the very prejudices, historical and sexual, that I seek to contest. This book is in part about the different terms by which the society *before* Plato conceptualized sexuality.

Sophocles' Antigone, the heroine of the Greek tragedy named after her, engages in an angry debate with Kreon, the tyrant of Thebes, who argues that she must obey his law and abandon her commitment to the unwritten laws of the ancient gods. Antigone, condemned to die for her rebellious and unwomanly behavior, witnesses the following exchange between Kreon and her sister, Ismene:

> ISMENE: What life is there for me to live without her?
> KREON: Don't speak of her. For she is here no more.
> ISMENE: But will you kill your own son's promised bride?
> KREON: Oh, there are other furrows for his plough.
>
> *Antigone* 566–69[4]

How are we to read this last line, which metaphorically names Antigone as a furrow? Is it merely a brutal dismissal of the doomed Antigone, a sign of Kreon's summary, tyrannical attitude toward what he sees as her criminal behavior? Is it the trace of the woman's castration, the marker of men's inevitable, universal, eternal perception that the female body is marked by lack, that it is wounded, deficient, defined by absence of the phallus?

This book means to explicate the metaphor used of Antigone's body—to see its otherness, to inhabit it, to read beyond easy dismissal of this passage—in the name of access to the strangeness of the Greeks, and to the arbitrary nature of our own ideas about sexual difference, gender, and the body. I will examine this metaphor in particular, its embeddedness in a larger network of metaphors used to allude to the female body, and I will then show how that metaphorical network alters over time and how it is contested and replaced with another way of understanding the relation between two kinds of gendered bodies.

This book is a critique of psychoanalytic theory and its ahistorical, universal claims about gendering. It is a description of an "other," the ancient Greeks, whose categories for thinking about gender undermine and disrupt psychoanalysis' claims to describe the past *and future* of gender difference. In the first part of this book I consider psychoanalysis' description of gendering and historicize the claims of Freudian and Lacanian psychoanalysis.[5] In part 2 I discuss Greek views on gender to demonstrate that the psychoanalytic model of phallocentrism and castration is inadequate for describing the ancient Greeks' views about gender difference and about male and female bodies. I conclude in part 3 that we must use psychoanalysis to analyze our position in the present but, at the same time, refuse its claims on the future.

In chapter 1, I briefly consider the psychoanalytic theory of the body and locate it historically, as a developing description of sexual difference appropriate in a particular historical moment. I contest the view of many psychoanalytic thinkers that their theory accounts for all cultures, all historical periods. Chapter 2 considers Freud's relationship to the Greeks and his strategy of confirming his clinical findings with reference to the texts and works of art of ancient Greek and Roman culture. In chapters 3 through 7, I trace a series of metaphors that the ancient Greeks used to refer to the female body, describing both a spectrum of such metaphors and changes in descriptive practices over time. In chapter 8, on Plato, I analyze the ways in which Plato, in the name of a new philosopher named Socrates, appropriates the traditional body of metaphors used to refer to women. Finally, in chapter 9, I argue that the Greek example disorients our culture's view of sexual difference as inevitably located in male and female bodies—one possessing a penis, one lacking; that a theory of gender based on deficiency is not universal but, rather, comes into being along with the beginnings of a monotheistic, idealist metaphysics; and that we, psychoanalyzed as we are, still inhabit this paradigm of gender distinction.

In making my argument, I find myself in the situation of the postmodern critic who both contests and uses the monolithic, monological theories of systematic criticism to create a new space from which to write about a newly fragmented subjectivity, about a new feminism that seeks to avoid the demands of orthodoxy and of that rigor which leads to paralysis, leaving feminism trapped within paradigms generated by a hostile or indifferent philosophical tradition. In the face of the monological, metaphysical tradition that abhors contamination by contesting discourses, I am glad to say that this book is contaminated with deconstructive theory, with Marxism, with psychoanalytic theory, in an attempt to use and refuse the systems of thought which have spoken us, which we inhabit so uneasily. This willful contamination involves a sense of both liberation and apprehension.

My object of study in these pages is not "the text," the single literary work marked off by its author, by its culture of origin, and by our own practices as the appropriate object of scholarly analysis. I have rather brought together many places in ancient culture where sexual difference is being generated: literary texts, ceramic vases, urban space, architecture, ritual practices, and agricultural production. Thus my object of study, as well as my theoretical orientation, is contaminated, fragmented, disparate. Classical civilization is, in fact, discontinuous with our culture; it is fragmentary and contaminated by centuries of interpretation and loss. To engage in a new way with psychoanalysis and with antiquity, with their representations of the body, I have violated the traditional practices of classical scholarship, even of literary criticism of classical texts, which, in America, has been the most open to new kinds of reading, to new theoretical orientations.[6]

My intention is to provoke: to ask feminism to think about history and historical difference; to ask psychoanalysis to acknowledge its ahistorical claims; to ask classicists to recognize that their work has traditionally ignored its own location in history, its relation to the culture in which it is produced, and its effects on the future. Classical scholarship, precisely because it is, as Nietzsche says, "unseasonable," can trouble and disorient our dominant modes of seeing, of theory, in the name of transforming our world.

I

THE WOMAN AS CLASSICIST

One

TO HISTORICIZE PSYCHOANALYSIS

> The process of algebrization, the overautomatization of an object, permits the greatest economy of perceptive effort . . . life is reckoned as nothing. Habitudinization devours work, clothes, furniture, one's wife, and the fear of war. . . . The technique of art is to make objects "unfamiliar," to make forms difficult, to increase the difficulty and length of perception.
>
> Victor Shklovsky

Critics, like artists, must "defamiliarize" the historical world for themselves and their readers. Otherwise we are operated by the assumptions, by the ideologies, of our own world, devoured by habitudinization, unable to think toward change because we accept the categories of our own ideological location. Our own *critical* practices, like artistic practices, are sustained ideological labor. Shklovsky, critic, artist, and writer, assumes in the epigraph to this chapter the inevitability of a habitudinization about "one's wife."[1] What of those who have no wives, who act out the scandal of women speaking? Our views about gender, like other categories of existence, must be defamiliarized, interrogated, not taken for granted as universal constructs.

Feminist criticism has sought to disrupt what we might see as the male narcissism of traditional scholarship, which considers only the role of the male in culture, by looking at women in history. We need now to ask not only how sexual difference works in history but also how it matters in relation to other kinds of mapping of the universe. And we need to interrogate and historicize our own desires, subjectivity, and ideological practices. Has the feminist desire to make the female visible been assimilated into an ideology that unquestioningly accepts the primacy of sexual difference and of the heterosexual dyad?

My argument is concerned in part with our ideology of gender and with some questions about our use of this term. We might well turn our critical attention to our own historicity as well as that of our objects. When the Greek poet Hesiod speaks of women, he inhabits a set of categories quite alien from our own. The *genos gunaikōn*—kind, gender, tribe, or race of women—is a genus, almost in the Linnaean sense, of a higher logical order than species, much more different from the race of men than the imperfectly oedipalized female of the post-Freudian family.[2]

I see my argument as both within and outside the discourse of psychoanalysis. It is not a plea to abandon psychoanalytic theory or practice. Psychoanalysis is one of the most valuable instruments we have for describing the processes of the mind, sexuality, gendering, and the production of the unconscious and the historically specific metaphysical binarism that determines our hierarchical logic. As a historically specific intervention within our culture, psychoanalysis not only describes but also contributes to reproducing its sexual and gender relations. By this I mean, for example, that people exhibit signs of the Oedipus complex in their lives not only because the family is the locus of rivalry between son and father for the mother, but also because we tell ourselves, or others tell us, the narrative of the Oedipus complex in order to help us understand and explain our personal, familial, and social histories; the Oedipus narrative orders much of our undifferentiated experiences. The family, educational institutions, advertising, and most other forms of acculturation take account of psychoanalytic theory in bringing us up.

A feminist cannot work without taking account of how people are produced as gendered beings in our culture. Gendering creates the binarism in relation to the phallus that then accommodates other forms of hierarchical power: racial and class differences as well as gender difference. Yet, as an instrument for producing gendered beings, psychoanalysis as a theory does not allow for a real transformation of sexual, racial, and class relations. To see outside the practice of psychoanalysis, to historicize its claims, to see it as an intervention within capitalism, means that we can be of it and yet not of it: we can conceive of a still further historical development in which gender hierarchy might not be the central defining category of the individual, in which we might undo the often crippling opposition between male and female, an opposition that has meant one must choose one of two sexual identities and suppress any contradictory or paradoxical tendencies.

Michel Foucault, in the first volume of his *History of Sexuality*, presents a powerful critique of the culture that produced psychoanalysis, arguing that the proliferation of such texts as Freud's in the nineteenth and twentieth centuries was not the throwing-off of repression but rather the production of discourses about sexuality, the result of power demanding that this former realm of silence be made to speak.[3] We are not conquering a barrier of shame and suppression when we speak of sexuality. We are rather complying with a demand that we produce speech about our sexual practices, fantasies, desires. This work of Foucault allows us to question psychoanalysis in a new way; he allows us to see it not as the uncoverer of buried, veiled truth but rather as a set of historically produced discourses embedded within a particular moment of capitalism.

The work of Gilles Deleuze and Félix Guattari in *Anti-Oedipus* similarly calls into question the assumptions of psychoanalytic theory, accusing it of reducing experience to a narrative of triangularity—"Daddy, mommy, and me"—thereby controlling and limiting the possibilities of erotic and social experience.[4] They see "oedipalization" as an instrument of repression and call for "schizo-analysis," a breaking-down of the oedipalized order.

These texts have begun to show, to me at least, how psychoanalysis, although an inevitable theory for the description of gendering in our culture, can be interrogated, especially from a historicist position. We must acknowledge the historically specific nature of our present version of gender opposition. And further, I believe, we must see that this description of difference is just one more transformation of a centuries-old binarism, one consistent with the metaphysical tradition of Western philosophy. Yet, even as we recognize our desire to undo the opposition between the sexes, to expose the implicit hierarchy of sexual difference, we must also recognize that each of us has gender, lived gender, which is always already socialized from the moment of the acquisition of language and is reinforced in daily life. Our paradoxical enterprise is to be both within and outside the sex/gender system, to see the ways in which it enables our being, but to call to the foreground its bias, its historicity.

Jacques Derrida, engaged in a new, subversive reading of the Western metaphysical tradition, points out the essentially theological orientation of Western metaphysics that began with Plato.[5] Binary thinking, the valuing of speech over writing, the conception of language as based on the sign (composed of signifier and signified), and structuralism—a recent manifestation of the tradition he is exposing—all are based on a metaphysics which claims purity for the idea without taking account of two of its features: that the existence of one element is conceivable only in terms of its *différance,* temporal and spatial, from the other; and that there is an implicit hierarchy in such opposition—that the signified is privileged over the signifier, speech over writing, presence over absence, and, I would argue, male over female. To say that gender opposition is a metaphysical construction is to say that it is an existent but not essential way of thinking about social relations, that it participates in a long tradition of disguised domination. Yet we cannot think of ourselves as human at present without foregrounding gender. Feminists especially are caught in the necessity of naming themselves as women even as they often seek to abolish the very category of gender.

Is it possible, given these constraints of categories and vocabulary, to talk about feminist theory? In *Powers of Desire,* E. Ann Kaplan asks, apropos of film, "Is the gaze male?"[6] I want to ask, "Is theory male?" Some feminists have claimed that it is. I want to look at *theōria,* the Greek word which first of all means "a looking at, viewing, beholding, observing, especially being a spectator at the public games."[7] In ancient Greece, *theōroi* (ambassadors or witnesses) were sent by city-states to the Olympian Games or to the oracle at Delphi as representatives of the state. Thus, the word "theory" is bound historically to the gaze in Western culture.

Theory, and the gaze, have been male. The observers, the witnesses, the beholders of the world have been both male and female, but only the male spectators, the *theōroi,* have been official ambassadors, named to see. They have seen, spoken, and written their desire. I want here to cite some famed theorists, seers of the body, and to contest their views.

Male theorists of the metaphysical tradition have most often seen sameness: Freud looks at little boys and little girls and sees only the penis—"strikingly visible and of large proportions."[8] Jacques Lacan, too, has eyes for the phallus, calling it "the most salient element in the real of sexual copulation."[9]

There are other kinds of ambassadors. The feminist ethnographer, for example, puts herself into question and recognizes her implication in the act of writing. She occupies a different position, looks from a different place, but is nonetheless a theorist, an observer. Rather than dismissing theory, we feminists need to create a new way of theorizing, to find a place from which to see, to observe not sameness but difference—historical difference (new narratives, not the same story at every historical moment) and material, corporeal difference (not presence and absence of the same).

The ideology about gender difference, which in capitalist culture supports all other versions of hierarchical difference, is a cultural product. Like all culture, it is related to the economic structures of society. I assume that the relations of domination we live with have been embedded in culture since the first sexual division of labor. They were produced historically, determined historically, but they persist through the recoding of difference in different terms in different historical moments.

The Privileging of the Phallus

In his essay "Some Psychical Consequences of the Anatomical Distinction between the Sexes," Freud makes a move typical of the metaphysical tradition for which he provides one more rationalization. He says, in speaking of children's differing reactions to the sight of the genitals of the opposite sex:

> They [little girls] notice the penis of a brother or playmate, strikingly visible and of large proportions, at once recognize it as the superior counterpart to their own small and inconspicuous organ, and from that time forward fall a victim to envy for the penis.
>
> *SE* 19:252

The little boy's reaction is very different. At first he "sees nothing or disavows what he has seen" (*SE* 19:252). Later, if he remembers the sight when he has been threatened with castration, he is forced to believe in the real possibility of the threat being carried out. He has "two reactions, which may become fixed and will in that case . . . permanently determine the boy's relation to women: horror of the mutilated creature or triumphant contempt for her" (*SE* 19:252). Freud's description of this stage of children's development ends with a dramatically phrased, theatrical assertion:

> A little girl behaves differently. She makes her judgement and her decision in a flash. She has seen it and knows that she is without it and wants to have it.
>
> *SE* 19:252

This strategy of mythicizing or fictionalizing the past of each individual by recounting a narrative consummated in a look, the gaze that determines the future, recalls romantic narratives like that of Dante catching sight of Beatrice. The child's past is retrospectively given meaning; her future, wanting to have it, and his future, horror or contempt, are both determined in this fictional moment of recognition. We all know this story and come to live our individual narratives in relation to it. Freud has given an explanation of gender difference, with a voice of assumed authority, that is embedded everywhere as a support for the dominance of the possessor of the penis.

Perhaps I seem to exaggerate the importance of psychoanalytic theory in our culture. I am writing out my difficulties with it, but I think anyone concerned with subjectivity and with sexual difference and with power and hierarchy must come to terms with this theory. Those who do not acknowledge its power—intellectual and institutional—are, nonetheless, to varying extents possessed by it, operated by it, produced by it.

Freud's writings, to differing degrees, support the "metaphysical" opposition of the two sexes, even when acknowledging the obstacles to individuals' achieving gendered sexuality, heterosexual normality. There is an assumed dualism here: some people have penises, some don't. We have the fiction of difference, of separate but equal status. Yet in fact we have *différance,* a barely disguised hierarchy between the two sexes. Freud demonstrates his own horror at women's fictional mutilation or, perhaps more obviously, his contempt for them. Speaking of the anatomical distinction in the same essay, he says:

> I cannot evade the notion (though I hesitate to give it expression) that for women the level of what is ethically normal is different from what it is in men. Their super-ego is never so

> inexorable, so impersonal, so independent of its emotional origins as we require it to be in men.
>
> *SE* 19:257

Here, too, we have a claim that what is being described is mere difference when in fact it is inferiority. The strong moral tone, a mood of censure, permeates the passage and reveals the contempt Freud feels. He is describing not two equal but differing beings; he is establishing a moral hierarchy, defining men's characteristics in opposition to, but superior to, those he describes as feminine.

One can find such arguments throughout the Freudian corpus; those who defend it tend to ignore such passages, wanting to see them as extraneous to the central theses, as unfortunate archaic vestiges from Freud's "Victorian" Viennese environment, or as defensible, accurate descriptions of gender difference. I would say that we cannot ignore such arguments, that they are essential to Freudian theory. The weight of Freud's insights is lost if we abandon the theory of castration, which is indissolubly linked to his description of sexual difference. Little boys would not fear castration, would not resolve their Oedipus complex, if they did not know of the existence of "the other," the castrated sex. Little girls serve to remind a boy that he must abandon desire for his mother and submit to his father in order to grow up to be a man and to have a penis and, therefore, to have a woman—not the same one but a woman, nonetheless, of his own. Nor can we dismiss this aspect of Freud's thought as an unfortunate remnant of the past.

The fetishized quality of the penis in Freud's text is quite evident. And I mean here not Freud's notion of fetishism but rather that of Marx. Penis envy is a desire created for a commodity. Marx describes capitalism in terms of the commodity form and the "fetishizing" of the commodity:

> We are concerned only with a definite social relation between human beings, which, in their eyes, has here assumed the semblance of a relation between things. To find an analogy, we must enter the nebulous world of religion. In that world, the products of the human mind become independent shapes, endowed with lives of their own, and able to enter into relations with men and women. The products of the human hand do the same thing in the world of commodities. I speak of this as the *fetishistic character* which attaches to the products of labour, as soon as they are produced in the form of commodities. It is inseparable from commodity production.[10]

I cite Marx on the fetishization of commodities not to draw a parallel between his use of the term "fetish" and Freud's. Rather, I want to emphasize that the possibility of conceptualizing the fetish in this way exists only within a world in which there is commodity production of the sort Marx describes, in which relations between people are understood as relations between things. In a psychoanalyzed world, the penis, like a commodity, takes on a life of its own. Only in a bourgeois economy, where the commodity form is highly developed and dominant, can the real of the body be conceptualized in such a way.

Thus the theory of gender that obtains within monopoly capitalism is a theory of the penis as commodity. The views of Marx and Lukács on production in capitalism coexist with and illuminate the theories of gender proposed by psychoanalytic theory and lived by all of us. As we move into multinational capitalism, as the "first" world becomes an economy not of production but of information, the theory of sexual hierarchy becomes a theory of the symbolic phallus.

The Marxist historical explanation allows us to account for psychoanalysis as a particular version of a tradition that justifies male supremacy and androcentrism by describing the economic system in which it is generated. The formulations by Marx and Lukács about the economic relations of capitalism, about the ways in which humans experience alienation and fragmentation, illuminate Freud's formulations about the penis as the isolated marker of sexual difference.

The work of the most important post-Freudian psychoanalytic thinker, Jacques Lacan, permits us to see the metaphorical quality of psychoanalytic discourse, its fictionality, so to speak. Lacan's description of the phallus can also be seen as falling within the terms of a discourse that describes the economic relations of the world we inhabit, a world very different from that of Marx and Lucács and Freud because it is at a different stage of capitalist development.

Lacan says of the phallus:

> The phallus is the privileged signifier of that mark in which the role of the logos is joined with the advent of desire.[11]

He describes the phallus as a signifier, as the privileged signifier that allows for the very possibility of speech (i.e., *logos*). It is speech that allows us entry into the symbolic community of human beings and that allows us to speak of absence, of that which we can never have. Lacan initiates a new phase of phallocentrism, of phallic cultism. The impossible desire to be or to have the phallus is analogous to the desire for the consumption of signs.

Our economy is one in which traditional forms of industrial production are diminishing as production is being gradually displaced to a "third" world of sweat shops and new forms of exploitation. We produce signs and information; we consume signs and information.[12] Lacan's gender theory, one that rewrites the archaic story of male domination, supports the old hierarchy of gender and race and class but this time by establishing the "name of the father" or the "paternal metaphor" as the principle of control. The family no longer has and no longer needs a present father; his function has been assumed by the symbolic phallus.

Lacan repeats the old story of male dominance:

> It can be said that this signifier is chosen because it is the most tangible [*le plus saillant*] element in the real of sexual copulation, and also the most symbolic in the literal (typographical) sense of the term, since it is equivalent there to the (logical) copula. It might also be said that by virtue of its turgidity, it is the image of the vital flow as it is transmitted in generation.[13]

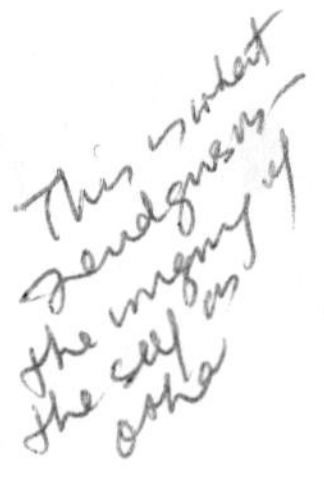

This is a typically maddening Lacanian pronouncement. It has all the obfuscatory power of Lacan's prose—the stenographic compression or condensation, the aphoristic, oracular tone. At the end of this passage, however, there is a break, revealing his investment in the celebration of the phallus that is like Freud's in the passage cited above. There Freud imagined himself as a little girl, seeing the massive organ of the little boy. This is the theatricality of his text: the taking of the place of the other, writing a part for her, dressing up, engaging in transvestism, in theory. Lacan, too, here imagines the woman for himself. He imagines the woman, or the one who takes the position of the woman, seeing and seizing the penis. It is "the most tangible element in the real of sexual copulation," the most salient, protruding thing.

Of course, for centuries the phallus has been conceived of as a detachable thing, worthy of reverence. Phalloi were carried in processions in the ancient world. Yet in antiquity there was a contestatory or complementary discourse about the body of the mother—the mother as earth, as a fertile field to be ploughed. By contrast, in the metaphysics of psychoanalytic theory, especially in the work of Lacan, there is emphasis on the phallus alone, on its presence or absence; it is a moveable symbol emblematic of castration, of separation and lack, of the possibility of absence, of language that speaks of need and establishes desire.

Lacan's theory rests not so much on the penis as a detached part of the body, as a commodified object alienated from the whole, but rather on the representation of the penis in the signifier "phallus," which *allows* language itself. Nonetheless, though Lacan wants to separate phallus from penis, he and other Lacanians have great difficulty in keeping the two terms separate.[14]

Lacan's re-reading of Freud has transformed psychoanalysis in part because that re-reading is so literary. Lacan, who reads Freud in part as a literary text, speaks his own extremely self-conscious poetic "writings." He allows us to see that Freud's arguments are fictions, just as his are; that the metaphors used by our culture are just that, metaphors; that culture produces language but never an unmediated relationship to what he calls the "real," a level of existence to which we have no access; rather, we have only language, symbolic practice, and the illusions of the realm he calls the "imaginary."

Lacan's reading of Freud lifts us off from a naturalized, immutable description of sexual difference, having and not having. No one can have the phallus; no one can be the phallus. The difference between male and female is not as natural, innate, and inevitable as it has seemed. Like a commodity, the phallus is an idea; it moves, is transferable, is not born, is not inherited, like landed property, into the possession of one sex or one class. In Lacanian theory, only the phallus, as the abstraction and reification of the sexual organ of the male, takes on the role of a commodity.

Lacan performs a sort of *sparagmos,* a dismemberment, of the male body as it has been thought of in Freud's work. In so doing, he initiates a new version of phallocentrism, of phallic cultism, but he also permits us to see the arbitrary nature of this worship, a worship that supports androcentrism. Those who worship the phallus, detached from the male body, demonstrate the ideological basis, the metaphysical overvaluation of the signifier of male supremacy. This view allows us to see beyond the thought of Freud as it describes and creates sexual difference; it allows us to see the historical specificity of psychoanalysis as a discourse even while it continues to define and limit us as persons with gender. At this moment, the issue of gender—this form of ideological, metaphysical difference—has assumed great importance for women, perhaps because it has reached the limits of its significance. Perhaps the definitions of sexual difference based on presence and absence, on possession and lack, have come to the end of their usefulness. The commodity form is no longer the dominant form of economic organization. The industrial West, especially the United States, no longer produces commodities to the extent that it did in the past; its economic dominance, which may be eroding, is based on services and on information. The penis as analogous to the commodity is being superseded. Yet the phallus is, like information, a bit of binarism; it is a new form of the old metaphysical justification of gender hierarchy. The crucial and hierarchical opposition of male over female may survive this transformation of its current ideological expression, especially if the transhistorical claims of psychoanalysis remain unchallenged.

My desire is to show that psychoanalysis is not a transcendent, universally adequate description of gendering. It is probably the most valuable discourse we have for understanding gender relations in our world, in capitalism. However, the critiques of psychoanalysis—those by Deleuze and Guattari, by Foucault, and especially by Derrida, and the early work of Luce Irigaray, in particular her book *Speculum*[15]—seem to me to show that we can begin, from within a world where psychoanalysis is the dominant explanatory discourse, to see beyond it: to a world where the insistence on gender difference, on the reproductive aim of heterosexuality, is no longer dominant; to a world where the sex/gender system, which psychoanalysis both analyzes and perpetuates, is seen as metaphorical, as metaphysical, as no longer natural, inevitable, universal.

Jacques Derrida has pointed out that Lacanian discourse, in its phallogocentrism, justifies a historically dominant androcentrism:

> One might be tempted to say: Freud, like those who follow him here [i.e., Lacan], does nothing else but *describe* the necessity of phallogocentrism, explain its effects, which are just as obvious as they are massive. Phallogocentrism is neither an accident nor a speculative mistake which may be attributed to this or that theoretician. It is an enormous and old root which must also be accounted for. It may then be described, as an object or a course are described, without this description taking part in what it operates the recognition of. To be sure. But this hypothesis . . . encounters . . . a very strictly determinable limit: the description is a "recipient" when it induces a practice, an ethic and an education hence a politics assuring the tradition of its truth. The point then is not simply to know, to show, to explain, but to stay in it and reproduce.[16]

It is this choice that Lacan makes and that Luce Irigaray and other feminists refuse. My text is meant to add to that refusal.

The claims of psychoanalysis, of Freud in particular, to understand and account for all culture, for ancient myth as well as ancient sexual practices, seem to me profoundly inadequate. And they point to the further claims of psychoanalysis to describe and to produce the future as well, a future defined by the same terms: castration, penis envy, lack. The desire to assimilate ancient and future cultures into our own, to assume a universal ahistorical version of socialization—the primal horde as prehistory and then, forever, civilization, discontented—seems to me naive and ideologically suspect. The conservatism of the psychoanalytic tradition, with some exceptions, leads to a view of civilization as immutable, yet to a sense of it as fragile, threatened by any sort of transformation in familial, social, or even class organization. To see the limits of psychoanalysis, to appreciate its historical specificity, is to attempt to free oneself from its radically pessimistic view of the future of civilization.

Psychoanalysis supports, is produced by, and is compatible with metaphysical, hierarchical, Western thought; it is the heir of Aristotelianism, of the logic of the great chain of being in which God emanates forth a series of beings arranged on a ladder of diminishing value and quality, from god to philosopher to master to husband to wife to slave to animal down through the oysters. One cannot read Freud without seeing the ways in which his works support this metaphysical tradition. To attempt to ignore the hierarchical nature of psychoanalysis—to ignore the argument that sexuality founds human existence, and that sexuality is founded on hierarchical gender difference—is to be complicit in its implicit defense of inequality.

My interest in historicizing psychoanalysis leads me to an analysis of gender description embedded in another economy, that of ancient Greece, in order to show how differently the sex/gender system was rationalized in a historically distant epoch, how even my feminist concern for the question of gender is conceivable only in our world, where gender has become such a vexed question precisely because its arbitrary metaphysical quality has been made visible. The ancient Greek world can represent an "other" world than our own, and this very otherness erodes the claims of psychoanalysis to be universally descriptive or explanatory.

I begin from my own narcissism, my own interest in the female body, an interest that Freud has both described and named. I recognize that my desire to see the female body in the otherness that is the Greeks is a product of my desire—the desire of a woman embedded within a certain version of sexual difference and defined by absence, by silence, by lack. It is this "lack," this requirement of deference to a system supported by both males and females that privileges those with a penis—those present, possessing, speaking—which drives me to a reading and writing of another world where other terms of otherness apply. These terms may prove to be more oppressive, but they will support an attack on the hegemony of psychoanalytic discourse and provide a way of challenging its assumed, implicit claims for universality. Even to begin to do historical work in this way is to attempt to acknowledge and begin to deconstruct the system of inequality that psychoanalysis supports. Our culture "psychoanalyzes" us as the first world underdevelops the third; I believe that feminists should historicize and criticize psychoanalysis rather than learn to "accept their own castration."

Two

DESIRING THE GREEKS

> They go so far as to accept a man who is *not affected at all* by some particular moment in the past as the right man to describe it. This is the usual relation of the Greeks and the classical scholars. They have nothing to do with each other—and this is called "objectivity."
>
> Nietzsche
> *The Use and Abuse of History*

Undermining and disrupting the claims of psychoanalysis to contain the future, to describe all cultures, to have verified its theories as transhistorical, I look with my feminist desire, as a fragmented, historically produced, subject-in-question, at the Greeks *as others* who can decenter our mythologies of sexual difference and who can illustrate the ways in which a culture's economic structure encodes its version of gender differentiation. In this chapter I contest Freud's colonization of ancient culture and offer another model for interpreting the Greeks, one which I believe to be less reductive, more historical, and consistent with feminism's emphasis on sexual equality.

Psychoanalysis and the Greeks

The Greeks of course have a privileged status in the history of psychoanalysis. Throughout his works, Freud refers to classical antiquity to authorize his findings about the psyche. Typically, he describes a theoretical or clinical finding and then finds a classical authority, a text, to justify his claims. For example, Freud finds both taboo and totemism (*SE* 13 : 137) in ancient Greece. Greek tragedy resembles "the scene of the totem meal" and evokes the "elimination of the primal father by the company of his sons" (13 : 155). The tragic hero "had to suffer because he was the primal father, the Hero of the great primaeval tragedy" (13 : 156). In the case of little Hans, Freud alludes to antiquity to support his understanding of this five-year-old boy: "The 'castration complex' has left marked traces behind it in myths (and not only in Greek myths)" (*SE* 10 : 8). Greek myth authorizes his view; he authorizes a certain reading of Greek myth by citing it here.

At times Freud recalls the particular figures of Greek mythology. In his *Five Lectures on Psychoanalysis,* he refers briefly to the Oedipus myth to account for the sexual life of children:

> The myth of King Oedipus, who killed his father and took his mother to wife, reveals, with little modification, the infantile wish, which is later opposed and repudiated by the *barrier*

> *against incest*. Shakespeare's *Hamlet* is equally rooted in the soil of the incest-complex, but under a better disguise.
>
> *SE* 11:47

This passage offers evidence concerning Freud's view of history. Antiquity is valuable because it allowed the undisguised representation of desire; as time went on, as civilization "progressed," the real nature of the human being was gradually concealed. Elsewhere he says:

> We assume that in the course of man's development from a primitive state to a civilized one his aggressiveness undergoes a very considerable degree of internalization or turning inwards; if so, his internal conflicts would certainly be the proper equivalent for the external struggles which have then ceased.
>
> *SE* 23:244

The value of studying antiquity is that it indicates the external correlates of modern man's internal struggles; the classical drama vividly represents conflicts that are repressed and buried in the psyches of present-day neurotics.[1]

In a characteristic gesture, Freud late in life finds confirmation for conclusions already arrived at in the words of an ancient authority:

> I am well aware that the dualistic theory according to which an instinct of death or of destruction or aggression claims equal rights as a partner with Eros as manifested in the libido, has found little sympathy and has not really been accepted even among psychoanalysts. This made me all the more pleased when not long ago I came upon this theory of mine in the writings of one of the great thinkers of ancient Greece. I am very ready to give up the prestige of originality for the sake of such a confirmation, especially as I can never be certain, in view of the wide extent of my reading in early years, whether what I took for a new creation might not be an effect of cryptomnesia.
>
> *SE* 23:244–45

He then gives an account of the work of Empedocles and equates the ancient philosopher's *philia* and *neikos* (love and strife) with his own "two primal instincts *Eros* and *destructiveness*" (23:246). The gesture toward cryptomnesia[2] and the willingness to grant originality to Empedocles might be seen as a screen for something else: Freud's colonizing attitude toward ancient civilization, by which he seeks to deny difference and historical distance and to demonstrate and eternalize his own views by proving their universality with this support from antiquity.

Freud visited Greece once, an event he recalls in "A Disturbance of Memory on the Acropolis: An Open Letter to Romain Rolland on the Occasion of His Seventieth Birthday" (*SE* 22:239–48). He recalls a depression curiously suffered by both him and his brother when they learned, contrary to their expectation, that they could in fact travel to Greece; furthermore,

> When, finally, on the afternoon after our arrival, I stood on the Acropolis and cast my eyes around upon the landscape, a surprising thought suddenly entered my mind; "So all this really *does* exist, just as we learnt at school."
>
> *SE* 22:241

Freud experiences a strange feeling of splitting or detachment, as if he were two people: one who believes in something he once thought doubtful; the other truly astonished that this thing's existence could ever have been doubted. He cannot see what is really there, or at least part of him cannot, because he makes what he sees into an aspect of his own history, his own relationship with his father, his own desire:

> . . . the whole psychical situation, which seems so confused and is so difficult to describe, can be satisfactorily cleared up by assuming that at the time I had (or might have had) a momentary feeling: "*What I see here is not real.*" Such a feeling is known as a "feeling of derealization" [*Entfremdungsgefühl*]. I made an attempt to ward that feeling off, and I succeeded, at the cost of making a false pronouncement about the past.
>
> *SE* 22:244

He attributes the experience of derealization to a defense; such phenomena "aim at keeping something away from the ego, at disavowing it" (22:245). Freud himself did not doubt the existence of Athens. "I only doubted whether I should ever see Athens. It seemed to me beyond the realms of possibility that I should travel so far—that I should 'go such a long way'" (22:246). He concludes his account of his trip, a gift from one old man to another, with the explanation of a feeling of depression at the prospect of such a trip:

> . . . a sense of guilt was attached to the satisfaction in having gone such a long way; there was something about it that was wrong, that from earliest times had been forbidden. It was something to do with a child's criticism of his father, with the undervaluation which took the place of the overvaluation of earlier childhood. It seems as though the essence of success was to have got further than one's father, and as though to excel one's father was still something forbidden.
>
> *SE* 22:247

Freud adds to this explanation of his depression and derealization another factor peculiar to his own situation in Athens:

> The very theme of Athens and the Acropolis in itself contained evidence of the son's superiority. Our father had been in business, he had had no secondary education, and Athens could not have meant much to him. Thus what interfered with our enjoyment of the journey to Athens was a feeling of *filial piety*.
>
> *SE* 22:247–48

Freud, at the site of ancient goddess worship, of the worship of Athena, has eyes only for the father. His depression, his sense of unreality, might be due to the material existence, the autonomy of the Acropolis, which, unlike the text of *Oedipus Rex* in his study in Vienna, disrupts the narrative Freud tells himself and refuses to be so easily appropriated into that narrative.

In *The Interpretation of Dreams,* Freud again uses ancient myth to support his claim for the universal existence of the Oedipus complex, the male child's "being in love with the one parent and hating the other" (*SE* 4:260).

> This discovery is confirmed by a legend that has come down to us from classical antiquity: a legend whose profound and universal power to move can only be understood if the hypothesis I have put forward in regard to the psychology of children has an equally universal validity. What I have in mind is the legend of King Oedipus and Sophocles' drama which bears his name.
>
> *SE* 4:261

The argument is circular. His discovery is confirmed by Oedipus' universal power to move; his assertion that it has that power is confirmed by his discovery of Oedipus. Once again his reading empowers what he then appropriates to empower himself. He attributes universality to the very thing that is alleged to grant universality to his views.

Freud recounts the legend of Oedipus and concludes:

> His destiny moves us only because it might have been ours—because the oracle laid the same curse upon us before our birth as upon him. It is the fate of all of us, perhaps, to direct our first sexual impulse towards our mother and our first hatred and our first murderous wish against our father. Our dreams convince us that that is so.
>
> *SE* 22:262

His remarks bear the trace of gender and of a particular, *historical,* desire to confirm, to find again in the ancient world, what we find in this one: the male child—his desire, his position in the family—as the exemplar.

Later in *The Interpretation of Dreams,* Freud cites other evidence from antiquity of "undisguised Oedipus dreams" (*SE* 4:398, n.1). Freud recalls

Julius Caesar's dream of intercourse with the mother and the oracle given to the Tarquins that Rome would belong to him who first kissed his mother, who in fact was to be understood as the earth. He also cites Herodotus on the dream of Hippias (discussed in chapter 4). All these examples concern sexual intercourse with the mother, earth. In context, they refer to the seizure of political power; the "mother" stands metaphorically for the earth, which signifies property, domination, sovereignty. Rather than offering proof of the universal desire for incest with the mother, these textual examples have political significance in particular ancient texts concerning a struggle for sovereignty.

Marx, another thinker with a nineteenth-century education, seems to believe, once he has shaken off his fantasy that the Greeks are the childhood of mankind, that earlier historical periods had complex religious, social, and political structures that masked the real relations of domination and exploitation, which became visible only in capitalism.[3] Perhaps for this reason Marxists have typically shown less interest in antiquity than psychoanalytic thinkers. They have evidently thought that one can better read back from capitalism the real structures of ancient society, which would not be especially illuminating about the present.[4] Psychoanalytic thinkers, on the other hand, find a source of undisguised truth, of raw, unrepressed material, in antiquity. Freud seems to believe that antiquity recorded, undisguised, the simple unrepressed desires of mankind. A feminist Marxism, a Marxist feminism, must read the sexual in the economic and see in antiquity not a veiled version of capitalism but a real otherness.

Freud should not be faulted for his nineteenth-century education and his desire to authorize his findings with evidence from antiquity, which was often understood to be an elite storehouse of ethical truths or of philosophical perfection. His readings of antiquity have the merit of ending an idealizing tendency, the search to find the apogee of human culture in classical civilization. He is not nostalgic for Apollonian idealism but rather fascinated with what he saw as the undisguised raw material of present-day repressed consciousness. To this extent, his use of classical culture for illustration has had a salubrious effect in clearing away a representation of the Greeks as disembodied Platonists engaged only in philosophical conversation.

Nonetheless, Freud, in his particular version of historicizing, seeing the Greeks as the unrepressed equals of ourselves, has left another legacy to readers of classical culture. Some read ancient texts simply to find confirmation of their clinical findings or analytic experiences or to verify their interpretation of modern neurosis by locating it "everywhere" in history, that is, in antiquity. The readings of classical myths that appear in psychoanalytic journals often fall within this category and repeat the Freudian gesture of appropriating the ancient world.[5] Others take seriously Freud's limited form of historicism and attempt, often in very sophisticated terms, to locate the Greeks as a stage in the evolution of mankind by using a developmental analogy, sometimes reading phylogeny as they read ontogeny, and interpreting history allegorically.[6] These scholars are perhaps less concerned with confirming Freudian principles than they are with demonstrating the universality of the patterns for reading ancient texts that they adduce from Freud.

Others see the Greeks not as representing a normal stage in the evolution of the psyche but as exhibiting deviant behavior. Some of the more interesting recent readings of ancient texts have been made on the assumption that the Greeks were "normally" neurotic, that their social organizations produced a character type marked by what we would see as neurotic behaviors.[7]

Feminists influenced by psychoanalysis have produced subversive and exciting readings in recent years; I think, for example, of Marylin Arthur's work on the Homeric Hymn to Demeter.[8] Such readings, produced from within the assumptions of psychoanalysis, begin to rewrite the male-centered psychoanalytic tradition in classical studies, challenging both the biases of psychoanalysis and its claims for universality of description.

All of these readings, however powerful and illuminating, remain within the field established by Freud. They do not really confront the work of Lacan and his emphasis on language, the phallus, and the splitting of the subject.[9] And these readings for the most part see the characters in classical literary texts as if they were patients in analysis; they colonize ancient culture in support of a psychoanalytic reading of the gendered body. They measure ancient culture by our own, seeing it as "undisguised," as an earlier stage of our present psychic state, as analogous to the development of the individual, and as characterized by its deviation from the norm established by our own culture. All of these readings, with the possible exception of the feminist one, are characterized by a desire to find the same in the past. This is the metaphysical gesture, the centering move, that establishes the tradition as sameness: we are the Greeks, they are we; or, rather, they are just like an analyst's familiar and neurotic patients.

With a sense of how polemical my own enterprise is in relation to the huge discourse of psychoanalysis, I challenge the heritage of Freud and his appropriation of classical culture not only in the name of another reading of Greek culture but also in the name of contemporary feminism. It is time to resist, to think critically and historically about psychoanalysis as an institution that both produces and describes our gendered subjectivity and that uses "the Greeks," whoever they are, to encourage us all to accept our own castration.

My version of the Greeks, created from my desire to see not sameness but difference, argues for a historical relativism. Ancient culture lets us try to think outside our culture, which is psychoanalyzed and commodified, lets us see psychoanalysis and capitalism critically, and offers a position that is not outside history but does allow a critical estrangement from our own practices and beliefs. To see the Greeks differently, to be unwilling to repeat the psychoanalytic or metaphysical gesture which colonizes the Greeks in a certain way, is nonetheless not an attempt to find *another* sameness in antiquity. I am not arguing that ancient Greek women were full of feminist rage, nor am I arguing for an Amazon republic or an ancient matriarchy. The fantasies of modern feminism have their uses, political and philosophical, but they do not lead me to imagine that the ancient Greeks embodied these utopian fictions. I argue for a historical perspective on the Greeks, seeing them neither as nineteenth-century philosophers nor as matriarchs.

If I find difference in the Greeks, it is not the same difference that simply confirms Freud's view of phylogeny and its recapitulation of ontogeny. My inquiry originates in a desire to locate historically a particular tradition of dualistic logic. A historicist can expose the particularly historical nature of certain binarist logics by arguing for a pre-Platonic logic, a logic not based on absence and deprivation or on estrangement from the divine One. The pre-Platonic world maps gender differently, not describing A and minus-A, man and defective man, that is, woman, but rather seeing difference, A and B, man and woman, almost as different species. Although they are certainly no less misogynist than later thinkers, the pre-Platonic Greeks offer a logic different from that of the post-Platonic metaphysical tradition, one of otherness that is not metonymic.

I do not believe that representing the process of change, from Homer to Plato, in representations of the female body need necessarily be the typically metaphysical history of a fall or a loss of presence. The Greeks' own ideas about production and reproduction change, but I idealize neither the beginning nor the end of this process. My argument does not seek to substitute the sameness of the female subject for the canonical sameness of the male subject but rather to historicize both contemporary feminist theory and ancient views on sexual difference. Nonetheless, it may not be possible to eradicate completely the traces of an evolutionary argument in telling a new narrative about ancient Greece. It is in the very nature of the metaphysical tradition in which we work that the language and terms we use are contaminated with a history; the past has already been inscribed for us in narratives of progress and decline.

The Classicist as Ethnographer

We can do cultural description differently, neither privileging the Greeks as origin nor seeing them nostalgically as some utopia of the presencing of Being, or of totality, or of matriarchal, Amazonian power. I want rather to interrogate the ahistorical, universal claims of psychoanalysis by relativizing them, by putting into question the adequacy of psychoanalysis as a theory for explaining historically distinct cultures, by pointing to its inability to posit a future of sexual equality, or of racial equality, or of democracy in general.

In recent years the self-critical stance of ethnography has produced illuminating reflections on the relationship between observer and the object observed, reflections that should be taken into account by anyone writing cultural history and theory, especially feminists, for whom engendered subjectivity is so determining. The model of ethnography is most interesting for me precisely because, unlike feminist history or even the new social history, ethnography has listened to Michel Foucault, Roland Barthes, Emile Benveniste and has put the place of the subject into question.[10] One of the consequences of the feminist movement has been to question the whole humanist tradition in which the "human" has always been assumed to be white, American or European, heterosexual, and male. The "other" —the female, the person of color, the homosexual—was always assimilated to this norm, either by being disregarded as deviant or by defining, by its difference, the rightness and superiority of the "human." In anthropology, the exposure of male bias, along with the consequences of the struggle between the forces of colonialism and national liberation, has revealed how much the sex, class, and imperial interests of the ethnographer affect his readings and writings of other cultures.

Experimental ethnography has undermined not only the authority of the white male heterosexual subject but also the authority of the author. Ethnographers, as opposed to empiricist historians, have begun to take account of an indeterminacy principle, to acknowledge that the observer of a culture affects the object of observation. Marjorie Shostak, for example, in *Nisa,* tries to efface her own subjectivity by letting the other speak, transcribing the words of a Southern African woman who has told her own story on Shostak's tape recorder.[11] Another strategy of experimental ethnography has been to foreground the identity of the ethnographer, to call to the reader's attention the presence of the observer in her text. Jeanne Favret-Saada's *Deadly Words* attempts to demonstrate how the speech acts of the ethnographer "perform" within the world studied, how the ethnographer is inextricably bound up in the reality in which she participates.[12] Such practices begin to acknowledge that the traditional rhetoric of ethnography, which attempts to efface the presence of the ethnographer or to mark it only anecdotally, has failed to locate the place from which the text is written. The assumption of transparency and common sense, of a shared identity between ethnographer and reader, is based on the very fiction of the "human" I mentioned before. To pretend to record empirical, unbiased observation is to obscure the real interests of the text, the effect of which is merely to add to the authority of the Western humanist tradition to speak for all. What is more, any ethnographic description is a text, and it is the product of a dialectic between two cultures or, rather, between the observer—but even to call her *that* is to participate in the fiction of the unmoved mover, of the theorist, so let us say: a dialogue between the ethnographer and the ethnos.[13]

The project of writing history, including cultural history, bears analogies with the processes being discussed by ethnographic anthropologists and their critics. Self-criticism is not the traditional stance of the cultural historian, who often sees himself as a "self" having unmediated access to another culture supposed to be perfectly visible and transparent. He works within a tradition of historiography seemingly innocent of interests and motives; thus he finds no epistemological or methodological obstacles to the application of common sense to culture.

My principal aim here is not to offer another, truer "reading" of classical culture. We can read the ancient world only from within our own world, our own desire. The very fact that some scholars have recently become interested in "woman," in the illiterate, in the irrational, and in the sexual practices of antiquity has more to do with our world—the feminist and Lesbian and gay movements, the failures of humanist scholarship, and the critiques of complacent classical studies—than with the ancient world itself. Every generation of theorists has its own view of ancient Greece, from that of serene Apollonian rationalism to orgiastic, hallucinating cults, to idealized pederasty, to the philosophical "usage of pleasures."

My interest *is* in the classical world *as an other,* as an alternative to our own, one in which we must recognize difference, about which we construct an allegory, an interested narrative that speaks to our own situation. Just as an ethnographer creates a textual dialectic between her own culture and that which she represents, so a writer concerned with the historicity of gender categories must recognize her interests in telling a certain story about the ancient world.

I anticipate my discussion of gender in ancient Greece by looking at a poem by Sappho, the Lesbian poet of the seventh century B.C. This poem is particularly interesting to me because I think it is consciously subverting the hegemonic discourse about gender difference, about heterosexual intercourse, in the Greek world. I will not offer a close reading of this poem but will rather point to the ways in which it seems deliberately to set itself against the reproductive heterosexual models of ancient culture that constantly refer to the metaphorical equation between the body of the woman and that of the earth. Sappho says:

> When we lived all as one, she adored you as
> symbol of some divinity,
> Arignota, delighted in your dancing.

Now she shines among Lydian women as
into dark when the sun has set
the moon, pale-handed, [*brododaktulos, i.e.,* "rosy-fingered"] at last appeareth

making dim all the rest of the stars, and light
spreads afar on the deep, salt sea,
spreading likewise across the flowering cornfields;

and the dew rises glittering from the sky;
roses spread, and the delicate
antherisk, and the lotus spreads her petals.

So she goes to and fro there, remembering
Atthis and her compassion, sick
the tender mind, and the heart with grief is eaten.[14]

Denys Page, a famed philologist, said of this poem:

> What is hidden we cannot judge; what is revealed we observe to be devoid of anything profound in thought or emotion or memorable in language. The occasion is commonplace enough; one girl has gone away, leaving a broken heart behind; that is nothing new.[15]

I believe Sappho's poem celebrates the female body as unploughed earth, as ground spontaneously yielding not grain but flowers; she aestheticizes the reproductive model she inherits with a vision of the earth as parthenogenetic. Her earth is nourished only by the female dew and flowers under the female moon, here called rosy-fingered in direct contrast to the dawn, also female but the precursor of the male sun, who nourishes the fields of grain. As in other poems, Sappho seems deliberately to take up the hegemonic language of Greek culture, of hunting, pursuit, militarism, and heterosexuality, and to offer a parallel universe, one that refuses the aims of the male culture.[16]

While Sappho describes the earth as blooming at night, unaided by sun and plow, the traditional heterosexual language of reproduction makes an analogy between the woman's body and a plowed field. In antiquity, ritual intercourse was practiced in fields to ensure the fertility of the land. Homer and Hesiod both describe the legendary intercourse between Demeter, goddess of the grain, and her mortal lover, Iasion, in a thrice-ploughed fallow field. And later, in Sophocles' *Oedipus Rex,* when Oedipus learns of his incest with Jocasta, he cries out for a sword to stab his mother/wife:

Give me a sword, I say,
to find this wife no wife, this mother's womb,
this field of double sowing whence I sprang
and where I sowed my children!

1255–58

In his anguish Oedipus repeats the paradigmatic language used for heterosexual reproductive intercourse in ancient Greek culture, language that makes the analogy between the body of a woman and a field to be ploughed by her legitimate husband. Her body, as a field for ploughing, is to produce a crop of children. This crop is ideologically equivalent to the grain that is the city's most important agricultural product during the predemocratic age.[17]

Sexual difference is encoded in ancient Greece in terms not of castration, of the presence and absence of the penis or phallus, but rather in terms that are analogous to those used of agricultural production. The ancient economy was based on agriculture controlled by a citizen population. The dominant metaphors of sexual reproduction in ancient culture are not recodings of the myth of female castration but are rather based on metaphors analogizing sexual reproduction and agricultural production. Hesiod describes the first entity after Chaos as Gaia, Earth, who gives birth parthenogenetically to her husband, Ouranos, Heaven. The female body is seen not as castrated but as full and self-sufficient. It is the earth, like the human female body, that can give birth parthenogenetically to all the goods that humans need. The earth first is seen as a full, closed surface, a meadow that is not yet a field, has not yet entered into culture. The female body is compared to the earth and to a vase full of oil, grain, or wine that must be opened.

The ideology of the woman's body as fruitful, spontaneously generating earth gives way in time to a cultural appropriation of the body that responds to and rewrites that primary image. Men claim that they must *plough* the earth, create fields, furrow them, and plant seeds if the earth is to bear fruit. They see female bodies as empty ovens that must be filled with grains and made to concoct offspring. They see the female body as analogous to a writing tablet on which they write: the stylus (plough) carving the lines (furrows) of letters (sown seeds) in the body of the mother. These metaphors, as expressed in texts, on vases, in the narrative of rituals, and in the spatial relations of architectual forms, are the subjects that I propose to study in the pages that follow.

All of these metaphors are rewritings of an original metaphor, an analogy made between agricultural production and human reproduction. Women in the *Iliad,* in Sophocles' *Oedipus Rex,* in ritual, and in spatial relations are associated again and again with agriculture. It is my argument, finally, that Plato, in the *Phaedrus,* represents the male philosopher as appropriating the agricultural metaphors, assuming the role of the earth, the field to be filled with the lover's seeds. It is only with the misreadings of Platonism, the literal, antirhetorical interpretations of the role of the philosopher, that Western culture rationalizes a system of binary opposition in which women are defined as not-A to the masculine A, or as A-minus-one to their A. The psychoanalytic language of the phallus, castration, and absence is a rewriting of this logic in terms of commodity production and the consumption of signs.

Sappho's poem is a text that seems to subvert the definition of women's bodies as fields to be ploughed. Yet even if I listen to Sappho as the ethnographer Marjorie Shostak listens to Nisa, I cannot innocently perform Sappho's gestures of refusal, which can be appropriated precisely because they remain within her culture's terms. In fact, Sappho's subversion of the dominant cultural metaphors is bound by those metaphors when she describes the woman's body as a field, even though it is flowering in the light of the moon rather than being ploughed by its master. She too accepts the connection made again and again by other poets between the body of the woman and the earth. Her representation remains within the culture's hegemonic language. Sappho's gesture of resistance is analogous to that of psychoanalytic feminists who celebrate the imaginary, the pre-Oedipal, *écriture féminine* in opposition to the symbolic, the Oedipal, presence and speech.[18] Like Sappho, they are still writing within the categories to which the culture names them: they choose to inhabit the space to which they are already assigned.

We can appreciate, through an allegorical reading of Sappho's practice, the appropriative power of hegemonic culture, the ways in which acts of subversion are caught up again in the logic of domination. Nonetheless, a different reading of Greek culture may decenter and defamiliarize our own ahistorical mythologies of gender hierarchy.

Metaphysics and Metaphor

> In the words of Phokylides: the tribes of women come in four breeds: bee, bitch, and grimy sow, and sinewy mare with draping mane. The mare is healthy, swift, roundly built and on the loose.
>
> The monster-looking sow is neither good nor rotten, and the bristling bitch lies snapping at the leash. Yes, the bee is best: a whizz at cleaning, trim and good in cooking. My poor friend, I tell you, for a bright, balmy marriage, pray for a bee.[19]

The binarism of metaphor and metonymy is a commonplace of structuralist thought after Jakobson.[20] It has been criticized in poststructuralism and defended, used, and abused in recent critical work.[21] Metaphor, it seems, is the privileged term in another binary set; metonymy really stands for all those rhetorical figures that are not metaphor, that do not have the superior status of "replacement." Metonymy is the "other" of metaphor, a figure that is logically a kind of metaphor, that is set against metaphor in order to define metaphor, but that is in fact inseparable from it.

I do not want to suggest some radical break in history here, some "world-historical defeat of womankind" in the change of description of the female body through metaphor, but rather to point to difference, to point to the consequences for gender of the philosophical investment in metaphorical substitution. I historicize these terms not to argue that there is no metonymy before Plato, no metaphor after Plato, but to suggest that we recode these rhetorical terms and use them historically. I see a transformation in the description of the female body in ancient culture, one that moves from metaphorical, analogical terms to a metonymic definition in the works of Aristotle.

And as I recode the synchronic use of metaphor and metonymy in historical practice, so too I would recode the implicit historical narrative in the works of Heidegger, traces of which remain in the work of Derrida, a narrative which attributes to Plato the invention of metaphysics in a moment in which we forgot how to think being. In *An Introduction to Metaphysics,* Heidegger says of the work of Plato:

> Being as *idea* is exalted, it becomes true being, while being itself, previously dominant, is degraded to what Plato calls *mē on,* what really should not be and really *is* not, because in the realization it always deforms the idea, the pure appearance, by incorporating it in matter. The *idea* now becomes a *paradeigma,* a model. At the same time, the idea necessarily becomes an ideal.[22]

If Heidegger sees the origin of our form of metaphysics in the Platonic text and finds in the pre-Socratics a less mediated access to the "presencing of being," there is for me something of value in this insight; an insight I would wrench from its utopian representation of the pre-Socratics and give a social and historical referent. There is a difference—a difference in logic, in perception, and in the representation of sexual difference—between the pre-Platonic and the post-Aristotelian worlds. Plato is in the center, making texts both metaphorical and metonymic, poetic and instrumentally logical. In the pre-Platonic literary and artistic works of ancient Greece, there is not an ideal, paradisaic representation of the female, but rather one radically different. The post-Platonic, metaphysical representation of woman sees her as a defective male, distinguished by absence and partiality. For both Aristotle and Lacan, the female body is defined in terms of metonymy. The female is the male, but lacking.

The pre-Platonic Athenians used metaphors to describe women's bodies, a series of metaphors that are often interchangeable and that are probably always already there in the language and vocabulary of sexual difference in Greek culture. I will describe some historical shifts in the use of these metaphors and talk about them synchronically, as a systematic vocabulary of interchangeable terms.

My list of these metaphors arises from my desire to understand Athenian culture and to put into question the phallocentrism I see as implicit in psychoanalytic readings and in those, like Eva Keuls's, that serve merely to authorize the authority of the phallus.[23] But my list is not an exhaustive one. In an earlier book, *Centaurs and Amazons,* I discussed the Greeks' view of woman as other, her role as the outsider in the house, her connection with animals, with barbarians, with the Amazons, and with others against whom the Athenian male citizen defined himself.[24] There I discussed the male Greek citizen's artistic and mythologizing practices, which were constituted along with the idea of the ancient city and the embodied representations of the Greek woman, along with barbarians, animals, and the other "others" of Athenian ideology.

Comparison

In the thinking of the democratic *polis,* as represented in tragedy, on vases, and on monuments, women were often compared analogically to animals or to human others—those barbarians, mythical and real, against whom the Greeks defined themselves. The Athenians frequently played at naming themselves and others in terms of likeness. Aristophanes alludes to such word play in *The Frogs* when Dionysus, addressing the tragedians Euripides and Aeschylus, tells them not to use comparisons:

> Get on with it, get on with it, and put your finest wit [*asteia*] in all you say, and be concrete, and be exact; and, be original.
>
> *The Frogs* 905–6[25]

They are not to use *eikones*—comparisons or similes.[26] Socrates also refers to the Athenian practice of likening:

> One thing I know about all handsome people is this—they delight in being compared to something [*khairousin eikazōmenoi*]. They do well over it, since fine features, I suppose, must have fine similes [*eikones*]. But I am not for playing your game [*ouk anteikasomai se*].
>
> *Meno* 80c[27]

But then he goes on to compare himself to a stingray (*narkē*), paralyzed and paralyzing. Although both these writers instruct partners in dialogue not to argue by comparison and are self-conscious about the practice, they continue to use comparisons, to define one thing in terms of its likeness to another.

In the *Rhetoric,* Aristotle discusses how one kind of likeness, metaphor, can be used implicitly to *evaluate* the object under discussion:

> And if we wish to ornament [*kosmein*] our subject, we must derive our metaphor from the better species under the same genus; if to depreciate it, from the worse.
>
> 1405b10

Argument by comparison can be used to praise or blame. In the case of women, their bodies, and their reproductive function, there is no direct motive, no address as in a debate, or even a dialogue; such representation is rather a general cultural practice of description and one that, in the case of the female body, tends more toward blame than praise as time goes on. The comparison of the body to the source of the autochthonous citizens, to the burgeoning earth, gives way to likening that body to a simple receptacle or a surface for inscription: a passive medium for the inscription of masculine culture.

I am concerned here with the specifics of the representation of the female body within Greek culture. But even within this system there are other possibilities, other metaphors different from the ones I have focused on. Sappho, for example, often compares women to flowers. Young girls are sometimes compared to animals; for example, they are likened to bears in an Athenian ritual performed at Brauron. The lyric poets of the preclassical period compare them to horses; Alkman writes:

> But our lovely choir leader
> will not let me praise her, nor
> say she is not fair.
> She knows well that she herself is
> something dazzling,
> just as if among a herd of
> cattle one should set a racehorse,
> sinewy, swift, and with feet full of thunder,
> creature out of a dream with wings.

This simile praises a beautiful girl; the likeness between girls and horses suggests erotic mastery, as in this lyric by Anakreon:

> My Thracian foal, why do you glare with disdain
> and then shun me absolutely as if I knew
> nothing of this art?
>
> I tell you I could bridle you with tight straps,
> seize the reins and gallop you around the posts
> of the pleasant course.
>
> But you prefer to graze on the calm meadow,
> or frisk and gambol gayly—having no manly
> rider to break you in.

Other poets liken women to animals in order to blame them, always excepting the industrious bee.[28] These metaphors are more common in the earlier centuries of Greek poetry than in the tragedy, comedy, and history of the fifth century B.C.

The dominant cultural metaphors describing women as opposed to girls allude to the reproductive function of women's bodies almost exclusively. They suggest initially that the woman's body is merely a container of the embryo, just as Apollo argues in these often-cited lines from Aeschylus' *Oresteia:*

> The mother is no parent of that which is called
> her child, but only nurse of the new-planted seed
> that grows. The parent is he who mounts. A stranger she
> preserves a stranger's seed, if no god interfere.
>
> *Eumenides* 658–61

This embryological theory, although contested in some Hippocratic texts, implicitly dominates the codes defining sexual difference in Athenian cultural life. Though the analogy between earth and the woman's body initially suggests otherwise—that is, that woman is the parthenogenetic source of life—as time goes by the function of woman as nurse of the seed becomes the predominant one, and, as will become clear in my discussion, the other metaphors used to describe the female body partake of and reinscribe this dominant function of the woman.

On Metaphor

In the *Poetics,* Aristotle gives the following definition:

> Metaphor is the application of a strange [*allotriou*] term either transferred from the genus and applied to the species or from the species and applied to the genus, or from one species to another or else by analogy [*kata to analogon*].
>
> *Poetics* 1457b

I discuss the metaphors *field, furrow, oven, stone,* and *tablet* because they are commonplaces of Greek representational practices, not only in literary texts but in ritual practices and in the production of graphic arts. These metaphors exemplify the transfer from species to species under the genus of container; for example, from woman to oven, two "species" of the "genus" container. They might also be understood as analogy, sometimes translated as "proportional metaphor," with four assumed terms a : b : : c : d; the plough, for example, is to the field as the penis is to the woman. The metaphors I have chosen form a system, one I have read out of the manifold possibilities immanent in the culture of the ancient Greeks. It seems to me particularly useful because it reveals, in a discrete series, the ways in which a representational system exists that encodes the female body on a spectrum of alienation from the earth. There is no absolute chronological progression in the employment of these five metaphors. They coexist, comment on one another, replace one another at times, and inhabit a contested site. There is a remarkable distance, not a chronological distance but a conceptual one, from the most organic, autonomous metaphor—the fruitful earth—to the most commodified, objectified, and passive receptacle—the tablet.

Aristotle makes clear the motive of domination implicit in the Greeks' penchant for metaphorizing, for analogizing, the woman's body. To compare a human body to an inanimate thing might be seen as a practice of abuse, unless the status of such a thing—the field of the fathers, for example—might not in some way have higher social status than a human being. The inalienable ancestral lands of the Greek family, connected as they were with hereditary status, with the worship of the ancestors and the Earth, might be seen thus to occupy a superior position to that of the interchangeable women of the culture, who could be replaced by remarriage if they died in childbirth or failed to produce heirs. In any case, to use these metaphors in this way, as the Greeks do, is eventually to instrumentalize the female, to reduce her to the status of a thing, an object to be manipulated, to be filled up, broken into, erased. . . .

Metaphor and Metonymy

This particular effort of domination, this desire, expressed by metaphor, to control, name, and produce the female by analogy, is historically limited and gives way to an alternate strategy of description. Although the dominant theory of the change in sexual relations from the fifth to the fourth and third centuries B.C. refers often to what is called a "feminization" of culture, suggesting greater freedom for women, a greater interest in them and in domestic life in general, I argue that the texts of the fourth century, rather than reflecting greater freedom for women, focus on women to anatomize and control them more directly.[29] If the fifth century sees women as another species—as the other, as foreign and unknowable, approachable only by analogical comparison with the known, the furrow, the tablet—the fourth century produces discourses about women that rely rather on metonymy, which describe women's place as lower in a hierarchical ranking, as I argued in *Centaurs and Amazons,* in relation to their superiors, men, and their inferiors, animals. The metaphorical relationships posited were not adequate to support an analytic discourse about women's place; in the *Politics,* for example, Aristotle is not content to compare the female body to the carpenter's raw material. He seeks a more prosaic and hypotactic form of explication that lays out the spectrum of possibilities of social organization.

A metonymic discourse, suggesting that, like men, women were human beings, and, like animals, were created for domination, sets them in their place within a hierarchy of beings and establishes a new order of kinds, one that suggests that they are already defined in terms of a "lack." We need not attribute to Plato the foundation of Western metaphysics, as Heidegger and Derrida seem to do, to see a radical transformation of logic and of the theory of social relations in the fourth century B.C. Plato represents rather a crucial transition, using metaphor and comparison to appropriate reproductive power for the male, while elaborating the so-called theory of the forms, in which the phenomena of the world metonymically partake of the perfection of the forms. The change from the description of women through metaphor to a definition by metonymy is related to the metaphysical project. That metaphysical project both produces and is produced by changes in the Greek world: the failures of democracy, the need for the Mediterranean economic community to be organized in a less fragmented political system. The same motives which lead characters in the Platonic dialogues to criticize Athenian democracy contribute to what we can see as a new monotheism, an imaginary monarchy, the monism of the good. In the time of Aristotle, Alexander brings into being, briefly but portentously, a supremacy which will become real monarchy in the Hellenistic, Roman, and later empires.[30]

Aristotle is the intellectual bound up with these changes in the Greek world. Although not referring to social relations, he expresses in the *Metaphysics* his dissatisfaction with a logical discourse too reliant on the trope of metaphor. Discussing the Platonic theory of the "forms," he says: "To say that the Forms are patterns, and that other things participate in them, is to use empty phrases [*kenologein*] and poetical metaphors [*metaphoras . . . poētikas*]" (*Metaphysics* 1079b25; cf. 991a20). He is critical of Plato's indulgence in poetic forms, in the dialogical fictional frame of what he views, perhaps, as systematic philosophical discourse.

In the *Politics,* Aristotle relies on what we might call a metonymic logic to describe and prescribe the ideal relations of domination between the master of the household and his inferiors:

> . . . it is natural and expedient for the body to be governed by the soul and for the emotional part to be governed by the intellect, the part possessing reason [*logon*], whereas for the two parties to be on an equal footing or in the contrary positions is harmful in all cases. Again, the same holds good between man [*anthrōpōi*] and the other animals: tame animals are superior in their nature to wild animals, yet for all the former it is advan-

> tageous to be ruled by man, since this gives them security. Also, as between the sexes the male is by nature superior and the female inferior, the male ruler and the female subject.
>
> *Politics* 1254b

Aristotle's metonymic strategy is a rewriting of the metaphorical. The female is subjected, weak, and inferior. In her subjection, weakness, and inferiority, though no longer like the parthenogenetic earth, she is nonetheless a human being, and therefore superior in her own right to other entities: to tools, to mute animals, to the things of the world.

As I have said before, mine is a polemical reading of the evidence from antiquity. There is for us no proper, no immediate access to the object, the real women of antiquity, no origin. For us, there are no women's bodies in the case of ancient Greece. There is no way for us to measure the relationship between the textual representations of women and the women themselves. There are only the textual choices, the analogies most often made by men in an ancient gesture of appropriation, of domination, of subjection. In the ancient world, with the exception of Sappho, it is always the male speaking, describing the object in language which is always a detour, and never an innocent detour, but a detour motivated by a desire to know, to control, to name. I mean here not to suggest some sort of patriarchal conspiracy, deliberate and premeditated, but rather that the culture located women in a position of silence and maintained them in a place of illiteracy and wardship without access to public forms of speech or writing. They were named by those who spoke and wrote. And we cannot know how they named their namers.

This is of course not to say that the real social conditions of the female were better in the pre-Platonic world. They may very well have been much worse. I mean not to be nostalgic about the fifth century B.C., nor to suggest that Plato's text is the site of the world-historical defeat of womankind. I rather describe what I see as a major transformation in the logic of sexual difference, an ideological transformation that is bound up inextricably with the dualism of Western metaphysics, with the valorization of the philosopher, the male, the good, in a set of categories and practices that are now being challenged not only by women but by people in places in the world once marginalized, subordinated—"feminized" in relation to a "first" world.

II

METAPHORS OF THE FEMALE BODY

Three

FIELD

> The Athenians observe three sacred ploughings: the first at Scirum in commemoration of the most ancient of ploughings, the second at Raria, and the third near the base of the Acropolis, the so-called Buzygius (the ox-yoking). But most sacred of all such sowings is the marital sowing and ploughing for the procreation of children. It is a beautiful epithet which Sophocles applied to Aphrodite when he called her "bountiful-bearing Cytherea." Therefore man and wife ought especially to indulge in this with circumspection, keeping themselves pure from all unholy and unlawful intercourse with others, and not sowing seed from which they are unwilling to have any offspring.
>
> Plutarch
> *Coniugalia praecepta* 144ab

Plutarch's remarks on the most sacred of Athenian ploughings were written long after the fifth century B.C., which is the major period under discussion here. Yet his emphasis on this metaphor, on the analogy between the field and a woman's body, gives voice to a persistent connection in Greek thinking about the body, about sexual difference, about intercourse. He reiterates the traditional view, appropriate to an agricultural economy, that agriculture and human reproduction are similar activities, that, like the fields of the earth, women must be cultivated, ploughed by their husbands, to ensure a new crop of children, which is like the crops of the fields.

In this chapter, I describe the place of the traditional metaphor of the field in Greek culture, its changes and development in relation to social and economic changes. This metaphor, associating the woman's body and the earth, which establishes a metaphorical connection between the field and her sexual organs, is a traditional analogy, as Plutarch demonstrates; it expresses a relationship that is not merely stereotypical but is so deeply felt by the culture that it appears everywhere: in literary texts, ritual practices, monuments, and in mythological narratives.[1] The metaphor of the flourishing field endures for centuries and is the basis for many rewritings in the critical democratic period, the fifth and fourth centuries B.C., the period of Athens' greatest literary productivity.

In this chapter, I set the earth/body metaphor in its historical context, the early history of ancient Greece, the economic, social, and political forms of organization from the eighth century B.C. to the fifth century B.C. I consider the representations of the earth and the field in the Homeric text; the ritual of the *hieros gamos* or sacred marriage; the creation of earth and the first woman; the analogy between the woman's body and an earthen vase; and the historical setting of these earliest representations of the metaphor linking earth and female body. It is this description that provides the matrix of the metaphors to be examined in the subsequent chapters, where I focus on other metaphors that reinscribe and transform the field metaphor. I trace a network, a system of metaphors that modifies and responds to this earliest metaphor and, in the course of the classical period, gradually rewrites the place of women in culture.

I consider first the representations of the earth-body analogy in the context of a preagricultural world, the traces of which endure in extant texts and artifacts, which, although probably themselves produced in agricultural societies, retain, in myth, ritual, and even in narrative elements, material related to preagricultural and artisanal production in earlier Greek culture. Following this evidence, mostly derived from epic poetry and from ritual, I will consider evidence of artisanal production and its effects on the traditional metaphors of the body, and then I will discuss those myths and religious practices that make most fully the analogy between agricultural and sexual practices. Each of these different modes of production leads to ambivalence concerning the female body; in particular, the notion of opening up the body, like opening the earth or the ceramic vase, gives rise to fears about that body's power, that body's capacity for withholding. Finally, I will discuss Solon's use of the earth-body metaphor, a reinscription that leads to a politicization of the analogy as a sign in debate and in the discourses of the *polis*.

The Preagricultural: Homer

Homer's epic poems were probably composed in the late eighth century B.C., when the Greek world emerged with new social forms from a period of devastation, emigration, and illiteracy. Scholars disagree about what period of history the poems describe; most now believe that the poems were composed orally and that the text contains stratified references to many different historical situations, from the Mycenaean, through the dark ages after the Mycenaean age, to the world of the eighth century B.C.[2] For example, the texts refer to several forms of land tenure, mostly obscure to us now, that are characteristic of different periods of Greek history. Homer's poems may at times allude not only to a preagricultural stage but also, for example, to a time of communal land ownership, and to a moment when the politically dominant figures and gods had land "cut off," in a *temenos,* for their special use, and to a period characterized by the inalienability of land.

Although the terrain of the battlefield of the *Iliad* is a plain marked by struggle and death, in the allusions to the world beyond the battle, we hear echoes of a preagricultural economy, of pastoral existence, and references to the earth's bounty. Homer uses a set of various, related epithets, formulaic expressions that characterize the earth as generous and welcoming. When Helen is looking out from the wall of Troy in the third book of the *Iliad,* describing the Greek warriors to Priam, she regrets that she cannot see her two brothers, Castor and Polydeuces. The narrator says that the *phusizoos aia,* the life-giving earth, holds them already. The earth that gives life is also the receiver of the dead. Using other epithets, Homer describes the earth as "much-nourishing" (*Iliad* 3.89, 265; 6.213; 8.277; 12.194; 16.418), as "grain-giving" (20.226–27, of the mares of Erichthonius in the genealogy of Aeneas), and as "much-feeding" (9.568).[3] Such epithets emphasize the earth's capacity to produce, give, and contain. Several figures for the relation of earth and human beings grow out of the basic concept reflected in these epithets.

The Hieros Gamos

Divine sexual union is associated with the productivity of the earth. When Hera seduces Zeus in book 14 of the *Iliad,*[4] their intercourse causes a flowering of the earth:

> . . . the son of Kronos caught his wife in his arms. There
> underneath them the divine earth broke into young, fresh
> grass, and into dewy clover, crocus and hyacinth
> so thick and soft it held the hard ground deep away from them.
> There they lay down together and drew about them a golden
> wonderful cloud, and from it the glimmering dew [*eersai*]
> descended. . . .
>
> 14.346–49

After their lovemaking, Zeus is overpowered by sleep and is thus distracted from the violence of the battlefield below him.

Homer here produces the topos of the *hieros gamos* or sacred marriage. In this section on the preagricultural period, I discuss some rituals performed in the later, classical period that illuminate the preagricultural world. Evidence about such rituals may come from even later texts, which cast light on the early poems because of the conservative nature of religious observance. The theme of the *hieros gamos,* for example, was a feature of ritual in classical, democratic *polis* culture. In the classical period, the marriage of Zeus and Hera was celebrated yearly in Athens during the month of Gamelion, the month of marriage. In the following month there was a great festival of Dionysus, called the Anthesteria, in which the Basilinna, the wife of an important official, apparently was "married to Dionysus and . . . united with him" in a *hieros gamos* in the center of Athens.[5] This performance of ritual intercourse may have been intended to ensure the fertility of the vines of the city; the woman's intercourse with a divine being suggests the analogy between the city's vineyards and her body. The vestiges of the *hieros gamos* in the ritual life of Athens indicate the connection between human and agricultural fertility that was characteristic of Greek thinking for centuries and that allowed for the metaphorical connection to be made between women's bodies and the body of the earth.

The Planting of Men

The Homeric description of Earth, especially in the epithets, seems to support the view that the earth is giving, containing; it is the giver of foods, the holder of the dead. In a famous description of genealogy in book 6 of the *Iliad,* Glaukos refers to the generations of men as similar to generations of leaves (*phullōn geneē,* 6.146), and here too are signs of a world where the labor of cultivation is not yet at the center of the relationship between humans and nature, where the earth produces spontaneously. In this allusion to autochthony, which prefigures more elaborate analogies between men and plants in later Greek texts, the earth is the source of the forest (*hulē,* 6.147) from which the leaves come in the spring. Homer seems here to regard history as a cycle of seasons in which men replace each other like the leaves of the tree.[6] The vulnerability of human communities is, however, indirectly suggested by the countless times the poets used the simile of the fall of a tree to describe the death of a warrior; for example, in the death of Simoeisios:

> He dropped then to the ground in the dust, like some black poplar,
> which in the land low-lying about a great marsh grows
> smooth trimmed yet with branches growing at the uttermost
> tree-top:
> one whom a man, a maker of chariots, fells with the shining
> iron, to bend it into a wheel for a fine-wrought chariot,
> and the tree lies hardening by the banks of a river.
> Such was Anthemion's son Simoeisios, whom illustrious
> Aias killed.
>
> 4.483

This analogy may be particularly common in the Homeric text because of its associations with autochthony. The seed is planted in the earth without the agency of another of the species. Earth is the receiver and nurse but has no part in the determination of the kinds of trees that grow, since all kinds grow out of her. The earth is a sort of promiscuous receptacle that receives all seeds and feeds all.

It may be that the analogy changes form when the once communal lands become privately owned fields. The forest in book 6 of the *Iliad* is indiscriminate; trees grow to be cut down by human effort for human use. But the produce of one's own fields must be one's property, just as one's offspring are. Human beings have the unfortunate necessity of planting seed in discrete earths, particular bodies; women's promiscuity thus is intolerable, since the nourished product of the planting must be identifiable as the offspring of a particular seed. In the world of the Homeric epics, one's descendants are not so much one's property as heralds into the future, guaranteeing immortality by committing acts worthy of the ancestors and perpetuating the family's name. The analogy between man and tree is common enough to establish an analogical pattern, one that will be valuable to consider when we talk about architecture and the analogy between the column and the human body. It also prefigures the many political myths of autochthony in the Greek world, among them those of Athens and Thebes, to be discussed later in this chapter.

Creation

The epic poet Hesiod probably wrote in the eighth century B.C. His work has many affinities with Homer's, although it may at times represent a more ancient stratum of myth than Homer's. Hesiod's social context seems to be not aristocratic, like Homer's, but a community of peasant smallholders dominated by an oligarchy. He is often concerned with origins, with the creation of generations, of gods, of women. Like Homer, Hesiod connects human creation with that of the natural world. Hesiod's third generation of mortals, made of bronze, are born from ash trees (*ek melian; Works and Days* 145), the source of spears.

Hesiod, in his *Theogony,* recounts the origins of the beings of the cosmos. After describing his inspiration by the Muses, he says that Chaos was first, then *Gai'eurusternos,* "Earth the broad-breasted," then Eros, and other gods: "Gaia now first gave birth to starry Ouranos, her match in size, [*ison heautēi*], to encompass all of her [*kaluptō*]."[7] This passage is significant here because it demonstrates the primacy of the maternal body for the Greeks. It is the male consort who is a supplement in Derrida's sense, that is, an addition and/or substitution. There is a scene of castration in the theogonic text (lines 178–81), in which Kronos castrates his father Ouranos. Nonetheless, the plenitude of the female body is primary. To read the narrative only in terms of the Freudian model of development is to miss the significance of a different system of gendering. Superimposing a reductive Freudian analysis, which sees only the "phallic mother," obscures the female primacy in the Hesiodic version of creation.[8]

Athenian Autochthony

The Athenian legends of autochthony also preserve the notion of preagricultural reproduction. The myth of Deukalion, like the story of Noah, may be traced back to Mesopotamia and to the great Mesopotamian cultures. Deukalion was the son of Prometheus. Zeus flooded the world, but Deukalion and his wife Pyrrha, who was Epimetheus' and therefore perhaps Pandora's daughter, survived. They were told by either Hermes or Themis to throw the "bones of their mother" over their shoulders. They interpreted this to mean that they should throw the stones of earth, "the mother of all," and from the stones of Pyrrha came women; from Deukalion's, men. Hellen, ancestor of all the Hellenes, was their descendant; from him came the founders of the Greek tribes, Dorus, Aeolus, and Xuthus, this last the husband of Creousa, who bore Ion, the ancestor of the Ionians. However, in one version of the legend, she bears Ion after being impregnated by Apollo. In this myth, two contradictory versions establish a conflict between the model of autochthony, with Hellen as the father of Xuthus, the father of Ion, and the model of divine origins, with Apollo as father of Ion. One version, moreover, establishes Earth as the parthenogenetic mother of the Hellenes, while the other allows for heterosexual reproduction.[9]

The most important myth of autochthony for the Athenians concerns the prehistoric kings of Athens.[10] Kekrops, the mythical first king, was born from the Attic earth (*autokhthōn*) (Apollodorus 3.14.1) and was often shown in art with a serpent's body below his waist. His wife bore him three daughters and a son, Erysichthon. The first two daughters' names, Pandrosos and Herse, are connected etymologically with "dew."[11] Kekrops was said to have instituted monogamy and the burial of the dead, to have invented writing, and to have sponsored a contest between Poseidon and Athena over Athens. Kekrops's grave was supposedly in the Erechtheion, a temple on the Acropolis. Without a living son, he was succeeded by Kranaus (Apollodorus 3.14.5); during his time the flood of Deukalion took place. He was expelled by Amphictyon, who was said by some to be a son of Deukalion, but others claimed he was autochthonous. After Amphictyon had reigned for twelve years, he was thrown out by Erichthonios. Both Pausanias and Apollodorus agree with the Athenian tradition that Erichthonios was born of Hephaistos (= Hephaestus) and Earth, with Athena's intervention. According to Apollodorus:

> Athena came to Hephaestus, desirous of fashioning arms. But he, being forsaken by Aphrodite, fell in love with Athena, and began to pursue her; but she fled. When he got near her with much ado (for he was lame), he attempted to embrace her; but she, being a chaste virgin, would not submit to him, and he

> dropped his seed [*apespermêen*] on the leg of the goddess. In disgust, she wiped off the seed with wool [*eriôi*] and threw it on the ground; and as she fled and the seed fell on the ground, Erichthonios was produced [*ginetai*].
>
> Apollodorus 3.14.6

The child Erichthonios is tended by Athena, kept in a box to be guarded and not looked into by Kekrops' daughter Pandrosos (*drosos* means dew, and it is the word Clytemnestra uses when speaking of the rain, the "dew," of blood from her husband's dying body [Aeschylus, *Agamemnon* 1390]). Kekrops' other daughter is Herse. The word *hersē* also means "dew," "raindrops," "foam" (like the mutilated genitals of Ouranos which create foam and give birth to Aphrodite), "honey" (*Theogony*), and, finally, "the young of animals" (*Odyssey* 9.222).[12]

In the Athenian civic ritual of the Arrephoria, young girls carried unknown sacred objects from the Acropolis to a place below and returned with other objects; two of the girls also participated in the weaving of Athena's robe.[13] The ritual is probably connected with one of the significant myths of Athenian autochthony, myths that contribute to or participate in the earth/body metaphor by suggesting that the Athenians were born not from woman but from earth.

Artisanal Production

Hesiod's text contains traces of an original, preagricultural production of earth and, in addition to its use of agricultural analogies, connects the creation of the female body with artisanal production. Hesiod describes the creation of the first woman.[14] Pietro Pucci very usefully describes the way in which woman is created as a "supplement" in Derrida's sense of an addition and a replacement. The misogyny of Hesiod's account is unmistakable. Pandora has a *kuneon te noon kai epiklopon ēthos,* "a shameless [canine] mind, and a deceitful [thieving] nature." Pandora removes the lid of a great jar and brings terrible doom on men:

> Earlier, human tribes [*anthrōpōn*] lived on this earth
> without suffering and toilsome hardship
> and without painful illnesses that bring death to men [*andrasi*]—
> a wretched life ages men before their time—
> but the woman with her hands removed the great lid of the jar
> [*pithou mega pōm'*]
> and scattered its contents, bringing grief and cares to men
> [*anthrōpoisi*].
>
> *Works and Days* 90–95

Only in the *Works and Days* does the account of Pandora's dispersion of evils occur. In the *Theogony,* it is she herself who is the evil. Hesiod says there: "From her comes the fair sex / yes, wicked womenfolk are her descendants. / They live among mortal men as a nagging burden / and are no good sharers of abject want, but only of wealth" (589–90). His text continues in misogynist complaint.

I am not so much interested in the well-known misogyny of Hesiod as in the analogy his text establishes between the ceramic vase and the body of the woman, an analogy I connect with the earlier evidence concerning the earth/woman metaphor. The two accounts of the creation of the woman Pandora are revealing in this regard. In the *Works and Days,* Zeus gives men (*andrasin,* line 56) a *kakon,* "an evil thing," in exchange for fire, which Prometheus has stolen on their behalf: "Then he ordered widely acclaimed Hephaistos to mix earth with water / with all haste and place in them human voice / and strength" (*Works and Days* 60–61). He is to form Pandora as he would form a vase. In the *Theogony,* Hesiod says: ". . . straightway because of the stolen fire he contrived an evil [*kakon*]" (line 570).

Hephaistos is the god of artisans and craftsmen; here he himself appears as a divine potter. I have discussed elsewhere the role the artisan god plays as creator of the world.[15] In book 18 of the *Iliad,* for example, Hephaistos forges the shield of Achilles and is like the Near Eastern artisan gods who create a world as they work. The analogy between the pot or vase (*pithos*) and the world Hephaistos makes elsewhere strengthens the ties which bind woman, earth, vase. As Pucci says, "She is molded like a vase by Hephaistos, and in the following lines Pandora is described as a container into which the gods put something (lines 61 and 67, *W and D*)."[16]

Particularly interesting in light of the vase/body analogy is the description of the crown made by Hephaistos, which is placed on Pandora's head by the craftswoman goddess Athena:

> It was a wondrous thing with many intricate designs
> of all the dreaded beasts nurtured by land and sea.
> Such grace he breathed into the many marvels therein
> that they seemed endowed with life and voice.
>
> *Theogony* 581–84

To this description of Pandora's crown, compare Hephaistos' work on the shield of Achilles in the *Iliad,* which may be likened to a creation myth:

> He made upon it a soft field, the pride of the tilled land,
> wide and triple-ploughed [*neion malakēn, pieiran arouran, eureian tripolon*] . . .
> The earth darkened behind them and looked like earth that has been ploughed [*arēromenēi eōikei*],
> though it was gold. Such was the wonder of the shield's forging.
>
> *Iliad* 18.541–42, 548–49

Hephaistos' work in the creation of Pandora's crown, as on this shield, has a living presence. His metalwork, like his pottery, has a divine energy.

Pandora's crown is connected not only with the richly ornamented shield of Achilles but also with the creatures painted on the vases of the Minoan Crete, the Mycenaean, and the Proto-Geometric periods. Although the representations painted in these different periods vary extensively, they nonetheless frequently embody the variety of creation, land and sea creatures, and present strong analogies to the figure of Pandora with her animated crown.[17]

Created by the craftsman god, the earthmaker, Pandora is analogous to earth and to ceramic vase. As Pucci says: "The reader would certainly like to know what Hephaistos does with this molded piece of earth, whether he bakes it or animates it without any further manipulation. There is not a word in the text that would enlighten us on this point, and we can only speculate that he probably does bake it."[18] The suppression or omission here is interesting. Gold need not be baked to assume a final form, so the other automata created by Hephaistos are not subjected to the baking process. However, the putative life of Pandora would be burnt out of her by a potter's kiln, so the analogy between her and vase cannot be made so explicit. The fact presents interesting problems in relation to the oven metaphor, to be discussed in chapter 6.

Hesiod calls Pandora *pēm'andrasin alphēstēisin* (*Works and Days* 82), "a scourge to toiling men." She is a terrible gift to men who must work for their bread, who must, among other things, cultivate the earth. There is a suggestion that, as she lifts the lid of the jar, she wastes the goods stored there. It is not only that she releases evils; there is also loss; and, if we consider the analogy previously mentioned of vase, body of the woman, and earth, she opens her own body in marriage to Epimetheus. She is herself then full of evils and plagues, and her closed body, like the earth before it, is opened by the plough, contains evils better left buried.

Vase

If the earth is seen as a vessel in which seed can be hidden, from which grain is offered, from which nourishment is obtained, and within which the dead are buried, it is seen also as analogous to those ceramic containers in which the Greeks stored grains, oils, wine, and in which they also buried the dead (see figure 1). Minoan *pithoi* contained all these things. A further association among vase, earth, and body is suggested by the nippled ewers found on Thera and elsewhere and common in the Minoan-Mycenaean period. The ewers, which have two erect nipples protruding from the shoulder of the vase, suggest a parallel between the woman's body and the ceramic shape (see figure 2). The protuberances, sometimes

FIGURE 1. Great jar, or *pithos,* of Crete, from the Mycenaean period (National Museum, Athens). Alinari / Art Resource, New York.

called *mastoi* (breasts), are found on very early vases from Thera and Crete and endure into the Proto-Geometric period, where the more stylized projections form part of the abstract design of the vase; they are still, however, located on the shoulder, so the analogy between the female form and the ceramic container is sustained. An analogical system, then, links vase, earth, and women's bodies; all are seen as hiding, containing, producing, and giving up substances that permit the continuation of human existence.

Agriculture: Demeter in the Field

Homer alludes to preagricultural production and makes an implicit analogy between sexual intercourse and the flowering of the earth in the *hieros gamos*. Elsewhere he alludes to the later canonical analogy between human intercourse and agriculture. In the *Odyssey,* Kalypso, ordered by the gods to let Odysseus go from her island, recounts a myth that suggests an ancient connection between the earth's fertility and that of the female:

> and so it was when Demeter of the lovely hair, yielding
> to her desire, lay down with Iasion and loved him
> in a thrice-turned field [*neiōi eni tripolōi*].
>
> *Odyssey* 5.125–28

Iasion is killed by Zeus, who strikes him dead with a thunderbolt. This event, the intercourse in the ploughed and fallow field, may be connected to the practice of ritual intercourse in fields to ensure their productivity, and it links the body of the goddess with the earth as it links human reproduction to agriculture.

Hesiod cites the same episode in the story of Demeter as evidence of the gods' jealousy over goddesses' connections with mortal men:

> Radiant Demeter, a goddess, and Iasion, a hero,
> coupled with passion on a field plowed three times,
> in the rich soil of Crete.
>
> *Theogony* 969–71

Here there is no mention of Zeus' anger or his killing of Iasion; the emphasis is rather on the wealth brought to man by the son of their union, Ploutos.[19]

Agriculture as Religious Practice

As Detienne shows, for Hesiod, agriculture is a religious practice.[20] When advising his readers on proper techniques for farming, for example, Hesiod says: "Pray to Zeus of the Earth and holy [*hagnei*] Demeter to make Demeter's holy grain ripen to fullness" (*Works and Days* 465–66). The gods keep their livelihood hidden from men: "Else you would easily do work enough in a day to supply you for a full year even without work-

FIGURE 2. Two views of an oinochoe with raised *mastoi* (breasts). Terracotta, late eighth century B.C. With permission of the trustees of the J. Paul Getty Museum.

ing; soon would you put away your rudder over the smoke, and the fields worked by oxen and sturdy mule would go to waste" (*Works and Days* 44–45). It is Prometheus' theft of fire that Zeus punishes, and the creation of Pandora, who opens the jar, is connected with the necessity of opening up the earth, of ploughing. Hesiod marks the difference between an economy of gathering and one of cultivation, and he stresses the way in which a gathering culture is given gifts by the earth and the way in which the cultivated earth seems to hide the seeds that are sown, perhaps even to begrudge farmers, in a poor season, the plants that grow out of her.

Hesiod describes agriculture as a reverent, sacred activity. The Greeks worshiped the goddess Ge (Earth) or Gaia, as she is called by Hesiod. She is addressed as Gaia, "mother of all," in Homeric Hymn 30, where she is represented as the source of all good: "Through you, O queen, men are blessed in their children and blessed in their harvests."

Mother and Daughter

The worship of Demeter and Kore likewise establishes a connection between human fertility and that of the earth, just as it links the earth and the female body (see figure 3). We have the example of the Thesmophoria, where elaborate rituals tend both the human body and the city's fields.[21] The myth of Kore and her abduction, which is presented in the seventh-century Homeric Hymn to Demeter, connects the loss and mourning of Demeter with the earth's winter and with sterility.[22] Hades is forced to surrender Persephone for part of the year after Demeter threatens to destroy humankind by "hiding the seed under the earth" [*sperm'hupo gēs kruptousa*] (353); "she would not let the grain sprout out of the ground" [*ou prin gēs karpon anēsein*] (332). Demeter, as goddess of the corn, the life-sustaining grain, has the power to end human culture, withholding, inside the earth's body, what human beings need for survival:

> . . . no seed
> in the earth sprouted, for fair-wreathed Demeter concealed it.
> In vain the oxen drew many curved plows over the fields,
> and in vain did much white barley fall into the ground.
>
> 306–9

The earth responds to Demeter's emotions, even though she herself is not the goddess of the earth. As the earth keeps her daughter hidden in the house of Hades, so she keeps the seeds hidden.[23] It is only when Kore is restored to her mother that the earth becomes fertile once again; the goddess is commanded to give up her mourning and to let the earth come alive (see figure 4). The poet says, in language like that of Homer:

FIGURE 3. Boeotian figurine of a seated woman wearing a pomegranate necklace associated with the worship of Kore and Persephone. Terracotta, early sixth century B.C. With permission of the trustees of the J. Paul Getty Museum.

FIGURE 4. Mixing bowl, or *krater,* showing the departure of Triptolemos from Eleusis (detail; Louvre, Paris). Alinari / Art Resource, New York.

> [she] swiftly made the seed sprout out of the fertile fields.
> The whole broad earth teemed with leaves and flowers.
>
> 471–74

The analogy between the goddess/body and the earth is probably very ancient; the theme of male death or sleep after intercourse may refer to the male loss of semen and of force, which is thus sacrificed to the earth in order to ensure its continued productivity. The goddess and earth are undiminished by their intercourse or by reproduction. Giving birth and receiving the dead seem to replenish them, while the male suffers only loss.[24]

The Eleusinian Mysteries

The central myth concerning Demeter, the corn goddess, and the loss of her daughter, Kore/Persephone, is recounted in the Homeric Hymn to Demeter and celebrated in the great ceremony of the Eleusinian Mysteries.[25] This festival endured at Eleusis for centuries. It reiterated the analogy made between agriculture and human reproduction, between the cultivation of the earth and human sexual practices. The ritual was celebrated in the fall, in the sowing season; the initiates gathered at Athens, bathed in the sea, and walked in a ritual procession from Athens to Eleusis. They fasted, drank a barley drink (the *kukeōn*), and then entered a grovelike hall, the Telesterion, one of the few closed ritual spaces in Greek cult, where they witnessed mystery rites whose substance is still unknown, although scholars believe that what was revealed may have been an ear of corn, the gift Demeter was supposed to have presented to humankind at Eleusis. The ceremonies seem not to have granted personal immortality to the initiates but rather to have offered a mystical insight into the cycles of production and reproduction overseen by Demeter, processes that guaranteed the continuity of human existence.

Theban Autochthony

In the myths of autochthony, as in the literary texts and the rituals of fertility, the body of the woman is the body of the mother and is metaphorically linked to the fields of the earth. In the Theban myth of autochthony, we encounter another narrative that links the birth of the citizens to a mother earth and also records features of other metaphors for reproduction, which I will trace in subsequent chapters. Unlike the myths and legends concerning Athenian autochthony, which stress the accidental or spontaneous birth of the original Athenians from the earth, the Theban myth focuses on sowing, the analogy between agriculture and the sowing of the first Thebans.

According to the myth of the origin of Thebes, Agenor, king of Tyre, had a daughter Europa, who was stolen by Zeus, who came to her as a bull. Kadmos was sent by his father, Agenor, to find Europa; at Delphi, he was told by the oracle to follow a cow and to build where she rested. There Kadmos founded the city Kadmeia, and there he sacrified the cow. The city's spring was guarded by a dragon, son of Ares; he was killed by Kadmos, who sowed the dragon's teeth in furrows. Warriors, sown and nurtured in the warm earth, sprang up. He pelted them with stones; they attacked each other until only five remained; they were called the "Spartoi," the "sown men." They were the ancestors of the noble families of Thebes. Kadmos, who came from Phoenicia, also brought the alphabet to Thebes and taught the Greeks how to read and write. The alphabet, marks carved into stone, bronze, wax, or wood, is, like seed, disseminated over a blank, receptive surface. The invention of writing is metaphorically equivalent to the sowing of the dragon's seed; the autochthonous Spartoi are reproduced like letters on a blank tablet.

Kadmos married Harmonia and had children, among them Semele, mother of Dionysus; Autonoē, mother of Aktaion, who was torn apart by his own dogs after being metamorphosed into a stag for seeing Artemis bathing; and Agave, mother of Pentheus, who tore him apart in a maenadic frenzy, thinking he was a lion cub. The *sparagmos,* the tearing apart that recurs in the Theban legend, is bound up with the themes of writing and sowing. Letters and seeds, like the dismembered parts of the body, can be cast about in ways that threaten the integrity of speech, the city, the family, and the individual. Women, the site of reproduction, are potentially violent and disruptive and promiscuous.

Kadmos and Harmonia were eventually turned into serpents, and the next dynasty was founded by Labdakos, who died and left as his heir his infant son Laios. Lykos ruled in Laios' place for twenty years, but was then exiled by Antiope's sons, Zethos and Amphion, who built Thebes' walls, moving the stones by the power of song. Laios in exile violently seduced Pelops' son, Chrysippos. This, according to legend, was the source of the curse on Laios' house. He regained his kingdom and married Jocasta, but an oracle warned him that he should not have children. One drunken night he impregnated Jocasta, who bore him a son. The child was exposed but survived and returned to kill his father, answer the riddle of the Sphinx, marry Jocasta, and become the tyrant of Thebes. His children, borne to him by his mother, were Antigone, Ismene, Polyneices, and Eteocles. After Oedipus discovered his parricide and incest and blinded himself, and before his death or apotheosis in the grove of Colonus near Athens, he cursed his sons. The sons had decided to share the throne of Thebes by ruling in alternate years, but when Eteocles was to surrender the city to his brother, he refused to give it up. Polyneices appeared with an army, led by the heroes called The Seven. These invaders were defeated, and the brothers ended by killing each other. Kreon, who took control of the city, ordered that the enemies of Thebes not be buried but be left to rot. Antigone was caught burying her brother and was herself buried alive. Her husband-to-be, Kreon's son Haimon, killed himself in her tomb, and Kreon's wife, Eurydice, then also committed suicide.

This story was a great source for literary and artistic texts throughout antiquity. It is particularly interesting here because it contains, in allusive form, reference to the metaphors I am discussing: the earth as the site of reproduction; the sowing of teeth, like seeds, in the earth; the inventor of the alphabet who sows letters, like teeth, like seeds; the stones of the city wall wooed by song, themselves like letters, teeth, seeds; the field as the incubator of the next generation; the earth as the site of burial. This myth, the source of some of the most important Athenian tragedies, will be discussed in later chapters.

Earth as Body

There is abundant evidence for the analogy made between the earth and the female body in the earliest texts and artifacts of historical Greece. Homer and Hesiod bear witness to the significance of the earth/body metaphor in early Greek culture. Homer provides material for the view of earth as giver or container. Vases suggest the identification between the feminine and the ceramic body. The poet of the Homeric Hymn to Demeter connects the body of the goddess and the earth. From Hesiod come the following important ideas: that Earth is the origin of differentiated kinds; that the first woman is created, like a vase, by the artisan god, from earth and water; and finally, that the labor of agriculture is a religious practice, that the success of the farmer depends on his proper attention to the divinities of the earth, especially to Demeter, goddess of the grain. These attitudes are significant especially for the background they provide for the attitudes of the later Greek thinkers, who inhabit a very different world, that of the *polis,* which, although it remained to a great extent dependent on agricultural production, was nonetheless estranged from the rhythms of a life lived among the fields and herds of Hesiod's narrator.

Hesiod represents parthenogenesis by earth, which suggests later fantasies of the spontaneously generative powers of the Nile delta. It is Earth who comes into being out of Chaos, and it is she who then gives birth to starry heaven "equal to herself" (*ison heautēi*) (*Theogony* 126), as well as the Mountains, and Pontos, the sea, "without sweet union of love" (*ater philotētos ephimerou*) (line 132). Only after that does she have sex with her "child"/husband/brother Ouranos. When Zeus wants to give birth, he must first incorporate the female, his wife Metis, in an act of cannibalism that prefigures Socrates' appropriation of the female in the texts of Plato that I discuss in chapter 8. Earth is thus seen, like the mother and the jar, as self-sufficient, self-generating, as giving or withholding; and the contradictory representation of Pandora as secondary, supplementary, fallen, is already an attempt to appropriate to the male the powers of cultivation, reproduction, thesaurization.

In addition, we see represented in Hesiod the first expression of the fantasy of male autochthony that long persisted in Greek thought, even though Earth, the goddess Gaia, is represented by Hesiod as the source of life. As Pucci says, ". . . the woman remains token and quintessence of the iron race, while man, in his common origin and life with the gods, represents the golden race."[26] Like the necessity of agriculture, bisexual reproduction is a product of the fall from divine presence.

There is much subsequent evidence for both of these views, evidence of reverence and awe for earth and woman and evidence of a desire to bypass the female, to appropriate her powers and to represent the male as self-sufficient. I mentioned earlier the poem of Sappho that seems to subvert the representation of the earth as reproductive, as nourished by the sun, and as analogous to the female body instrumentalized in heterosexual ideology. Her work is unique in its refusal of the traditional analogy; throughout the literary, ritual, and artistic traditions, the metaphorical association between earth and body is reiterated. Furthermore, each of these models for analogizing the female body to the earth—the preagricultural, the artisanal, and the agricultural—has concomitant dangers associated with it; the ambivalence of the earliest Greek thinkers toward the earth, who might withhold her bounty, is also expressed toward the female body analogically.

Openings

I do not want to indulge in the metaphysical gesture of considering all this evidence as conclusive of a paradise lost, a moment of feminine presence and wholeness in pre-*polis* culture. All of the representations discussed are produced in a culture already marked by agricultural and artisanal practices, already "fallen" from a state of unmediated connection to the earth. The Greeks themselves, even before Plato, represent the stage of the preagricultural as a lost, irretrievable moment, and thus they contribute to a narrative of decline within which they often create poetic and artistic texts. And even within a nostalgic representation of the spontaneously generating earth, there is strong ambivalence and fear concerning the power of the earth and the parthenogenetic mother.

If the grain-giving earth, like a vase, also contains the bodies of the dead, then there is a danger in opening it. We might compare the later ritual associated with Dionysos, the Pithoigia, in which the ceremony of the opening of wine jars is attended with apprehension as well as with rejoicing. The Anthesteria, during which the Pithoigia was celebrated, was concerned both with wine and with the "spirits of the unseen world."[27] The juice of the grapes had been stored in *pithoi* (like the one Pandora opens) and fermented until the ceremony of the opening, when wine was taken to the shrine of Dionysos in the Marshes. Aristophanes' chorus of frogs, associated with the passage to the underworld, sing in these same marshes. The opening-up of the underworld, like the opening of the jar and the opening of the virgin's body, is a liminal event associated with ritual precaution. The drinkers of the new wine prayed as they drank that the wine would not harm but rather benefit them.

The next day of the festival was the Feast of the Choēs, a type of pottery with "a generously curving belly, a short neck that merges into the body, and a trefoil mouth."[28] (The modern description preserves the analogy between the animate and the ceramic body.) It is only on this day, according to Demosthenes (*Neaira*), that the sanctuary of Dionysos was opened to receive offerings made by the wife of the Basileus, the Basilinna. The drinking of wine from the *choēs* was accomplished in ritual silence; the opening of the mouth to drink was not accompanied by its opening for speech. Supposedly, these ritual rules originated in a desire to protect the Athenians from contamination by the matricide Orestes.[29] The emptied *choēs* were garlanded and handed to the priestess at the shrine of Dionysos. On Chytrai, the last day of the festival, a meal was offered to Hermes for the dead, a meal "meant to placate the hostility of the departed." On this day "the spirits of the dead were free to come up to the land of the living and roam about. So householders . . . smeared their doorways with pitch." "The sanctuaries of Athens were closed."[30] (During this festival, slaves were allowed to celebrate with the free.)

All these ceremonies are associated with the dangers of opening. A further aspect of the Anthesteria involved a chasm, supposedly the place where the waters had gone after the flood of Deukalion. Pausanias says that annually an offering of honey mixed with wheat flour, a typical offering to the dead, was poured into it. According to Parke, "the chasm was originally identified as an entrance to the underworld."[31] This offers an interesting parallel with notions of ritual intercourse, since honey may perhaps be seen as a bodily product, analogously connected with seminal fluid, and wheat with *sperma* or seeds.

All this evidence from the ritual calendar of classical Athens, although anachronistic, will serve to demonstrate that these rituals associated with openings support the analogy made among vase and body and earth, and that Pandora's opening of the *pithos* may be associated with her connection to Epimetheus, who foolishly receives her as a gift, presumably opens her body, and reaps the consequences. There is potential danger involved in ploughing, sowing, and harvesting the earth. Opening it up may unleash dangerous substances, and it may anger the one opened, the female body of the earth who is thus split.[32] This "cutting into" is very different from Freud's "cutting off." If the hymen is the part analogous to the lid of the jar, then its breaking is recounted in Pandora's own action of lifting the lid, and the opening of the earth/body/*pithos* is displaced onto the female. The earth may stop giving spontaneously after Pandora's act of opening; ploughing and cultivating are fallen acts compared with gathering.

Demeter at Athens

The earth/body metaphor figures also in the art and the social and religious practices of the cities, which grew in the period following the feudal, epic stage of social organization in ancient Greece. An important Hellenic ritual associated with Demeter was the Thesmophoria, celebrated in the archaic and classical periods in Athens and elsewhere. Zeitlin contrasts Dionysiac with Demetrian rituals as they serve as models for the female in the city. She points out, incidentally, that the rituals associated with Theseus, celebrated during the same period as the Thesmophoria, were politicized and "particular to Athens and to the development of his historical identity. . . . For the male, return to origins is return to the model of Theseus, the founder of the city. For the female, return to origins is return to the model of Demeter and Kore that operates on an earlier and more generic basis in keeping with the more ancient *aition* of the rite."[33] Here, as in Sophocles' representation of Antigone, women were archaized elements, representative of a conservative, prehistorical position within the complex ideology of the city. "The 'citizens,' well-born women, who celebrate the Thesmophoria, have no 'history'."[34] In this festival women were made to represent an archaic time, by living in tents, sleeping on the ground, eating primitive foods. They hauled up the remains of piglets, which had been thrown into ditches (called *megara*) in an earlier ceremony, as well as models of snakes and phalloi; the remains were placed on altars and mixed with the city's seed-corn and sprinkled in the fields to ensure their fertility. The site of the women's encampment, reached in the first day, called the Anodos or "going-up," was near the Pnyx, the place of the Assembly's meetings. The second day was called the Fast or Nesteia; Parke says, "on it the women abstained from solid food and sat on the ground" and uttered abuse at each other.[35] The last of the days was Kalligeneia or "the day of fair offspring." "This time the reference is not to agriculture or even to animal husbandry. The Greeks typically associated together all natural birth, and Demeter though chiefly goddess of the corn-crop also presided over human fertility."[36] Thus the analogy between the fields of the earth and the woman's body, with its hidden, internal spaces, is reinforced by the series of rituals of the Thesmophoria. Zeitlin discusses the processes of emptying out and filling up which underlie the ritual practices of the Thesmophoria.

These rituals have further ideological implications. If the religious practices of the city, including worship of Ge and especially of Demeter, involved an indissociable bond between the seed corn and fair human offspring; if the traditional religion thus makes an implicit analogy between the woman's body and the body of the earth, between the field's productive powers and the citizen-wife's reproductive powers; if women's effect on the earth and their ritual encouragement of their own fertility are set in some mythical, prepolitical, prehistorical time, then the restriction of women to these realms must be felt as a contradiction when that same city experiences itself as a temporal, historical, political entity whose economy is no longer that of a self-sufficient oligarchic family or kinship group but is based on strategies of import and export, of monetary and financial manipulation. At stake is not only the food supply of the city, to a great extent imported, but also the link between agricultural and human reproduction.

The rituals, myth, and ideology, defining metaphors of sexuality and gender, must either be transformed in light of these political and historical changes, or the citizens must acknowledge a deep split, as they seem to have done at Rome, between traditional religion and the realities of fallen political existence. Can we see Aristophanes' *Thesmophoriazousai,* for example, not only as parodying and preserving traditional gender and generic categories but also as betraying anxiety about the categories' values?

The Earth Enslaved

In the centuries leading up to the classical period—the fifth century B.C.—the city of Athens changed from an oligarchy, dominated by a small group of aristocrats, the hereditarily powerful, to a democratic *polis,* in part through the efforts of the poorer citizens who were for some time constantly in danger of being overwhelmed, even enslaved, by the aristocracy.[37] Let us look at the text of the poet Solon, the sixth-century lawgiver of Athens, whose reforms did much to enable the peculiar democratic form of the Athenian *polis.* Long after the time of Hesiod, as the city formed and conflicts arose between wealthy and poor citizens, Solon was asked to arbitrate the "class" struggle of the Athenians. He ended citizen enslavement for debt and the practice of forcing sharecroppers to give a sixth of their crops to the wealthy. He said of his own accomplishments:

> My purpose was to bring my scattered people back
> together. Where did I fall short of my design?
> I call to witness at the judgment seat of time
> one who is noblest, mother of Olympian
> divinities, and greatest of them all, Black Earth.
> I took away the mortgage stones stuck in her breast,
> and she, who went a slave before, is now set free.
> [*mētēr megistē daimonōn Olumpiōn*
> *arista, Gē melaina, tēs egō pote*
> *horous aneilon pollakhē pepēgotas,*
> *prosthen de douleusousa, nun eleuthera.*]
>
> Plutarch *Solon* 15.5

The lines refer to the *horoi,* "mortgage stones," which were probably markers placed to record the cultivators' debts. The attitude toward Earth expressed here is particularly interesting because it uses the metaphor of slavery. Earth was marked, bound, enslaved by these markers. Is the very notion of property an offense to Solon? We know, for example, that in some ancient Greek communities land tenure was inalienable; it was thus excluded from the new world of commerce and exchange that was to become the norm in Athens. A. Andrewes, in his discussion of the *hektemoroi,* the sharecroppers Solon freed, concludes:

> For the *hektemoroi,* cancellation can only mean that the payment of sixths was abolished, and Solon's boast about the *horoi* points in the same direction. That would leave the *hektemoros* on the land he cultivated, with no remaining limitation on his rights over it, rights that would easily develop into ownership in the Classical sense.[38]

Interestingly, Boisacq, in the *Dictionnaire étymologique de la langue grecque,* says that the word *horos* originally meant "furrow"; its original meaning is a furrow which marks a limit, which is ploughed to show the bounds of a space. It is, of course, quite likely that these *horoi* were phallic, like the herms, and that Solon is referring to some kind of phallic enslavement of Earth, from which he has freed her. There is some scholarly controversy concerning not only the form of Solon's innovations but also the significance of the *horoi.* M. I. Finley, for example, says that *horoi,* at first boundary stones, had a second use as "markers placed on farms in order to make public the fact that these particular holdings were legally encumbered."[39] Rather than indicating that land was sharecropped, the *horoi* may have been records of mortgage. In any case, Solon freed the land—which in his poem is deified—from enslavement.

French argues that Solon's reforms not only freed the land from mortgages but probably also freed the excess population from subsistence-level existence on farms of low productivity and sent them to port and city in search of work. "The remission of debts was not a prelude to a period of social harmony, but to an era of internal strife in which the city population appears for the first time as a political force of increasingly formidable dimensions."[40] French records the gradual shift from a self-sufficient economy based on grain production to the development of foreign trade by the Athenians. Their foreign trade raised the price of oil and wine, so farming changed from production of Demeter's grains, which were finally imported on a large scale, to the higher-priced export crops, the liquids of Dionysus.[41]

The sixth century thus witnessed a dramatic change in the productive life of the Athenian *polis.* Peisistratos, the sixth-century tyrant or self-made monarch, who contributed greatly to the evolution of the Athenian economy, was probably supported by what French calls "the lower orders of the free population," the landless.[42] His own fortune was probably based on mining and was therefore more mobile than those of the more traditional "landed" aristocrats. During his reign he encouraged the production of exports, increasing the value of mobile wealth vis-à-vis the property of the hereditary nobility, and decreasing the importance of agriculture to the ancient city and its political organization.

The Persian Wars of the early fifth century also had a permanent effect on the Athenian economy. The ability of Attica to support itself entirely by agriculture was greatly lessened. Athens became dependent on imported cereals, and much of the religious practice of such agricultural festivals as the Thesmophoria came to have an archaizing character. I do not want to exaggerate or claim that Athens became a purely financial, silver-exporting city. Nonetheless, the features of Greek religion that emphasized agriculture as the worship of the earth divinities were to some extent archaic, referring back to a period of autarky and oligarchic citizen-farmers, an ideal which was held up as politically significant in the fifth century by such thinkers as Sophocles.[43]

The Politics of Metaphor

What is perhaps most interesting about all these data, which will be elaborated in subsequent chapters, is the way in which the description of the female by the male who sees her, who is the "theorist," varies according to the demands and needs of culture. The rewriting of the particular metaphor earth/woman's body is transformed over the centuries, and, as we will see, it is contested by other metaphors that dominate at other moments. My emphasis is on the contestation, the challenging and putting into question of cultural "sets." There is always a vocabulary of possible signs to be used, transformed, and generated, and the choices made by individuals—poets, dramatists, vase painters, urban planners—must be seen as choices within situations of conflict. When Solon speaks of Earth being enslaved by the *horoi,* he is using the earth/body analogy to serve particular political ends. And he calls on particular resources to support his position. He evokes the old myths of Earth as the mother of all, the myths of autochthony that name all Athenian citizens as children of Earth. All human beings are products, finally, of Earth's primal creation after Chaos; all human beings are derived from the production of the first woman, like a vase, from earth (*gaiēs*) and water. The Athenians, even more specifically, are descended from the seed of Hephaistos, which impregnated Earth. In the political struggle of the sixth century, Solon uses these ancient claims to show the wrong of enslaving other Athenians, and the wrong of enslaving Earth, mother of all. He sets these claims against the rival political myths of aristocracy and the rights of the wealthy to accumulate, to gather the land of others. Myths of stratification and dominance are exemplified by such texts as Hesiod's sequence of ages, where the heroes, from whom the aristocrats might claim descent, once lived on earth. The text of Hesiod thus contains contradictory elements in a synthesis that provides contesting political groups with the mythic vocabularies they can use to argue for dominance or for sharing; for *isonomia* (equal rights) or for *eunomia* (good order), the aim of the oligarchs.

What will be most apparent from our oblique perspective, which is our interest in the metaphors used to describe the female body, is how flexible, generative, and fertile these myths are; how much their content is the occasion for radically diverse claims about the nature of sexuality, reproduction, and social existence. It is always men (except for Sappho) who see women and define them in metaphor and "theory," and their descriptions, always ideologically charged, vary according to historical demands. To focus on several different moments in the transformations of the earth/body metaphor is to see how variable it is, how it is made to accommodate changing conditions, from an archaic culture to an agrarian economy and then, beyond that, to an imperial and commercial world.

Four

FURROW

> Beside the oracular wall she [Season] saw the first tablet, old as the infinite past, containing all things in one: upon it was all that Ophion lord paramount had done, all that ancient Cronus accomplished: when he cut off his father's male plowshare, and sowed the teeming deep with seed on the unsown back of the daughter-begetting sea.
>
> Nonnus
> *Dionysiaca* 12.42–47

This chapter is concerned with a rewriting of the most traditional metaphor for woman's body, the earth. Even within the paradigm established by the Hesiodic model of parthenogenetic reproduction, of Earth as the source of all life, there are modifications. In Homer's text, for example, the earth and the woman's body are already conceived not so much as "earth," as a vase full of goods, but as a field, as space marked off by culture, by human labor. In the further elaboration of this analogy, the field is further marked, cut into, and ploughed by the cultivator; the body of the woman is not only the property of her husband but also the space in which he labors, a surface that he breaks open and cultivates, the terrain where his heirs are produced (see figure 5).[1]

In this chapter, I discuss examples in which the metaphor of the field becomes the metaphor of the furrow, especially in the writings of the Greek tragedians. Such examples are particularly evident in those tragedies concerned with the legend of Thebes, in which the sowing of the dragon's teeth is the origin of the Spartoi, the sown men, from whom the citizens of Thebes claimed their descent. Sophocles brings this metaphorical network to its most developed point in his tragedies about Oedipus, and he passes on to Euripides a contaminated, incestuous version of the ploughing and autochthony mythography. The relationship of the Athenians to their land changes in this period as I point out in this chapter. My argument is that their alienation from their land, the loss of the traditional economic and religious relationship to their fields, contributes to the estrangement of the metaphor. Women's bodies, which were once taken for granted as resembling the fathers' fields, are now seen as cultivated furrows. The anxiety about the citizens' alienation from agriculture may be translated into an anxiety about traditional representations of sexual difference.

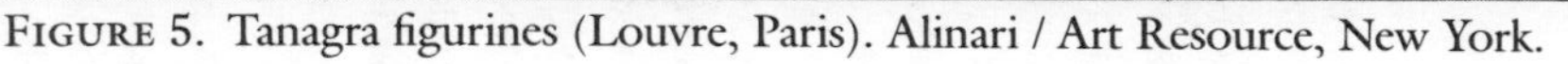

FIGURE 5. Tanagra figurines (Louvre, Paris). Alinari / Art Resource, New York.

The Ploughing of Medea

Pindar, who wrote in the early part of the fifth century B.C., composed poems in honor of athletic victories.[2] The Greek world underwent a stage of political aristocracy and oligarchy as the nuclei of the classical cities formed. Although democracy was being prepared for in Athens, in other cities aristocracies retained their traditional power. Pindar was a poet of this age and was aristocratic in sympathy. He, in particular as the poet of victors from far-flung colonies of the Greek world, was affected by the great efforts and successes of Greek colonization, spurred in part by land hunger in the mother cities.

Pindar's *Pythian Ode* 4, apparently delivered to the North African city Cyrene with the aim of convincing its king to bring back the aristocrat Demophilos from exile, interestingly combines certain features of the metaphorical complex that associated earth and the female body while, at the same time, stressing *plowing* that body. The parthenogenetic body, the containing earth, has become the site not of spontaneous generation but of cultivation. The central myth of *Pythian Ode* 4, of Jason and the Argonauts, includes the themes of plowing and sowing; the ploughing with adamantine plough was one of the labors of Jason:

> But now Aietas threw down before him
> the adamantine plow, and brought out bulls
> snorting streams of blazing fire through their jaws,
> pawing the earth with brazen hooves.
> Single-handed
> he led them to the yoke, tied them in, and drove them
> plowing the furrows straight, digging a fathom deep
> into the earth's brown back.
>
> 4.224–28

The activity of ploughing is associated implicitly with intercourse with Medea and brings Jason the golden fleece. In the next section of the poem, the account of the Lemnian women, Pindar uses the language of sowing to refer to intercourse:

> On that eventful day or in the nights of love
> the seed of your greatness fell
> in foreign furrows . . .
> [*kai en allodapais*
> *sperm'arourais toutakis humeteras aktinos olbon*
> *dekato moiridion amar ē nuktes*]
> for then it was that Euphamos' race
> was sown [*phuteuthen*] to endure forever . . .
>
> 4.254–57

The metaphor of sowing the female body is active in Pindar's time in the aristocratic, even antidemocratic, circles associated with epinician poetry, which is ideologically distant both from the social and ritual world of Athens and from the literary innovations of democratic theater.

The Fifth Century

By the fifth century B.C., Athenian culture had been radically transformed politically, economically, and socially. The Greeks defeated the Persian invasions, and the Athenians played a major role in their victories. The class struggles of the sixth century, evident in the reforms of Solon and Kleisthenes and in the tyranny of Peisistratos, led to a new form of *polis,* the *dēmokratia* (democracy) in which the *dēmos* (people) assumed more power than ever before. The place of women in this new political and social situation had altered also; citizen-women became the guarantors of citizenship for male lineages, and greater and greater emphasis was placed on their sexual purity.[3] They were guarded as vulnerable possessions of their households, traded among citizen-families, hoarded within families without male heirs.

In a transformed social world, the earth/body metaphor, which had reciprocally described both agriculture and reproduction, was reinscribed and transformed as well. The emphasis on the earth as an autonomous being—as full, generous, and capacious for production and storage of goods, seeds, flowers, even human bodies—changed to an emphasis on cultivation. The furrowing of the earth, the labor and effort of the fathers who broke open the earth—now seen as more passive, awaiting cultivation—became a primary metaphorical structure.

In the rituals of the city, the women were set in a particular relationship to the *polis;* they were made to represent and to act out a certain version of social existence. Zeitlin has shown how the cultic models of Dionysus and Demeter offer different versions of female identity, but it is significant that her discussion places far greater emphasis on the rituals of Demeter than on those of Dionysus.[4] In Euripides' *Bacchae,* we get a sense of the place of Maenadic cult outside the city late in the fifth century during the great social, political, and military crisis at the end of the Peloponnesian War.[5] But the citizen-women repeat, year after year, the ritual of the Thesmophoria, which, as Ileana Chirassi-Colombo has shown, restricts the women to a realm that is sacral, mythic, and atemporal or, rather, that associates them with archaic forms of economic production and links their reproductive function to a transcended agricultural stage.[6] Women are, in the religious life of the city, made "prehistoric," as Clytemnestra is in the *Oresteia;* like the Eumenides, they are buried, made insignificant in the political life of the city. They embody a metaphor that is seen and marked as archaic and that functions as long as the city can support this version of their identity. Eventually, however, especially in the context of tragedy, women break their silence; they can no longer be contained in the metaphor. The contradictions of both speech and the economic changes in the city's functioning—the declining emphasis on cereal agriculture, the growing dependence on the exportation of wine and oil, on silver, on taxes on the port, on mercantile enterprises of all sorts—meant that the metaphor reached a limit of signification. This is most deeply felt in Sophocles' work. By the time of Euripides, the metaphor has been overcoded and no longer signifies the body. It becomes a sign of archaism, of a conservative religious and political position that becomes the target of Euripides' irony, especially in his texts touching on the great myths of autochthony, like the *Ion* (discussed more fully in chapter 5).

Metaphor and Tragedy

The metaphors employed by the Greeks, flexible and mutable as they are, are called into question by history. One of the most powerful challenges to the earth/body metaphor comes through tragedy, itself a product and a producer of democracy. If the woman's body is like the earth, if she produces children like plants, if she is like a vase—an earthen container holding and giving up the goods of life—then how can she speak?

Jean-Pierre Vernant, in a brilliant essay, describes how tragedy exemplifies and creates the practices of the democratic city.[7] Tragedy is born with the *polis,* with the tyrant Peisistratos who breaks the power of the aristocracy and enables the democracy to claim its existence as a body of equals. Vernant shows how the "chiastic" form of tragedy exemplifies the ideology of the city. The chorus, an anonymous body of citizens, speaks in the elevated, metrically elaborate and dictionally archaic forms of lyric poetry, while the characters of the tragedies, drawn from myth and legend and representing the aristocratic, archaic past of the city, speak in the relatively simple metrical forms of iambic trimeter and use the speech of everyday Athenian life. Thus tragedy, even in its form, seeks to resolve the contradiction between the people and the aristocracy and enables the city to "make itself into a theater," to act out in another way the legal, political, and social contests it lives with every day. And for the city, the vocabulary of metaphors inherited from the archaic, aristocratic, kinship-oriented past includes the ideological equation between the earth and the mother's body.

Aeschylus, for example, used the ploughing imagery in his Theban play *Seven against Thebes.*[8] The chorus, in describing the terrible curse on the house of Oedipus, sings of Laios' crime:

> . . . but he was mastered by loving folly
> and begot for himself a doom,

father-murdering Oedipus,
who sowed his mother's sacred womb,
whence he had sprung himself,
with bloody root, to his heartbreak
[*hoste matros hagnan*
speiras arouran, hin'etraphē, rhidzan haimatoessan
etla].

750–55

Aeschylus associates sexual intercourse, Thebes, and ploughing; the story already contained the theme of the Spartoi, the sown men. Laios' and Oedipus' intercourse with Jocasta was a repetition of the same deadly sowing, seeds planted in earth that sprout only to war on one another. The enmity of Eteocles and Polyneices simply repeats the battle of the first sown men, and Jocasta, like the earth in which the dragon's teeth were sown, produces accursed autochthonous warriors (*Gēi te mētri; Seven against Thebes* 16, cf. 412–13).

Fertilizing Blood

The scene of a woman fertilized by her husband's blood dominates Aeschylus' *Agamemnon,* when Clytemnestra, emerging from the palace having struck dead Agamemnon, exults:

Thus he went down, and the life struggled out of him;
and as he died he spattered me with the dark red
and violent driven rain [*drosou*] of bitter savored blood
to make me glad, as gardens stand among the showers
of god in glory at the birthtime of the buds
[*diosdotōi, / ganei sporētos kalukos en lokheumasin*].

1388–92

Aeschylus makes Clytemnestra into a reader of the Frazerians, of the Cambridge school myth of the dying god who is sacrificed to the mother goddess. It is her grandiosity, her exultation in the sacrifice, in the blood rain, which must be controlled by Orestes and regulated, with the Erinyes born from Ouranos' blood rain, by the laws of the *polis* and the masculinized goddess Athena. The laws of pollution that would condemn the murderess as impure have no effect on Clytemnestra here.

In the *Oresteia,* Aeschylus takes the scene of the fertile field and estranges it. He sets it back, archaizes it, so that the metaphor is associated with the Mycenaean age, with the dark past of the Trojan War, with the kinship worship of the Furies, who see only mother-right, only the ties of blood between mother and child. They refuse the connection of Orestes to Agamemnon and focus on Agamemnon's crime against Iphigeneia, which is seen as a crime against Clytemnestra, justifying her murder. Aeschylus sets against their "primitive" cult of blood rain, human sacrifice, and mother-right, the reason of the court of the Areopagus, the *logos* of the city, the masculinized, virgin goddess Athena, who is no longer a goddess of earth, but, born from her father's head, a refusal of the old myths of matriarchy. Aeschylus thus refuses the metaphor of earth and female body, supporting Apollo's view that the female body is not the source of life but, rather, that it is a receptacle, a temporary container for the father's seed. The metaphor is in fact far distant from Hesiod's parthenogenetic Gaia, who is the first thing and who generates offspring from herself. Apollo sees the mother purely as a container. Aeschylus uses the ideology of male parthenogenesis to transform the inherited metaphor.

Incest and the Tooth of Hippias

Although it is not a tragic text, the *Histories* of Herodotus shares in the cultural matrix in which the Athenian tragedies were produced. Herodotus records the dream of Hippias, son of Peisistratos, a dream which connects the events of the fifth century with the mythical metaphors of sowing teeth and of possessing the land as a woman that we find in the Theban legend. During the Persian Wars, Hippias assisted the Persians before the battle of Marathon, hoping to be restored to power in Athens.

"The previous night Hippias had dreamed that he was sleeping with his mother, and he supposed that the dream meant that he would return to Athens, recover his power, and die peacefully at home in old age" (*Histories* 6.107).[9]

Heartened, Hippias leads the Persians to Marathon, but:

> While he was busy with all this, he happened to be seized by an unusually violent fit of sneezing and coughing, and, as he was an oldish man, and most of his teeth were loose, he coughed one of them right out of his mouth. It fell somewhere in the sand, and though he searched and searched in his efforts to find it, it was nowhere to be seen. Hippias then turned to his companions, and said with a deep sigh: "This land is not ours; we shall never be able to conquer it. The only part I ever had in it my tooth possesses."
>
> *Histories* 6.107

The Persians lost the battle and the war, and Athens had no more tyrants, except tyrants like Oedipus on the tragic stage.

This anecdote recalls the myth of the Spartoi, men sown as dragon's teeth. The tooth would consume, would eat up the land. It is like a seed, like a dragon's tooth, but it has fallen into sand and is without issue. It is perhaps meant to signify the fruitless tooth of an old man, his impotency, to link the vain hopes of the tyrant's son with Thebes, and to condemn him further in his hopes for monarchic domination over the city of Athens, like the Spartoi's struggles for control of Thebes.[10] The anecdote demonstrates the power of the mythic material—the metaphors for the body and the land—which the historian uses to express the old man's vain aspirations for power.

Sophocles

Sophocles draws on the associations between female body and earth made by Homer and later poets and by rituals of human and agricultural fertility. He further estranges that metaphor by dwelling on it obsessively. The younger tragedian Euripides thus inherits not a living web of associations among women, fields, ploughing, and intercourse, but rather an estranged, perverse set of associations that link the metaphor with incest, with the Theban stories of repetition and contamination, with an abandoned social and political structure that is struggling within the troubled democratic city to regain economic and ideological hegemony.

Sophocles uses the mythic complex when he tells the story of the house of Oedipus. Early on, in the *Antigone,* the first of his three remaining plays concerning Thebes, the tyrant Kreon says that his son Haimon, who loves Antigone, can marry another woman; I cited this passage in the introduction as an example of metaphorical discourse that is likely to be appropriated by today's readers either as a trivial, incidental metaphor, or as a bit of evidence in the construction of a psychoanalytic reading of ancient tragedy. Kreon says of Haimon: "Oh, there are other furrows for his plough" [*arōsimoi gar kh'aterōn eisin guai*]" (*Antigone* 569). Haimon too is descended from the Spartoi. The language suggests the legend of autochthony and the link it implicitly makes between life and death, sowing and burial. Polyneices, who is above ground, is out of place; Antigone (and Haimon) will die underground, out of place, but unlike their autochthonous ancestors, incapable of creating new life. The old mythic language of autochthony does not apply, nor does the old version, recounted by Homer, Hesiod, and Sappho, of the earth spontaneously flowering, giving birth, rendering gifts to humankind. Here the field has been reduced to a furrow, and the function of the female is to receive the seeds of her husband and to nurture his crop. The metaphor is not simply one among many; it has a privileged status, as we have seen, in the representations of women in Greek culture. The transformation of the fertile earth, the naming of the woman as a furrow, is an important reinscription of the inherited paradigm, a reduction of her potential, a mastering of her fertility. She is no longer the parthenogenetic source of all nurturance, but property, marked and bounded, ordered by cultivation.

Deianeira, wife of Herakles, uses this same language in the first speech of Sophocles' *Trachiniae,* lamenting the long absence of her husband. An obedient wife, she calls herself a field:

> We have had children now, whom he sees at times,
> like a farmer working an outlying field,
> who sees it only when he sows and when he reaps
> [*kaphusamen dē paidas hous keinos pote,*
> *gēitēs hopōs arouran ektopon labōn,*
> *speirōn monon proseide kaxamōn hapax*].
>
> *Trachiniae* 31–33

She yearns for his return but ends by poisoning him unwittingly. I will discuss this play further, when considering the metaphor of the tablet, but it is significant that Sophocles represents Deianeira in this way, since usually this language is used by men of women's bodies and of the act of legal, marital, procreative intercourse. Clytemnestra, who sees herself as a field, need not be ploughed; she is fertilized by the dewy drops of blood. Deianeira is a fascinating character, a wife who internalizes her location in Greek culture, who accepts her place as the static field to which Herakles intermittently returns, but who nonetheless destroys her husband.

Castration and the Oedipus Rex

Sophocles' *Oedipus Rex* is a fundamental text for psychoanalysis. Part of the task of rereading classical literature from a different place from that of Freud is to reread *Oedipus Rex.* To read it means to desire it in another way, not to seek confirmation of the universality of the incest and castration theory but to read its own metaphors differently. I do not mean to suggest that the Greeks had no castration anxiety. Any reading of Hesiod's *Theogony* must reveal how the generations of the gods succeed each other in a cyclical pattern of castration or displacement, until the arrival of Zeus. Nonetheless, it seems clear that if we take seriously the Greeks' representations of sexual difference in the body, the castration of the female is not the sign of difference. The female is not the equivalent of the castrated male, although the castrated male is represented as defeated, overwhelmed, superseded. The woman is rather seen primarily, in a move that allegorizes the body in a system different from our own, as the equivalent of a work space, of the place of agriculture, of cultivation. The violent and unsettling metaphors used of Jocasta's body, comparing her to a field plowed by her husband, by her son/husband, by the "fathers," can best be understood in terms of the sex/gender system and the economic, social, and political relations of the ancient city.

The most intense and literal use of the ploughing metaphor occurs in *Oedipus Rex,* where it is so frequently repeated that it takes on the character of an obsession. Jean-Pierre Vernant has written a powerful and polemical essay against the psychoanalytic reading of the play.[11] My reading of the female body as it occurs in this play and elsewhere in Greek culture, which is indebted to Vernant's work on Hestia and Hermes, supports his refusal of the psychoanalytic reduction of this text.[12] Vernant argues that Oedipus does *not* want to commit incest; equally important is the sense of potential fertility and parthenogenetic powers of the female who, like the earth, is seen as self-sufficient. The theory of incestuous desires inhibited by fear of castration emphasizes the power of the father, the law of the father, his ability to prohibit, punish, and castrate; but in the Greek text the emphasis is on the mother's autonomy, on the troubled relationship of the male to the female, and on the fear generated by the audience's estrangement from the earth. I do not argue that one can necessarily reconstruct "the meaning present within the work," as Vernant suggests, but rather that another desire, one not confined to psychoanalytic categories, can read *Oedipus Rex* otherwise. In fact, the psychoanalytic reading filters all of Greek tragedy through a phallocentric desire, sees only Oedipus. I read in *Oedipus Rex* the metaphor of ploughing and a crisis in the ideology of sexual differentiation.

The Earth Sickened

The pattern of imagery concerning ploughing and sowing in *Oedipus Rex* begins with the priest's complaint to Oedipus, in phrases which link the sickness of women, of crops, and of herds. The priest, addressing Oedipus in supplication at the beginning of the play, says of the city:

> A blight is on the fruitful plants of the earth,
> a blight is on the cattle in the fields,
> a blight is on our women that no children
> are born to them . . .
> [*phthinousa men kaluxin egkarpois khthonos,*
> *phthinousa d'agelais bounomois tokoisi te*
> *agonois gunaikōn*]
>
> 25–28

The plague of the *Iliad* was caused by the possession of Chryseis. She was "opened" by one who has no right to her, and the result was wasting disease. In *Oedipus Rex,* it is Jocasta who is the furrow, who has been opened by her son/husband. The earth itself, analogous to her body, is sickened. In the priest's list, the earth, herds, and women's bodies are all made equivalent in suffering. The priest's speech, formal and hymnlike, unites the forms of reproduction essential to the city in an elegant triadic structure. The plague poisons all. The play begins, then, with the shadow of Laios' curse and with the traditional harmony between earth and women replaced by disastrous, unproductive sickness in both. Oedipus, as king, calls the suppliants children (142); he is the cause, now, of their disease. The chorus repeats the association between the earth's fruits and women's children: "There are no growing children in this famous land; / there are no women bearing the pangs of childbirth" (171–74). The chorus compresses the triadic phrases of the priest, eliminating the herds, and focuses on the sympathetic relationship between earth and the mother's body.

Oedipus then ominously recalls the language of Aeschylus in *Seven against Thebes,* in which his warring sons, Polyneices and Eteocles, are called *homosporoi,* "sown together" (*Seven* 804): " . . . they have thus perished by hands that dealt each other death, hands from the self-same seed" (*Seven* 930–32). *Homosporos* can refer to offspring from the same parents or ancestors. (Pindar, in *Nemean* 5.1.43, uses it to celebrate the kindred of the victor Pytheas.) So this reference to Polyneices and Eteocles could simply mean that they are brothers, but it also alludes ironically to the fact of their incestuous conception. In Sophocles' text, Oedipus claims a connection with Laios which justifies his pursuit of the latter's murderer, believing that they both had Jocasta as wife: "[I] who possess his bed and the wife who bare seed to him" [*ekhōn de lektra kai gunaik' homosporon*] (*Oedipus Rex* 260). Vernant points out how profoundly ambiguous the language of the text is, and he discusses Sophocles' use of the word *homosporos* and the language of ploughing.[13] Here Oedipus means that both he and Laios "sowed" in Jocasta, but the word means ironically that Jocasta his wife is also his kin, his mother; that he sowed in her, but that he was also himself sown. He curses those who disobey him, linking again the crops of the field with the women's offspring; he prays that the gods send them: "no crops springing from the ground the plough [*aroton . . . gēs*] / nor children to their women" (270–71). The earth, in the genitive (*gēs*), and women, also in the genitive, are made rhetorically parallel, while children are equivalent to the harvest, in a figure appropriate to this heir of the Spartoi.

When Teiresias enters, he at first refuses to answer Oedipus who compares himself to a stone: "You would provoke a stone! [*petrou*]" (334–5). His words recall the myth of Deukalion and Pyrrha, who sow the stones, bones of the mother, and reap human beings. Human beings would be stones, if they could only be immortal, like the columns of a temple. Oedipus is angry, and Teiresias ends by telling him who he is: "He shall be proved father and brother both / to his own children in his house; to her / that gave him birth, a son and husband both; / a fellow sower [*homosporos*] in his father's bed / with that same father that he murdered" (457–60). Teiresias glosses Oedipus' earlier unwitting use of *homosporos;* here it means clearly that he is a sower in the same furrow in which his father sowed. Oedipus does not understand him.

Later, when the messenger from Corinth comes to report that Oedipus' supposed father is dead, Jocasta tells him not to worry about the prophecy of sleeping with his mother. "Before this, in dreams too, as well as oracles, / many a man has lain with his own mother. / But he to whom such things are nothing bears / his life most easily" (981–83). This remark is often thought to refer to the dream of Hippias reported in Herodotus (*Histories* 6.107). The words connect Jocasta, as Bernard Knox has shown, to the intellectual, secular, rationalizing atmosphere challenging the traditional values of the Greek *polis*.[14]

Jocasta as Furrow

Oedipus the tyrant, having learned from messenger and shepherd who he is and what he has done, rushes into the house, and in this section of the tragedy the imagery of ploughing becomes especially dense and brutal. Oedipus has realized that he has committed parricide and incest. The chorus sings a long ode, lamenting the fate of human beings, recapitulating the past successess of Oedipus and speaking of his present disaster. They say:

> O Oedipus, the famous prince
> for whom a great haven
> the same both as father and son
> sufficed for generation,
> how, O how, have the furrows ploughed
> by your father endured to bear you, poor wretch,
> and hold their peace so long?
> [*iō kleinon Oidipou kara,*
> *ō megas limēn*
> *autos ērkesen*
> *paidi kai patri thalamēpolō pesein,*
> *pōs pote pōs poth'hai patrōai s'alokes pherein, talas*
> *sig'edunasthēsan es tosonde;*]
>
> 1207–12

Jocasta is called a great harbor (cf. 420, 423) and then furrows, which bore Oedipus and endured him in silence. The double metaphor evokes a traditional doublet, the totalizing opposition of land and sea that covers all the cosmos. Here the doublet also suggests a traditional political opposition between those bound to the land, the land-owning citizens of the old city, and the new merchants, rowers in the fleet, all those who formed part of the democratic resistance to traditional forms of land-owner power. The doublet evokes the political debate in Athens between those who defended land, army, agriculture, and those, frequently of another social status, who argue for reliance on an Athenian navy, on the naval empire, the thalassocracy of the city, for the commerce and tribute which characterized the period of greatest prosperity in the city.

The body of the mother, of the woman, is associated here not only with a safe harbor but also with the safety of the land and with the cultivated earth; her husband ploughs her, breaks the surface of the land (1257, 1485, 1497). This is a distinctly different metaphor from the ones suggested by Freud's reading of the little girl's body as castrated, deprived, missing some crucial part. Freud's description proceeds by means of comparison, Sophocles' by assimilation. Jocasta is associated with the traditional practices of agriculture and the paternal furrows. She is the fathers', Laios' field, but also the field in which Oedipus, father of his children, sowed. The chorus asks her how she could keep silent, suggesting that she knew his identity, or that the female body should recognize one who had been there before, even if the woman Jocasta did not recognize her son. It suggests too that she was already ploughed, already open; this is perhaps implied in the use of the plural, "furrows," here.

The second messenger reports the suicide of Jocasta, silent now forever, and Oedipus' blinding; Oedipus sought her with a sword:

> begging us always: Give me a sword, I say,
> to find this wife no wife, this mother's womb,
> this field of double sowing whence I sprang
> and where I sowed my children!
> [*mētrōian d'hopou*
> *kikhoi diplēn arouran hou te kai teknōn*]
>
> 1255–57

He calls her "the mother's double ploughland"; this highly condensed phrase makes her his mother and the mother of his children, doubly ploughed, by both his father and himself, and earth, the arable land, the tilled ground. He seeks to furrow her again, with his sword, but he finds her hanging inside. It is as if *she* were the pollution that must be eliminated because she received both him and his father. Not killing himself but seeking her out, he finds her already dead, and still he does not kill himself. She is pollution; he will end, in *Oedipus at Colonus,* conferring blessing on Athens. He here blinds himself with the pins from her garments, and blood falls from his eyes, a black rain (*melas / ombros*). (We recall Clytemnestra and the death of the marital partner associated with blood rain.) He laments the birth of his children, using language suggestive of their autochthony: "born as mine were born" (*blastoous' hopōs eblaste,* 1376); *blastanō* is properly used of plants and means "to bud, sprout, grow" (cf. *sperma* [seed], 1405).

Once again the language of ploughing and sowing dominates the imagery. He calls himself "a father seeing nothing, knowing nothing, / begetting you from his own source of life" (*hos humin, ō tekn'outh'horōn outh'historōn / patēr ephanthēn enthen autos ērothēn,* 1484–85). He uses the passive *ērothēn,* from *aroō,* "to plough"; the metaphor of field and furrow is here stretched to its limit as he imagines himself sowing where he was sown. The word is strong and shocking; the text distances him from the memory of Jocasta's body, from the experience of her body, by associating his act with ploughing. He committed incest—but he was only a plough that ploughed where it had been planted. He is refusing her humanity, using the metaphorical language and the mythic material about autochthony to deny her status as a human being. She is a furrow cut into the earth.

The movement of the trope, the transfer from woman to earth, is an operation of metaphor. The earth cannot die and must know all ploughs, therefore there is no crime in ploughing there. Oedipus repeats this language, speaking of his daughters' miserable future: "Your father killed his father / and sowed the seed where he had sprung himself / and begot you out of the womb that held him" (*ton patera patēr / humōn epephne; tēn tekousan ērosen, / hothen per autos esparē . . . ,* 1496–98). His repetition of this same metaphor is compulsive and terrible; it is as if he must return again and again to his crime, but always in this metaphorical language that distances him from Jocasta. He says his daughters will have no husbands: "clearly you are doomed / to waste away in barrenness unmarried" (*khersous phtharēnai kagamous humas khreōn,* 1502). He uses the word *khersos,* "barren," referring to dry land. Indeed, Antigone goes out to perform burial rites for her brother Polyneices on the land called "dry and barren ground" (*stuphlos de gē / kai khersos, Antigone* 250–51); and she is buried alive, "unploughed."

Jocasta is like the earth, the fathers' fields, silent, enduring. What implications does the reference have politically? The autochthonous *homosporoi,* the Thebans, are contaminated, too closely related; there is already no otherness in their breeding. Here the incest simply repeats Kadmos' act of sowing the dragon's teeth in the earth; the result is war, violence, fratricide. What does this mean for the autochthonous citizens of Athens, likewise sprouted from the earth? Are they associated with the unmixed lineage of the autochthonous Thebans, with their violence and repetition, or are they set apart from the haunted, disastrous Theban situation? What significance does this have for the economic and ideological conflicts of the city in the 420s?[15]

The Ideologeme of the Furrow

What the Russian formalists might call the "ideologeme" of the furrow as a metaphor for the female body emerges from the nostalgic vision of the earth as mother of all, provider of all things, which need not be cultivated to produce the satisfaction of all human needs.[16] The intercourse of Demeter and Iasion in the thrice-ploughed fallow field, a *hieros gamos* that encourages the earth to produce, is a half-human mimesis of the *hieros gamos* in the *Iliad* that causes the earth to flower. The earth, which once spontaneously provided and generated new beings, is the source of differentiated existence in Hesiod's *Theogony.* Only after the punitive manufacture of Pandora, the first woman, must men labor in the fields. The metaphor of ploughing survives only to become restricted in the fifth century, as its field of reference centers more and more on the myth of Thebes, its version of autochthony, its archaism, and as the city changes its relation to the traditional practices of agriculture and reverence for the ancestral lands.

The Thebes of Herodotus

Other fifth-century texts touch on the metaphor of the furrow. Herodotus has much to say on the subject of Thebes, and all of his account of the Boeotian city is colored by the account of the Egyptian city of the same name. Egypt seems to occupy a paradisaical position in Herodotus' topography; he says of those who work near the Nile:

> As things are at present these people get their harvests with less labour than anyone else in the world, the rest of the Egyptians included; they have no need to work with plough or hoe [*hoi oute arotrōi anarrēgnuntes aulakas ekhousi ponous*], nor to use any of the ordinary methods of cultivating their land; they merely wait for the river of its own accord to flood their fields; then, when the water has receded, each farmer sows his plot, turns pigs into it to tread in the seed [*tote speiras hekastos tēn heōtou arouran esballei es autēn hus, epean de katapatēsēi tēsi husi to sperma*], and then waits for the harvest.
>
> 2.14

The delta of Egypt barely needs intervention for reproduction. The labored, cultivated earth of Sophocles' Jocasta, a work space overworked by the incestuous practices of the house of Thebes, is set against the utopian fields of ancient Egypt.

The Ion

In the *Ion,* probably written in the 410s, Euripides treats the myth of Athenian autochthony and cites the traditional earth/body metaphor extensively and ironically.[17] The myths of autochthonous generation are exposed as contradictory and politically interested in the context of the various references to the myths of Athenian autochthony in the play. Ion interrogates his mother Creusa, unknown to him, and asks curiously about the story of Erichthonius: "Your father's ancestor sprang from the earth?" (*ek gēs sou progonos eblasten patēr,* 267). He uses the verb *blastanō,* "spring, bud, sprout, grow," properly used of plants. (His inquisitive tentativeness suggests that of the chorus in *Oedipus at Colonus.*) Xuthus, husband of Creusa, obeying the Delphic oracle after he has also consulted Trophonios and been promised a child, exits from the temple and embraces Ion. The boy asks who his mother is, and Xuthus says he doesn't know.

> ION: Earth then was my mother?
> [*gēs ar' ekpephuka mētros;*]
> XUTHUS: Children do not spring up there.
> [*ou pedon tiktei tekna*]
>
> 542

Xuthus is a skeptic, a rationalist who seems to refuse the whole myth of the autochthony of his wife's family, while Ion is eager to believe himself a sprout of the divine Earth. They turn to reason (*logōn allōn,* 544), and Xuthus tells Ion of his youthful sowing of wild oats, of his adventures with Maenads before his marriage at Delphi, which might account for Ion's being his son. This plausible conjecture satisfies them both and allows for the rationalist position to be represented, just as in the *Bacchae* the poet sets Kadmos and Teiresias discussing possible rationalist interpretations of the myth of Dionysus' birth.

The device of the *dea ex machina* at the end of the *Ion* calls attention to itself as a device and exposes Apollo as a lecher and coward and hypocrite. Athena briskly sums up his revelations (1570ff.). They are like prizes for keeping quiet, although Ion will hold the throne because he is descended from Erechtheus. "Apollo then / has managed all things well" (1595); Xuthus is to know nothing. With this very unconvincing divine performance, the playwright is obviously skeptical and mocking. The Athenian claims for autochthony are questioned and rendered almost ludicrous.

Nicole Loraux's reading, arguing among other things for a dating of the *Ion* around 411, rests on the assumption that "chez Euripide le tragique est distorsion systématique des valeurs dominantes."[18] The tragic renders ambiguous what Athenian law makes clear—on parenthood, on citizenship—and blurs categories throughout, placing its events in Delphi, while ambiguously pointing toward Athens, its present, its past, its topography, and myths of autochthony. Autochthony itself is rendered ambivalent, as Creusa shares attributes of Gorgon and snake;[19] she is likened as well to Athena and Persephone and Demeter herself. The traditional myths of parthenogenesis and autochthony, male rulers springing from earth, are treated here as if they were corrupt elements of propaganda, to be set in relation to the equally dubious Theban version of autochthony represented ironically in the *Phoenissae.*

The Phoenissae

Jocasta begins Euripides' *Phoenissae* by recounting the oracle given to Laius, which warned him against having children: "Sow not that furrow against divine decree" (*mē speire teknōn aloka daimonōn bia,* 18). She reports that drunk, he did "sow a child" (*espeiren hēmin paida,* 22), and having sown (*speiras*) a newborn, he gave the child away to be exposed. The repetition here at the opening of the drama serves as an emblem of the whole legend, perhaps particularly the tragedians' treatment of it. Euripides cites, almost parodies, Aeschylus' *Seven against Thebes.* He even recalls the misogyny of Aeschylus' Eteocles (*Phoenissae* 201). The chorus recounts the tale of Kadmos' foundation of the city (638ff.): he followed the heifer and slew the dragon of Ares:

> [he] struck the blood head with the blows of his monster-slaying arm
> sowing its teeth in the furrows deep [*bathusporous*], at unmothered [*amatoros*] Pallas' bidding.
> Then earth sent up armed terror over its surface.
>
> 666–68

Later, the chorus contrasts the rites of Bacchus, revels of fawnskin and thyrsus, with Ares' desire for war (784ff.) and speaks of Thebes' origins again: "Earth, you bore, you bore / —I heard the news in my foreign home, I heard it well— / the race that grew from the teeth of the crimson-crested monster" (*tan apo thēro trophou phoinikolophoio drakontos / gennan hodontophuēi,* 818–20). Teiresias enters and mentions the Erechtheids, to whom he has just given victory (852ff.), linking this Theban story to Athenian myths of autochthony, including the victory over Eumolpus that required the sacrifice of the king's daughters. Here he announces that Kreon's son Menoeceus must die to save Thebes. Ares desires vengeance for the death of the earth-born dragon (*drakōn ho gēgenēs,* 931, 935), a bloody libation:

> If earth gets fruit for fruit [*karpon*] and human blood
> for her own offspring, then this land shall be
> friendly to you, she who sent up the crop [*stakhun*]
> of golden-helmeted Sown Men [*spartōn*]. One of their race,
> child of the dragon's jaws, must die this death.
>
> 937–44

There is here a sinister pun on *genos/genus*: race, family, lineage/jaw. Menoeceus is the last unmixed offspring of the sown men on both his mother's and father's side.

Menoeceus, like Iphigeneia at Aulis, decides to sacrifice himself for the city against his father's will. He swears by Zeus and Ares "who set the sprouting offspring of this land / to be its rulers" (1007–8). The earth is thirsty for blood (*xērand'endeuon gaian haimatos rhoais,* 1152); they (the warriors) drenched the dry earth with streams of blood. Euripides is engaged in rivalry with Aeschylus here.[20] The brothers kill each other; Jocasta kills herself; Oedipus appears only to be expelled by Kreon. Antigone, forbidden to bury Polyneices, threatens to kill Haimon in their marriage bed (675) and leaves in exile with her father.

By the time of Euripides' *Phoenissae,* (possibly 412, 409, or 407 B.C.), the metaphors fraught with meaning for Sophocles have become signifiers for signifiers. The allusions to ploughing, for example, connote not so much an intense association between human and agricultural fertility but a reference to Sophocles' tragedies and those of Aeschylus, which generated a metaphorical vocabulary consonant with the social and economic institutions of the early democratic *polis*. In Sophocles's text there is already tension, even crisis, about the equation of earth and body; Euripides uses the trope to refer to his literary predecessors, ostentatiously alluding to a cultural past and building an overcoded, stratified, self-conscious work that by its very form calls into question the genre of tragedy itself as well as its place in the city. If the tragic theater is a locus where the city put itself in question, mirrored and produced itself, created social, legal, political relations and texts through which to understand its own institutions, then Euripides' text refuses reference and speaks of the exhaustion of metaphor, the impossibility of structure, the inevitability of contamination, and the slippage of meaning. He responds to the political and cultural crisis by echoing and then further estranging traditional metaphor. The place of the woman and the earth/body metaphor must change with history.

Holding the Earth

How are we to understand these passages in tragedy, these references to the ancient metaphor, the analogy between the field, furrow, and woman's body? The translation from field to furrow and the association of the planting analogy—the autochthony myths—with Thebes speak of a disruption of the traditional analogy between the woman and the field. This is related to the social and economic crisis at the end of the fifth century brought about by the Peloponnesian War, by Athens' abandonment of Attica to the marauding Spartan troops, and by fears about the rootedness of the citizens of the city. I believe that there is not only a literary dialogue occurring in these moments of tragic drama but that, as Vernant has argued, there are relations being posited which touch on, enact, engage the political and social issues of the city, which is the audience of tragedy.

Finley provides evidence of the importance of land-holding to the citizens of ancient Athens, although he does not allude to its religious consequences. He points out that "in large measure land and money remained separate spheres."[21] Noncitizens could accumulate money but could not buy land, except with special enactments. A strong traditional tie existed between land-ownership and citizenship in classical Athens. "In so far as land was in fact preferred to other kinds of wealth, the choice was a psychological, social and political one: land was the proper wealth for a self-respecting gentleman and citizen."[22] In the democratic city of the fifth century B.C., land-owning was linked to the citizen class, especially to the wealthier members of that class.

There is an important political issue here as well; the fifth-century Athenian leaders who decided to give up the territory of Attica were bent on saving the *polis* as an idea, but doing so meant sacrificing the *citizen* as an idea held by a certain "class" of Athenians. When the Persians invaded Greece at the beginning of the fifth century, the oracle at Delphi gave two discouraging and enigmatic oracles to the Athenians. The first seems to refer to the city itself as a body:

> Why sit you, doomed ones? Fly to the world's end, leaving
> home and the heights your city circles like a wheel
> [*lipōn gaie / dōmata kai polios trokhoeideos akra karēna*].
> The head shall not remain in its place, nor the body,
> nor the feet beneath, nor the hands, nor the parts
> between.
>
> Herodotus *Histories* 7.140

The city is first called round, like a running wheel, circular; it is given a head, body, feet, hands, and "parts between." The evidence confirms Vernant's vision of the classical city conceived of as a circle of equals.[23]

The Athenian envoys are so discouraged by this first oracle that they refuse to leave the temple until they die unless they receive a more promising message. The second oracle at first suggests that the Acropolis of Athens will be ravaged, which it was, but it then speaks of a wooden wall (*teikhos . . . xulinon,* 7.141) to be given to Athena's charge by Zeus. Themistocles urges the interpretation that the citizens should abandon the acropolis and take refuge in their wooden ships (7.143). In fact, the citizens did evacuate to Troezen, Aegina, and Salamis, (*Histories* 8.41), and the Athenian fleet defeated the Persians at Salamis. The Athenians were the more willing to leave the city itself after it was learned that the snake that lived in the temple on the Acropolis had not eaten his or her monthly honeycake, since they interpreted this to mean that the goddess herself had left the Acropolis (8.41). Themistocles, in urging the other Greeks to fight at Salamis rather than abandoning it, in anger says to the Corinthians that, as long as the Athenians have two hundred ships, they have a city and a land (*kai polis kai gē*) greater than the Corinthians', and he threatens to leave Greece with all the Athenians for a colony in Italy (8.61–62). The willingness to abandon the land of Attica, expressed by these popular democratic figures—Pericles as well as Themistocles—may be seen as an ideological position that appeals to the poorer, landless citizens. Even though the version of the Persian invasion that Herodotus records is that Athena herself approved of the abandonment of her citadel, their departure risked offending the religious principles of the more traditional thinkers.

We cannot calculate, of course, the ways in which the abandonment of the land affected those land-owners who had deep familial ties to their holdings. For many of them the practice of agriculture was religious as well as economic. In commenting on the costs to Athens of the Peloponnesian War, French catalogues the physical devastation:

> This entailed, in broad terms, the sacrifice of the entire farming community outside the vicinity of the city walls. As a result of the annual invasions, and the systematic destruction of the crops, Athens temporarily forfeited much of the rural income which had, until the developing of her mining and commercial sectors, been the sole financial support of the state. In addition, the capital value of the land was heavily reduced by the burning off of cover crops, the cutting down of vines and olive trees, and the dismantling of farm buildings. In 431 the Attic farmers are said to have objected to the evacuation of their land on the grounds that they had only recently recovered from the effects of the Persian occupation fifty years before.[24]

The traditional position of reverence for the land, of undisturbed worship and continuity with the ancestors, and of autochthonous privilege was radically shaken by the events of the fifth century.

The Earth in the Text of Thucydides

Thucydides indicates the changed relationship of the Athenians to their land, a letting go that was initiated by Themistocles during the Persian Wars. The Spartan king Archidamos, discussing the possibility of war with the Athenians, tells his people, in a striking reversal of Solon's imagery of the enslaved earth, that he fears the war could last for his children to fight: "the Athenians have too much pride to become the slaves (*douleusai*) of their own land, or to shrink back from warfare as though they were inexperienced in it."[25] He expects them to do as they did before when they were confronted by a superior land power—evacuate the city. Pericles' advice is like that of Themistocles. Pericles insists on Athens' naval strength, its superiority at sea, and its power to extend its empire: "we must try to think of ourselves as islanders [*nēsiōtai*]; we must abandon our land and our houses, and safeguard the sea and the city" (*War* 1.143). He says the citizens must not lament the loss of houses and land (*gēs*) but of men, because only men can beget more men. His language works against the traditional autochthony fantasies and pushes the city toward a rational, secular strategy.

Yvon Garlan has discussed the break this policy made with previous ideas about defense. In an important article on the defense of territory in the classical period, he says, "on peut donc dire que l'importance croissante accordée à la défense de la ville par rapport à celle du territoire a contribué à la crise de la cité: elle tendait, en effect, à détacher le territoire du corps civique, à le 'dépolitiser' au sens étymologique du terme."[26] Attica, he says, was sacrificed for the other bases of Athenian power, her ships, tribute, and democracy. The choice was necessary for the development of the city's artisanry, commerce, and imperialism.[27] The development of exchange weakened the economic restraints that had been crucial in the previous period when the emphasis was on "autarky," the self-sufficiency of the traditional household, kin-group, or *polis*. With the changed economic structure, the fortified city came to be valued over the productive land or the "territory" of the countryside.

Garlan's language, the use of *corps civique,* suggests the anxiety expressed in Sophocles' text that Pericles' choice was felt almost as an amputation, a mutilation, a terrible estrangement from the earth, "mother of us all." The city followed Pericles' plan. Anxiety about its potential effects may be seen in *Oedipus Rex.* Sophocles' description of both the abandonment of traditional military policy and religious reverence for the land, cult, and deities and the choice of the democracy for a mobile, thalassocratic policy expresses both concern about the old dependence on the land and dread that the new policies will end in a terrible disaster, like the plague that the city of Athens had just recently experienced.

At the end of the war at its lowest point, after the defeat of the Sicilian expedition, Thucydides' general Nicias reiterates Pericles' views in a moment of disaster, attempting to hearten his retreating, fleeing troops: "Reflect that you yourselves, wherever you settle down, are a city already [*autoi te polis euthus este hopoi an kathezdēsthe*]" (*War* 7.77). These are the men who are to die in the quarries of Syracuse. The defeat of the Athenians in the Peloponnesian War—the dramatic changes in political and social life that ensued—guaranteed the reinscription of the place of woman and of the earth/body metaphor in a new social text.

Five

STONE

> Your duty will be to remain indoors and . . . to receive what comes in, and distribute so much of it as should be spent, and watch over whatever is to be kept in store, and take care that the sum laid by for a year not be spent in a month.
>
> Ischomachus to his wife
> in Xenophon, *Oeconomicus* 7.35–36

The stones are the bones of the mother. Earth is the mother of us all, the first being in Hesiod's account, the source in autochthonous myths of several Greek cities, including the most prolific artistically—the Athenian. And if earth is the mother, then the stones of the earth are her bones. Deukalion and Pyrrha correctly deduced this when told to throw their mother's bones over their shoulders; these stones, like the teeth of the slain Theban dragon, are seeds from which sprout human beings.

Stone/Rock

The Greeks had many words for what we call stone, and I want all of them to resonate here in this the least textbound of my chapters. Woodhouse lists under "stone": *lithos, petros, laas, khermas, oloitrokhos, lithidion, stēla;* under "rock": *petra, akra, krēmnos* (crag), *lepas, spilas, agmos, skopelos.*[1] There are many kinds of stones, especially in Greece. In this chapter I go through a disparate set of texts and objects, stopping here and there to focus more intensely on some than on others, attending less to the chronological sequence of texts than before in order to touch on a wide variety of metaphorical uses of stone.

Another list, this time of some uses made of stone: Stones are cut into and made into seals for impressing into wax, for sealing up *deltoi.* Marble is mined out of the earth and used to build the artificial caves, the miniature interiors mimetic of the earth's interior, which are temples. Marble is mined and carved into sculpture, representing male and female, human and animal, and hybrid creatures. Metal is mined from the earth, taken out of its interiority, forced into service, made into receptacles and pressed into inscribed coins. Stones make up city walls and the enceinte of a fortress, protecting the enclosed space within, seen to be like a woman's body in Homer. Sometimes stones are magically transported by music. Stones are used for throwing at people, for "lapidation," and for *pharmakos*-like rituals. Achilles is in danger of being stoned in Euripides' *Iphigeneia at Aulis;* Creusa is to be stoned to death in *Ion.* Stones can be weapons.

Stones are mountains. Sometimes they assume the shape of human beings, transformed from human flesh to stone. The gaze of the Gorgon Medusa can turn human beings to stone, and this process of metamorphosis is magically linked to the making of statuary, of stone images.[2] Hephaistos makes moving beings from gold; Daedalus makes statues like living beings. Kronos swallowed a stone in the place of his son Zeus. Prometheus was bound to a stone hillside and tormented by Zeus' eagles; Typhoeus is bound under a mountain that erupts with his violence. Stone can be humanized, made to serve human needs; it can also be part of the earth—undying, hard. The most important decrees of the classical city were inscribed in stone rather than on wood and were left in view like part of the landscape to adorn and instruct, to allow access to the law to all the citizens of the democracy. There was an effort to make stone into buildings, to decorate the gods' and goddesses' space, to imitate the hollowed spaces of the earth, to use stone to create negative, empty space that had the potential fertility of the earth.

The connection with the womb, with intercourse, with procreation is less evident in the case of stone than in the metaphors of earth and oven. Stones are an extension of earth, but they are hard and unyielding. A man cannot penetrate a stone; he can fill an oven or plough the earth. Stone is associated with virginity, as in Antigone's case, or with the end of fertility, as in Niobe's. Yet there is a desire to work stone, to make it yield, to force it into spaces not of productivity but of receptivity, like the interior of a temple, or, as Charles Segal has shown, like the invisible, hidden space behind the facade of the theater.[3]

At the most general level, the metaphor of stone seems to represent an inversion of the fertile earth, giving a contrasting emphasis to the entreasuring capacities of the earth's interiority. It suggests the unfulfilled, latent potentiality of the woman as earth, a negative counterpart to the fruitfulness of the earth and the female, as well as suggesting the female's power to hoard and to protect the goods of the community.

Medusa

My interest in petrifaction forms part of my debate with psychoanalysis. Freud was interested in the Medusa myth and in the relationship between this myth and castration. Philip Slater also focuses on this myth.[4] The idea that women can turn men to stone, either by making them impotent or by giving them multiple erections, fascinated Freud. He saw the snakes of the Medusa as related to the theme of castration; the mother has many phalluses. Medusa was decapitated—castrated—but her head was seething with snakes. Freud chose *Oedipus Rex* as the one tragedy that mattered, out of all Greek tragedy. His choice was based on his desire for confirmation of the eternal relevance of his notions about incest, castration, and repression. He similarly chose, out of all Greek mythology, the myth of Medusa and read it out of its mythic and social context. My reading of the Medusa myth locates it within a complex of myths about petrifaction and other artistic practices. I see it not as a discourse about castration but rather about the association of the female body with the earth. The earth is full of stones, which are seen by the Greeks as her bones, as seeds of human beings; the earth is also the place of burial. To be turned to stone by the gaze of the mother is to return to the earth.[5]

Gorgons

The Gorgons' birth is described by Hesiod in the *Theogony:*

> To Phorkys Keto bore the fair-cheeked Graiai. . . .
> then the Gorgons . . .
> Sthenno, Euryale, and ill-fated Medousa,
> who was mortal. . . .
> Dark-maned Poseidon lay with one of these, Medousa,
> on a soft meadow strewn with spring flowers.
> When Perseus cut off Medousa's head, immense Chrysaor
> and the horse Pegasos sprang forth.
>
> 270–83

Keto also gives birth to the monster Echidna: "divine / and iron-hearted, half fair-cheeked and bright-eyed nymph / and half huge and monstrous snake inside the holy earth, / a snake that strikes swiftly and feeds on living flesh" (*Theogony* 298–300). She bears various appalling monsters, including Kerberos who eats raw flesh, the Hydra, and the Sphinx who destroyed the Kadmeians (326). The last offspring of Keto and Phorkys is a snake: "who guards the apples all of gold in the secret places of the dark earth of its great bounds" (334–35).[6] Thus Medusa's family is associated with monstrosity, with females old when they are born, with a nymph who never ages, with snakes in the recesses of the earth. The creatures of the sea, Keto and Phorkys, create these terrestrial monsters.

The Graiae are young and old at same time, aged children; their femaleness is appropriate, since they embody the paradoxical connection of the earth with the mother's body, with birth and death. (Hesiod says that Zeus will destroy the people of the iron age when their babies have gray hair at birth, *Works and Days* 181.) The snake, although obviously a "phallic symbol," was associated with the mother. This is another bit of evidence against a castration theory for the female body in antiquity. The recesses of the earth, like caves, like the recesses of the house and of the mother's body, were the haunts of the snake who served her, just as the snake of the Acropolis lived in the recesses of the Erechtheion. It is the female body that is primary; the male phallic snake is subordinate, lost in its depths.

Hesiod does not mention the petrifying power of the Medusa's look. She is mortal while her sisters are divine. She mated with Poseidon in a meadow and gave birth from her severed head. In the *Iliad,* Homer says Hektor has the eyes of the Gorgon in battle (8.349); Agamemnon bears a Gorgon on his shield:

> And circled in the midst of all was the blank-eyed face of the Gorgon
> with her stare of horror, and Fear was inscribed upon it, and Terror.
> *Iliad* 11.36–37

Athena's aegis also bears the terrifying image: "and thereon is set the head of the grim gigantic Gorgon, / a thing of fear and horror, portent of Zeus of the aegis" (*Iliad* 5.741–42). This time the head stands alone, severed from the body, and is all the more horrible. Often in art—on vases, on the metope at Palermo, on the pediment at Corfu—the Gorgon is represented as a huge staring head, a monstrous face with extended tongue, glaring frontally, while her body is presented in profile, with the legs crooked in the running position. She is an apotropaic figure, mortal or not, a terrible head who drives away the warrior who sees her (see figure 6).

According to the legend as told by the second century A.D. mythographer Apollodorus, Perseus was sent by Polydectes, the king of Seriphos, to get Medusa's head. Perseus took the one eye and one tooth the Graiae shared and forced them to help him. Apollodorus says of the Gorgons: "they turned to stone (*lithous*) those who beheld them" (*The Library* 2.4.2). "So Perseus stood over them as they slept, and while Athena guided his hand and he looked with averted gaze on a brazen shield, in which he beheld the image of the Gorgon, he beheaded her" (2.4.2). Because his mother Danaë had been persecuted by Polydectes, Perseus used the Gorgon's head, averting his own gaze from it, to turn Polydectes and his friends to stone: "and all who beheld it were turned to stone (*apelithōthē*), each in the attitude which he happened to have struck" (2.4.2). Perseus gave Athena the head of Medusa, and she put it in the middle of her shield.

The Pindaric Medusa

Pindar, in *Pythian* 12, sings of the snaky heads of the Gorgons when he tells how Athena invented a song for Medusa's death:

> . . . he [Midas] has conquered all Hellas by his skill
> in the art Athena once invented,
> when she wove
> the grim death chant of the cruel Gorgons,

FIGURE 6. Mask of Medusa. Sixth century B.C. (Acropolis Museum, Athens). Alinari / Art Resource, New York.

which she heard pouring out
in streams of bitter anguish
under the maidens' repulsive serpent heads
[*tōn partheniois hupo t'aplatois ophiōn kephalais*],
when Perseus cried out in triumph, bringing
the third of the sisters to Seriphos,
death to the people.

Pythian 12.11–21

Pindar, although he refers to the Gorgons' snaky locks and the flute's many-headed melody, does not here specifically mention the petrifying powers of Medusa's glance. But he uses the same pun Homer used, when Achilles spoke of Niobe's people as *laous de lithous* (people/stones, *Iliad* 24.611). Pindar uses only the word *laoisi,* which evokes both *laos* (people), and *laas* (stones). (Cf. *Olympian* 13.63).

Pindar recounts the whole narrative more explicitly in *Pythian* 10, his account of Perseus' adventures:

He slew the Gorgon then,
and brought her head
decked in serpent curls,
a stony death
to the men of Seriphos
[*kai poikilon kara*
drakontōn phobaisin ēluthe nasiōtais
lithinon thanaton pherōn].

(Pythian 10.46–50; cf. *Nemean* 10.4)

This female's head, with its crown of snakes, returns human beings to the earth from which they came.

Medusa appears on the pediments of buildings and is omnipresent on Corinthian vases of the orientalizing period. Like the Sphinx, she is a hybrid monster; the snakes of her hair make her not a woman but, like her sister Echidna, a snake-woman. Is this the "phallic mother," an earth goddess equipped with snakes, the mother provided with a phallus to reassure the boy/man that castration does not occur?

I claim rather that the whole culture is concerned with this image of the mother who is parthenogenetic, like the earth, or who is androgynous, equipped with a snake/phallus. This mother is omnipotent, adequate in herself, not needing the male. This is one perception of the female body and of the mother: that she is self-sufficient; it is consistent both with the view of the earth as parthenogenetic and with the view of the dangerous interiority of the earth. To see this as an inevitable phase in the evolution of the child, and therefore as an inevitable stage in the evolution of humankind, is to make the same error Marx makes when he says that Greek art appeals to us because it comes from the childhood of mankind (as well as, it would seem, making the same claim for phylogeny recapitulating ontogeny that MacCary makes). The Greeks saw the mother as the earth, as self-sufficient, because they were agrarian cultivators and consumers of grain, oil, and wine. Their ideas of sexual reproduction are modeled on agricultural production. The earth was "mother of us all." Even uncultivated, she produced the food that sustained human existence. The plough increased production, but it did not cause it; the human beings dependent on the earth experienced ambivalence toward that earth, capable as it was of denying them their livelihood.

Apollo's embryology in the *Oresteia* marks an important moment in the discourse of male supremacy. As they were further alienated from direct agricultural work, using slaves for manual labor, living in the city as absentee land-owners, artisans, or merchants, the Athenians' ideology of production and reproduction was transformed. Human beings produced artifacts that were sold for food; grain came from the countryside or was imported from far away. The earth, the Earth goddess and her gifts, was replaced by man the maker. The myth of Medusa is a myth of fear of women, fear of their archaism, their self-sufficiency, their buried power.

On the *Ion*

Stones appear again and again in the *Ion,* the tragedy of Euripides concerning Athenian autochthony. When his mother Creusa's plot to kill Ion is discovered, she is to be stoned to death (*thanēi petroumenē,* 1112). It is interesting that stones—"the bones of the mother" thrown by Deukalion and Pyrrha; stones which produced Hellen, father of Xuthus—are to be used to kill the autochthon Creusa, as a *pharmakos* or scapegoat was stoned.[7] The god, however, refused to be defiled (1117–18) by such an execution. This passage brings up the notion of mixture, of *contaminatio;* the citizens of an autochthonous creation share a pure lineage and refuse exogamy because it estranges them from their direct descent from earth.

Ion sees Creusa as a hybrid, serpentine monster and uses a bizarre image, as if she were the Gorgon with snaky, tangled locks: "Take hold of her and let / Parnassus' tops, when like a quoit she bounds / From rock to rock, comb out those perfect tresses" (1266–68). There is a play here on *plokous* (locks of hair), and *plakes* (flat hill-tops), which reinforces the Medusa theme; by a transfer of quality, the stones of the mountain share the stoniness of her hair; her hair—unshorn, uncared for, delicate or wild, both at once—will be at once combed and shredded by the rocks, which will make her into a rocky discus as she, the Medusa, makes them rock (*autēs tous akēratous plokous / komēs kataxēnōsi Parnassou plakes, / hothen petraion halma diskēthēsetai*). Creusa, implicated in the autochthony myth of the Athenian people, is a variant of the Medusa figure and contaminates the Athenian legends with some of the misogyny and ambivalence associated with that figure.

Woman Turned to Stone

Niobe was daughter of Tantalos; her father cooked and fed her brother Pelops to the gods, or stole the gods' food. Thus he was admitted to the banquet of the gods, ate with them, and was one of them before the division between gods and men, which was brought about perhaps by Prometheus (Pindar, *Olympian* 1.60 ff.). Niobe was married to Amphion, son of Zeus and Antiope, daughter of the river Asopus or Nycteus king of Boeotia. (Amphion and his brother Zethus walled the city of Thebes as Amphion moved the stones with the notes of his lyre. Thus the musical notes of the lyre, and the words of poetry, are like the stones that make up a city wall—discrete, mobile, protective, hard, yet responsive to human desire.) She bore six sons and six daughters and boasted that she was equal to Leto, who had only two children—Artemis and Apollo. The two avenged their mother by killing all of Niobe's children.[8]

The first mention of Niobe occurs in the *Iliad,* where Achilles, having refused sleep and food as he mourned for his dead comrade Patroklos, receives Hektor's father, Priam, and agrees to surrender Hektor's body. In this strange interview that seems to take place in the land of the dead, outside of time and the rage of the battlefield, Achilles gives up his anger and grief and consoles the father of his dead enemy:

> Now you and I must remember our supper.
> For even Niobe, she of the lovely tresses, remembered
> to eat, whose twelve children were destroyed in her palace,
> six daughters, and six sons in the pride of their youth, whom Apollo
> killed with arrows from his silver bow, being angered
> with Niobe, and shaft-showering Artemis killed the daughters;
> because Niobe likened herself to Leto of the fair colouring
> and said Leto had borne only two, she herself had borne many;
> but the two, though they were only two, destroyed all those others.
> Nine days long they lay in their blood, nor was there anyone
> to bury them, for the son of Kronos made stones out of
> the people [*laous de lithous poiēse Kroniōn*]; but on the tenth day the Uranian gods buried them.
> But now she remembered to eat when she was worn out with weeping.
> And now somewhere among the rocks, in the lonely mountains,
> in Sipylos, where they say is the resting place of the goddesses
> who are nymphs, and dance beside the waters of Acheloios,

> there, stone still [*lithos*], she broods on the sorrows that the gods
> gave her.
> Come then, we also, aged magnificent sir, must remember
> to eat.
>
> *Iliad* 24.601–19

Apollo, who sets in motion the plot of the *Iliad* by striking down the Greek camp with a plague, here ends the poem with his sister killing the children of Niobe. Like Priam, who boasted fifty sons, Niobe once proud becomes an emblem of parental grief.

The people (*laos*) become stone (*lithous* or *laas*), a pun that recalls the myths of autochthony—of Deukalion and Pyrrha, of Kadmos. The myths of origin tell of people born from stones; here the people are turned back into stone. These myths of petrifaction may also be a justification of political privilege for those who are said to have been born autochthonously from the stones of the land; they have rights to which later immigrants are not entitled. Human beings who are born from the mother earth are buried again in her. Their bones become like stones in the earth. As Achilles tells the story, it is meant to console Priam; other parents have survived their children, as Achilles' father will survive his son. The children will be buried, as Hektor is buried, in a great barrow, as Achilles was said to be buried in a tomb that Alexander the Great visited. And the mother herself—once the earth, Ge, Gaia, the origin—becomes again a mountain, part of the landscape, still mourning her loss.[9] As Nagler points out, the Niobe exemplum connects her with Achilles, whom Patroklos accuses of being water and rock (*Iliad* 16.33–35), and with Patroklos himself, who weeps in a stream of tears like water from a rock (16.3=9.14).[10] Nagler believes Achilles is bringing in his own genealogy with the mention of the nymphs of Acheloios.[11] Further, he says, "the same strange combination of the rigid (rock) with the flowing (water) recurs when the divine horses stand stock still '*like a funeral stele*' and *weep* for Patroclus (17.434)."[12] Nagler sees the masculine as rigid, feminine as flowing; Achilles "now represents the ideal of masculine firmness and feminine tenderness"; "the image of rock and water becomes a focus for the themes of unyielding strength and compassion, immortality and the cyclical flow of birth and death, when they come to a climax as *consolatio* material in the Niobe tale."[13] The weeping Patroklos is like a woman, a little girl, as he weeps. As Kakridis has argued, he represents a final stage of supplication for the hero:

> . . . in a common form of the Embassy motif the hero would resist all his male suppliants but finally yield to a closely related family figure, for example, his wife or mother. Now, no female figure comes forward to answer to Cleopatra in Phoenix's para-

> digm in Book 9, but in Book 16 Achilles fancies that Patroclus is playing just this role when the latter supplicates him. . . .
> *tipte dedakrusai, Patroklees, ēute kourē/nēpiē* . . .
> "Patroclus, why are you crying like a little girl?"[14]

Women weep. Achilles, comparing Priam to Niobe, and obliquely to himself perhaps, weeping for Patroklos, and his father, weeping for him; all these men are seen in light of another return, not the return to battle, or the return home to Mycenae or Ithaka, but the return to earth which is burial, when the hero himself becomes part of the man-made mountain, the barrow, part of the earth as Niobe is. Man is born of earth and of woman's body, and returns.[15]

If, for Homer, Niobe is a figure of grief, of the parent who survives her children, of the mother, Earth, who endures and weeps forever, in Sophocles' *Antigone* she is once again spoken of as an exemplum in a rhetorical figure; Antigone herself evokes her. As she is being led off to her burial, for an execution that protects the executioner from shedding blood, Antigone speaks of her predecessor:

> [I have heard (*ēkousa*)]
> Pitiful was the death that stranger died,
> our queen once, Tantalus' daughter. The rock
> it covered her over, like stubborn ivy it grew [*tan kissos hōs atenēs/petraia blasta damasen*];
> Still, as she wastes, the rain
> and snow companion her.
> Pouring down from her mourning eyes comes the water that soaks the stone.
> My own putting to sleep a god has planned like hers.
> *Antigone* 824–31

The lines are ironic, because Niobe is killed for boasting of her many children, while Antigone will have none; doubly ironic since in fact both end alone, childless. Antigone calls herself "without bridal bed" (*alektron,* 917).[16]

Antigone has *heard* of Niobe. That is, she received the tale through the ear, as an illiterate must, one who cannot place Niobe in time or in a text. Because she is unlettered, she cannot establish a chronology for herself, one which would place Niobe in time long ago; she sees her not as part of a song or a literary exemplum, but as a person, a foreign stranger. The chorus has just said that Antigone is alone (*monē*) in going as a mortal woman to the land of Hades. She thinks Niobe to be mortal like herself and confuses time and history and genre.

The growth of stone, the rocky plant, like the ivy that is the plant of wandering Maenads (cf. line 1132, on Dionysus), and the deathly Dionysus overpowered Niobe; she is like an animal or a Homeric bride—"tamed," worn down, worn away by rain and snow. Again, Antigone cites her source, *phatis andrōn* (the word of men). She insists on the oral transmission of her knowledge of Tantalos' daughter. She has snow and rain for her companions instead of her children, and she weeps; the ridge of hills are like her brows. Antigone's daimon puts her to bed in the same way.

Antigone does not mention Niobe's children, her boast, the gods' murder, or the children's lack of burial, which must recall her brother Polyneices. She sings only of the tamed woman, conquered by rock as Antigone will be; Antigone will never be the *damar,* the tamed Homeric wife, but she is to be tamed nonetheless in the tomb. The Dionysiac ivy that the dancing Maenads used to adorn themselves becomes a sign of death and paralysis. This Niobe is not alive; the rain and snow weep for her and cause the mountain, which forms her brows, much bewept, to cry again.[17]

Electra, too, uses the exemplum of Niobe in a way that illuminates Antigone's special formulation of the topos; Electra says to the chorus, in her lament for her murdered father:

> And Niobe, that suffered all, you, too,
> I count god
> who weeps perpetually
> in her rocky grave.
>
> Sophocles *Electra* 150–53

She considers Niobe to be a god, to be one of the blessed, because she is petrified in grief, because in her rocky grave she weeps forever. Electra envies her concentration; her own obsessive desire to mourn would only be satisfied with revenge or with this attitude of frozen, perpetual grief. And Electra is conscious of the literariness of her allusion, which occurs just after a mention of Itys, the cannibalized child. Like Procne, Niobe, and Antigone, Electra is *ateknos* (childless, 164) and, of course, *alektron.*

It is Antigone who cannot separate a rhetorical figure from the texts, who cannot read the *Iliad* or know the distance between herself and the creatures of story. She is caught up, like all illiterates—many women, perhaps—in a world without a linear sense of history. She cannot distance herself from legend, from the gods, from the stories she has heard all her life. In this she is an archaic figure, one who knows the old stories, the old gods, the old "unwritten" laws (*agrapta,* 454). She assimilates herself to Niobe in a gesture that celebrates the goddesses of the earth—the mother, the children of the same mother—the stories heard that have no relation to the painstaking chronologies of the *polis,* of a historian like Herodotus.

If the metaphor of stone is an inversion, or negative counterpart, of the earth analogy, then the myth of Niobe is illuminating for its suggestion of the deathly space that is the earth. She is the origin of all these children, twelve or fourteen, half male and half female, thus in some way the origin of all. The family of human beings is large, half female, half male. All die; genocide is a persistent fear, related to the flood myths of Deukalion and Pyrrha and of Noah. The myth of Niobe repeats the theme of destruction by turning the people into stones. No one is left alive but the weeping mother. Yet the myth also provides a covert means of regeneration; the stones are the source of life in the myths of autochthony, and Niobe becomes part of the earth, the origin and mother of all.

Caryatids

Stone is an element of earth, but a nonproductive one, except in the myths of autochthony. So Achilles, the hard warrior, even seeing himself as a mourning mother, is a stony one. And Antigone, the childless virgin, sees herself becoming the stone of her tomb. Stone is the virginal aspect of earth, or the postmenopausal earth, no longer reproductive, like the Pythia at Delphi. The ploughed field is fertile earth; the mountain at Sipylos can only weep.

The Homeric Hymn to Aphrodite that celebrates that goddess' union with Anchises begins with a catalogue of the divine virgins, whose virginity makes her reproductive powers possible. Hestia and the *korai* who keep the treasuries and guard the Erechtheion are, like Athena, virgin stone, protecting an interiority that remains chaste. If the stony women, Niobe and Antigone, are nonsexual, guaranteeing the fruitfulness of their opposite Aphrodite, who is not perhaps the ploughed field but the garden of Adonis, then the temple space, created of stone in the landscape, is like Niobe's body—a human shape that becomes stone, that becomes part of the seen world, that becomes like its mountains.

The caryatids are stone figures of women's bodies that support the temple space. The first columns were probably trees, reminiscent of the legendary dryads. The peristyle columns of Ionian temples were like a grove set aside for worship. Just as Atlas supports the earth, as Herakles becomes a column on the Olympian metope, so the whole space of the temple, its interiority, is like the space inside the body of the mother.

One temple in particular seems to exemplify not the infertility of stone as contrasted with the earth but rather the capacity for keeping safe, for entreasuring—features that stone structures and the earth share and that are extended metaphorically to the female. The Erechtheion on the Athenian Acropolis was a complex of enclosures that held various treasures that were valuable to the Athenians as significant of their past (see figure 7). The second century A.D. traveler Pausanias says it housed altars to Erechtheus, Boutes, and Hephaistos, and that sea water sent forth the sound of waves. "On the rock is the outline (*skhēma*) of a trident" (*Description of*

Greece 1.26.5). The word *skhēma* means "form, shape, figure"; the building now called the Erechtheion supposedly had a hole in its roof above a mark that was said to have been made by a lightning bolt. Pausanias continues in a rather rambling fashion, describing an image (*agalma*) of Athena: "A legend concerning it says that it fell from Heaven" (1.26.6).[18] He says that in the Temple of Athena Polias, which is thought to be one of the rooms of the Erechtheion, is a wooden Hermes and a folding chair made by Daedalus, more Persian spoils.[19] Then he says, disjointedly, "About the olive, they have nothing to say except that it was testimony [*marturion*] the goddess produced when she contended for their land" (1.27.2). The very day the Persians burned Athens the olive grew back again. Continuous with this temple is that of Pandrosos, the daughter of Kekrops who did *not* look into the chest which contained Erechtheus. Here Pausanias describes the Arrēphoroi, who descend "by the natural underground passage" through the enclosure of Aphrodite in the gardens, carrying an unknown burden given them by Athena's priestess and, leaving their burden below, bringing back something else.[20] Near the temple are statues, one of Erechtheus. "There are also old figures of Athena [*agalmata arkhaia*], no limbs of which indeed are missing, but they are rather black and too fragile to bear a blow" (1.27.6). They were burnt by the Persians.

Homer mentions the worship of Erechtheus in the temple of Athena (*Iliad* 2.549–51), and in the *Odyssey,* Athena leaves Scheria and comes to Marathon and Athens: "And [she] entered the close-built house of Erechtheus" (*dune d'Erekhthēos pukinon domon, Odyssey* 7.81). The brilliant, utopian description of Alkinoos' palace immediately follows. The temple of Athena and the house of Erechtheus may have been one temple, burnt by the Persians and rebuilt at the end of the fifth century. Detailed inscriptions remain, recounting its construction.

The relationship of the building now called the Erechtheion to Pausanias' description has been much debated. Frazer says only the part of the building dedicated to the worship of Erechtheus should be called the Erechtheum (cf. Plutarch *Life of Lycurgus* 843e; cf. Herodotus *Histories* 8.55). He points out that Pausanias said the building was "double" (*diploun,* 1.26.5); it is interesting that he seems to mean here an inner and an outer room. According to Frazer, it was through the inner room that one reached the salt sea and the mark of the trident, "the indentations in the rock," although the cistern, identified by Frazer with the sea, was under the western porch and the marks "in the crypt under the north porch." Thus, the *muchoi,* the inner recesses of the building, the hidden places, were salt water and the trident's mark: the female genitalia, salt secretions, and an opening in the earth. In addition, the Pandroseion is the place of dew, *drosos.*

Although Pausanias does not mention the caryatid porch, Vitruvius the

FIGURE 7. The Erechtheion, with the Caryatid portico (Acropolis, Athens). Alinari / Art Resource, New York.

Roman architect recounts its supposed origin. In his introductory remarks on architecture, he says an architect must be a man of letters, draftsmanship, mathematics, optics, arithmetic, and finally of history:

> For example, if anyone in his work sets up, instead of columns, marble statues of long-robed women which are called caryatids, and places mutules and cornices above them, he will thus render an account to enquirers. Caria, a Peloponnesian state, conspired with the Persian enemy against Greece. Afterwards the Greeks, gloriously freed from war by their victory, with common purpose went on to declare war on the inhabitants of Caria. The town was captured; the men were killed; the state was humiliated. Their matrons were led away into slavery and were not allowed to lay aside their draperies and ornaments. In this way, and not at one time alone, were they led in triumph. Their slavery was an eternal warning. Insult crushed them. They seemed to pay a penalty for their fellow-citizens. And so the architects of that time designed for public buildings figures of matrons placed to carry burdens; in order that the punishment of the caryatid women might be known to posterity and historically recorded.[21]
>
> *On Architecture* 1.1.5

Vitruvius goes on to describe how the Spartans, after defeating the Persians, built a Persian colonnade at Sparta, placing the statues of their captives, dressed in barbaric costume, to support its roof, and their example has been followed by other architects.

This account does not necessarily illuminate the caryatid porch of the Acropolis. Athens may not be referred to; its caryatids were called *korai,* girls; the Athenians did not celebrate triumphs, as the Romans did. This is an explanation after the fact, which may be relevant to other caryatids, for example, those at Delphi, or to none (see figures 8 and 9). But it gives a reading of the architectural element, one that interprets the human body column as a sign of just punishment. The caryatids' burden is seen as heavy, as a warning.[22]

Rather than reading the caryatids as victims of just punishment, I see them as treasurers. Helene Foley's work on the *Odyssey* discusses the early and crucial relevance of this aspect of women's existence: "Household economics does not require men or the establishment of a sexual hierarchy and women's control over this sphere is seen as natural, unproblematic."[23] Women preserve and maintain the goods brought to them by the men of their households. "The household, as in the analysis in Xenophon's *Oeconomicus,* processes and makes useful and permanent goods produced by men through agriculture and herding."[24] Women transform raw materials (almost as ovens transform grain and earth to bread and ceramics), and

FIGURE 8. Bronze mirror with Caryatid. Sixth or fifth century, B.C. (National Museum, Athens). Alinari / Art Resource, New York.

FIGURE 9. Dancing nymphs as Caryatids. Fifth century B.C. (Delphi Museum). Alinari / Art Resource, New York.

they are the treasurers of those materials when they have been transformed. Like Hestia, who is connected with the oven—the fire that transforms things brought inside, that warms the house and connects its interior space with the outside—the wife as treasurer ensures the prosperity and endurance of the home.

In his argument in defense of Orestes, murderer of his own mother, Apollo points to Athena, born from the head of her father Zeus, "not nursed in the darkness of the womb" (*en skotoisi nēduos, Eumenides* 665). The real parent is *ho thrōiskōn,* the masculine, the mounter, the impregnator, the leaper, the one with the seed, the semen. The female *esōsen,* preserves, saves, keeps alive. The mother is the *treasurer* of the seed, of the young sprout. As she keeps safe the goods her husband brings to the house, so she keeps safe his seed.

In Xenophon's *Oeconomicus,* mentioned by Foley and frequently referred to by Foucault, Ischomachos the husband discusses how he trained his young wife in her role as keeper of his house. He recounts his lessons in ordering their common goods, instructing their slaves, preserving and maintaining foodstuffs and clothing. She becomes a faithful treasurer, contributing to the well-being of their *oikos* by remaining in her place—inside, guaranteeing the contents of the house, vigilant, careful, frugal, and, of course, chaste. The order of the household is a sign of her containment within her place; she is the opposite of the wild Maenads running amok on the hillsides, consuming wild things instead of preserving, cooking, transforming the wild into domestic consumables.

Xenophon's Ischomachos recalls for Socrates how he trained his fourteen-year-old wife by explaining the division of labor and the necessity for protecting and treasuring the goods of his household:

> . . . those who mean to win store to fill the covered place, have need of someone to work at the open-air occupations; since ploughing, sowing, planting, and grazing are all such open-air employments; and these supply the needful food. Then again, as soon as this is stored in the covered place, then there is need of someone to keep it and to work at the things that must be done under cover. Cover is needed for the nursing of the infants; cover is needed for the making of the corn into bread, and likewise for the manufacture of clothes from the wool. And since both the indoor and the outdoor tasks demand labour and attention, god from the first adapted the woman's nature, I think, to the indoor and man's to the outdoor tasks and cares.
>
> *Oeconomicus* 7.20–22

He goes on to recount how he taught her to order and cherish and tend their possessions.

FIGURE 10. The Erechtheion, with a detail of the Caryatid portico (Acropolis, Athens). Alinari / Art Resource, New York.

Like Hestia and Athena, virgins whose chastity guarantees the sanctity of the household and of the interior space of the *polis,* the Athenian caryatids act as treasurers for the city. The caryatids are not abject, not humiliated, not led in triumph. They are stable, balanced, and proud (see figure 10). This is one representation of the female: as contented guardians, as the support for sacred space, for a "treasury" of the most ancient and precious of the city's objects. Their billowing robes conceal their rounded bellies, emblematic of the hidden interiority of their bodies and of the Erechtheion's sacred spaces. The Acropolis had no Atlas figures; no Persians were made to act as columns (although the Persians are represented in combat on the temple of Athena Nike). Instead, these *korai,* like the buried votive *korai* and the images of Athena—the great bronze Athena Promachos, the "Lemnian" Athena, the chryselephantine Athena within the Parthenon, the very ancient wooden *xoanon*—these are the virgins who occupy the city's most holy ground. The Parthenon itself is a great hollow, a space kept empty and potential as if to guarantee the sanctity, purity, untouchability of the city and its prosperity. It must have seemed a sacrilege when the Persians entered the enclosure at the top of the Acropolis, burning and destroying as they went. Instead of holding to the agreement to leave the sacred space in ruins, as a reminder of Persian violence, the Athenians buried the *korai* and rebuilt the sacred enclosures within the enceinte of the Acropolis itself.

The north side of the Acropolis was associated with very ancient cult practices, probably originating in the late Helladic period, since they seem to have grown up around the Mycenaean *megaron*. Pericles' building plan included the Erechtheion, but it was probably not completed until 408 B.C. and was then damaged in 406 by fire (Xenophon, *Hellenika* 1.6.1). The building is atypical of Greek architecture, in part because it contains several different chambers, and in part because the foundations of the south and east walls stand more than eight feet higher than those of the north and west walls.

A frieze extended around the building, except at the roof of the north portico; its subject is not known, but it consisted of Pentelic marble figures attached to a background of Eleusinian dark stone. It is difficult to sort out the various chambers' functions, since Pausanias' description is confusing. (One piece of evidence is the account by Philochoros [Fragment 146] of a dog who violated the sanctuary.) The magnificent north porch, with an Ionic colonnade, a frieze in blue Eleusinian marble, paneled ceiling, and decorated door, protected the marks in the stone and had an opening overhead in the roof. The sacred snake, fed on honey cakes, may have lived here near the tomb of Erechtheus. The asymmetrical southern portico is the caryatid porch, which has a marble wall founded on the peristyle of the old temple of Athena, probably dating from the Peisistratid era (529 B.C.). This old temple was wrecked by the Persians. There are four caryatids in front and two behind, each one different from the other, balancing their weight on the outside leg so that the porch, although closed by their bodies, unfolds in two. The porch faced the north side of the Parthenon and was entered through the east wall.

The interior of the whole Erechtheion complex is labyrinthine, with its various enclosures, uncentered doorways, different levels, interiors within interiors, and a basement at a level below that of the lowest floor. The building has *mukhoi,* or interior recesses, like those of the body, and the *korai* seem to protect the building on one corner while from other directions it seems to invite entry. Perhaps the most important feature of the building is its treasury-like status; it is a complex receptacle, a container of treasures, and in this sense the caryatid motif copied from the Delphic treasuries is most appropriate. In addition, as I have said, it is not a simple rectangular space, like the interior of most temples, or even a rectangle within a rectangle, but rather a recessed, complex, rather tortuous space, perhaps resembling the famous Maltese structures that are thought by some to be sites of labyrinthine ritual rebirth.[25]

The Greeks have a generalized notion of containment or enclosure, of the fruitful inside, linked in turn to an agricultural economy; the stone temple and the treasury even more are emblematic of the filled receptacle. Pierre Vidal-Naquet has shown how the Homeric wife was in charge of thesaurization, of guarding over the booty acquired by her husband.[26] Xenophon too stresses this aspect of women's work (*Oeconomicus* 7.35–40). The treasuries at Delphi are like the storehouses watched over by women. The caryatid structures, very prominent at Delphi, may have evolved from a felt connection between the treasury of the *oikos* and that of the city at this international shrine.

The Erechtheion would be seen as a sort of city treasury, a storehouse, a container of valuables. The caryatids are Athena's guardians, watching over the olive tree, spring, *xoanon*—the oldest treasures of the *polis*. This temple, then, is a model of the idea of temple, a container of sacredness, of the aura surrounding holy images, not to be entered, necessarily, but to be kept apart from secular space.

The fact that the caryatid porch is only one element, part of a side of a complicated structure, is modified by its situation as the facade facing the Parthenon and the figure of Ge; it is the element that faces the main axis of the Acropolis space. The position, too, of the *korai* is significant; they present a closed yet open rank, steady, constant, yet with space between them, and balanced not so as to mass themselves at the center of the porch, the possible entrance, but weighted away, toward an opening up of the space. The actual entrance was off to the right side; it seems not to have been used as a public entrance. It is the smallest of the porches, yet the most visible from *inside* the *temenos;* from below the Acropolis, it would not be visible. Thus the citizens, the ritual celebrants would see it as the face of the Erechtheion, while from below, in the more profane city space or *agora,* the north side would be most visible.

Ge, Athena, and the caryatids were at the center of the Acropolis sanctuary; the Pandroseion was probably the enclosure next to the caryatid porch, with its olive tree, while next to it was the Kekropeion, with the tomb of Kekrops. Zeus, Poseidon, Erechtheus were on the outer north side, Kekrops was buried in the inside; the "female" space then is in the interior, perhaps the negative space, created by the Parthenon and Erechtheion and containing the open space between them. The hyperbolic structure of the Propylaea would be a hymen, a threshold, protecting the interiority and receptivity at the center of the Acropolis.

The Body as Treasury

Is there a historical pattern of evolution from a view of the earth as self-sufficient, to the earth as a space of fertility needing semination, to the earth as a mere receptacle? I would rather see this whole ideological set as an arena of struggle, with the differing representations of the female body's place in reproduction changing according to class, historical context, and political persuasion. In any case, the dominant perception does not seem to be Freud's infantile theory of sexual difference—that is, castration—but rather a view of the woman's body as a site of labor, production, reproduction, or as a space for entreasuring things of value.

What is compelling about the stones metaphor is its connection with virginity, autochthony, and thesaurization. Antigone compares herself to Niobe; most important to her is her own transformation into stone, but what matters perhaps more to the audience, besides her inability to distinguish between herself and divine or semidivine legendary figures, is her childlessness. Niobe had children but lost them; she will have no more. And Antigone will die unwed and childless, buried in stone. It may be the contrast with the living earth that is most important. Earth the mother produces growth, plants, trees, animals. She need not even be ploughed or labored over, broken into by men. But stones normally yield nothing; thus, they perhaps stand for women like Hestia who choose virginity over marriage, or women like Antigone and Niobe, who are prevented from raising children.

Hestia, the virgin, is the guardian of the hearth, the fire at the center of the house. The interiority of the woman's body is echoed by the enclosed space of the *megaron*. The stone temples, which are the houses of the gods' images and which contain their potentiality, are like caves, hollows in the body of the earth, the mother. A temple like the Erechtheion, with its complex inner space, particularly resembles the *mukhoi,* the recesses of the woman's body and of the earth. And the caryatids, petrified women, are its guardians, treasuring and protecting that inner space, that potentiality, just as the Homeric and Xenophonic and all Greek wives were meant to guard and hoard and protect the stores of their husbands' houses.

The analogy with intercourse, present in the acts of ploughing, writing, baking, is not present here. Rather, the culture emphasizes untouchability, unavailability. The sacred threshold cannot be crossed, just as the virgin Athena cannot be touched. This is another aspect of the female body, the asexuality of presexual and postsexual female. The Pythia at Delphi was to be postmenopausal. Hestia, the goddess of the hearth—the center of house and city—the goddess of fixity, is a virgin.[27] Some women must remain pure potential, never having their interior filled up by sex or pregnancy, so that other processes of thesaurization can occur. There must be a protected interiority. Athena throws the seed of Hephaistos to the ground.

Ordinary people, it seems, did not enter temple space; it was conceived of not as a shelter for a worshipping community but rather as a home, as an outer skin, of the god or goddess. The idea of the internal space is best preserved ideologically by having such privileged space, *temenos,* a space cut out from the secular world to stand for insideness, for the emptiness that endures and waits. The male gods had their temples too, but perhaps we can read them as based on the earthly female analogy, that their empty space—like Kronos' swallowing his children, like Zeus' swallowing Metis and giving birth to Athena or being pregnant in the thigh with Dionysos—is analogically based on the female power of reproduction. Their power, implicit in the temple space, is interiorized like that of women's bodies, and, if Vincent Scully is correct about Minoan religion and architecture, it is based on the model of goddess worship.[28]

Not all of these images are of interiority. Stones have differing degrees of mobility. Some reinforce the idea of female genesis, or parthenogenesis. If stones are the mother's bones, and they are seeds of men, then the earth is reproductively self-sufficient, and the autochthonous peoples are matrilineal. The mobile stones that protect city and fortress are associated with the boundary-marking interiority, as are the mined marble and metal that is used to make containers like temples and funeral urns. Stones thrown are weapons; the bones of the mother can be used for ritual sacrifice like the *pharmakos* rite. Niobe the mountain is a part of the landscape—once absent, nonexistent, but now immovable. The great temples, like the Parthenon, become part of the landscape. They are not transformed human bodies, but they are the products of human labor and are emblematic, especially the Parthenon, of virgin interiority and sacred space. The sculptures that decorate the temples have a further degree of mobility; they are attached but are sometimes conceived of as separate entities made to adorn. Many sculptures surrounded but were not attached to the temples, as were the caryatids of the Erechtheion. Some stones were inscribed and set up in sacred and political space. They bore all sorts of inscriptions—details of temple construction, dedications, laws, decrees. Unlike the *deltos,* such stones were visible, as Pelasgos, in Aeschylus' *Suppliants,* proudly announces about the inscription ensuring the safety of the Danaïds. The inscribed stones were set up, made part of the public landscape. Stones for throwing were the most mobile of all; in the autochthony myth, they are seeds, like the teeth/letters/seeds of the Kadmos myth. Maria Gimbutas has published images of goddesses from Old Europe with seeds pressed into the clay. The figurines suggest inscription—the decoration of the body with signs, insemination, the sowing of the body with seeds—and, perhaps, construction, an analogy between the making of a figurine, a statue, and a building adorned with sculpture.[29]

The Greeks continued the ideological process, the attempt, in response to economic and social change, to reinscribe the female body under the sign of the husband and father. Unlike Freud's castrated little girl, or female-receptacle, the earth-mother of the Greeks is dangerously self-sufficient. It is their proximity to agricultural production and to the concomitant goddess-worship, that determines the Greeks' radically different perception and conceptualization of the female human body. The body is like the earth, autonomously productive; like stone, part of the earth's landscape, guardian, virginal. The metaphors—earth, stone, oven, tablet—coexist with each other and with others, representing different stages of the alienation of the female body with the possibility of parthenogenesis, the possibility of self-sufficiency and autonomy like that of the earth herself.

Six

OVEN

> Sosibius, in the third book of his commentary on Alcman, says that *kribana* is the name given to certain breast-shaped cheese-cakes.
>
> Athenaeus
> *Deipnosophistae* 3.115

The analogy between the female body or, more particularly, the uterus and an oven is, like other analogies already described, a commonplace of Greek thought. What is most interesting about this metaphor is that it implies a view of offspring not only as the fruits of seeds planted or the contents of a vase, but also as food—a strange notion but one consistent with such myths as that of Kronos, who devours his children, and that of Pelops, the boy cooked and served to the gods as food.

The metaphor of the oven seems to have strong affinities with the furrow/earth metaphor. It links the processes of plant reproduction and their attendant agricultural and botanical imagery with the work of the artisan and the cook. It minimizes, however, the possibility of parthenogenesis or autochthony, since in the representation of the woman's body as an oven there is an assumption of passivity, the passivity of a receptacle. If the male inserts his loaves, his seeds, his penis, his seminal fluid, in an action analogous to the process of baking, then the female receptacle contributes nothing but heat and the space in which the loaves rise and bake. Thus, there is an implicit and ideologically powerful rewriting of the metaphorical construct associated with agriculture; here we have a reinscription that retains continuity with the earth metaphor but that determines the situation of the woman as space, as a topos, very differently. In the network of substitutions that I am describing, the oven metaphor represents a further stage of alienation from the representation of the woman's body as an autonomously fertile field. As a human artifact, the oven is as ancient as the vase; it can be seen in archaic culture as another reinscription of the earth metaphor, but it has a neolithic prehistory that may precede agricultural production as well as the notion of property. The oven is a human artifact, made of earth or stone, but shaped by human agency and set in the cultural space of the house or the courtyard. The oven is like an earth in which the seeds of the cultivator are placed or a fixed, productive point in the *oikos*. The oven is also sometimes seen as a miniaturized earth, a possession at the service of the master of the house, a portable, mobile bit of property that may resemble the interior space of the household itself.

In this chapter I closely examine some almost contemporaneous uses of the oven metaphor and then look further at a chronologically distant text, one that describes a famous shrine of the ancient world, to note that the language of the oven and of baking has a long history, that the analogy between the oven and the earth has been connected for centuries with the view of the earth as analogous to a woman's body.

The Granary

There is interesting early evidence not only for the representation of the woman's body as a sort of entreasuring receptacle but also for its connection with grains. A. M. Snodgrass points to a rich woman's grave found in Athens in 1967, dating from the later tenth or earlier ninth centuries B.C. This female cremation contained both a large model granary and a chest made of clay, the lid of which was decorated with more such model granaries.[1] The extravagance of the grave goods may indicate not only the wealth of the dead woman, and her connection with a particular source of wealth, but also the appropriateness of the connection between the entreasuring female body and its capacity for production.

Periander

The fifth-century historian Herodotus metaphorically alludes to the reproductive powers of the woman's body; for him, although there are traces of the earth metaphor in his representations of the female, the woman is most often associated with corn, with grain, and is the producer of the cooked. He describes her body not as a field giving up grain, not as a furrow to be ploughed by her husband, but as an oven concocting offspring.

The oven metaphor occurs specifically in one of the tales told by Herodotus about the Corinthian tyrant Periander. Telling the story of the Kypselid dynasty of Corinth, he recounts the hiding of the child Kypselos in a chest when a rival family, the Bacchiads, tries to kill him.[2] His mother hides him after their first attempt fails, "in fear lest the second time they got hold of her baby they might feel differently and actually destroy it, she hid it in a chest [*es kupselēn*], which was the most unlikely place she could think of" (*Histories* 5.92). This chest, for which Kypselos is named, is like the chest in which Danaë was locked up with her son Perseus and set adrift in the sea by her father Akrisios.

Periander was Kypselos' son, a blood-thirsty tyrant whose adviser was Thrasyboulos, another tyrant who himself once silently demonstrated to Periander's herald how best to govern by cutting off the heads of the tallest stalks in a field of corn (*Histories* 5.92). Periander understood from this gesture that he too must kill the "highest" of Corinth's citizens. Herodotus illustrates his brutality with the following story:

> . . . anything that Cypselus had left undone in the way of killing or banishing, Periander completed for him. Once, on a single day, he stripped every woman in the town naked, on account of his wife Melissa—but let me explain: Periander had mislaid something which a friend had left in his charge, so he sent to the oracle of the dead, amongst the Thesproti on the river Acheron, to ask where he had put it. The ghost of Melissa appeared and said that she would not tell, either by word or sign; for she was cold and naked, the clothes, which had been buried with her, having been of no use at all, since they had not been burnt. Then, as evidence for her husband that she spoke the truth, she added that Periander had put his loaves into a cold oven [*epi psukhron ton ipnon*]. The messengers reported what they had seen and heard, and Periander, convinced by the token of the cold oven and the loaves (because he had lain with her [*emigē*] after she was dead), immediately issued a proclamation to the effect that every woman in Corinth should come to the temple of Hera. The women obeyed, crowding to the temple in their best clothes as if to a festival, and Periander, who had hidden some of his guards for the purpose, had them all stripped—every one of them, mistresses and maids alike—and their clothes collected into a pit and burnt, while he prayed to the spirit of his wife Melissa. After this he sent to the oracle again, and Melissa's ghost told him where he had put whatever it was that his friend had left with him.
>
> *Histories* 5.92

What can this particular anecdote tell us about the relations between the sexes in the fifth century B.C.? First, Periander was known to have killed his wife Melissa, deliberately or not. His uxoricide was the source of his son's alienation from him. Murder of one's wife was not a common crime, so far as we know, although in one of the most famous legal speeches of antiquity, against Eratosthenes, a cuckolded husband defends himself against the charge of having murdered his wife's lover *in flagrante delicto.*

Periander consults Melissa concerning this deposit, this *parakatathēke,* which is called *xeinikēs,* that is, of a guest, a friend, a stranger, a foreigner. A *parathēkē* is a laying down and is a financial term, perhaps, but it also suggests the placing of something somewhere and thus parallels the deposit Periander made in Melissa. If it is a financial deposit, there is a hint of a further parallelism, since the term for interest, *tokos,* is the same as a word for offspring and comes from the verb meaning to give birth. A financial deposit, like a deposit of semen, might lead to interest, to profit, to increase; in this case, the deposit in the dead wife, like the lost deposit, has no issue.

Periander sends messengers to an oracle that uses the dead, a *nekuoman-*

tēion; the word suggests the very bodies of the dead. The river Acheron is associated with the land of the dead and, although it was localized in Thesprotia, belonged to the realm below the earth, that of the buried. Melissa shivers there and complains, like the dead comrade Odysseus met when he encountered the dead, a companion who begged for burial. Melissa complains not to Periander himself but to a messenger, a mediator who is like the herald who visited Thrasyboulos. She is naked. Her clothes were not buried or burned with her, as we shall see, because Periander undressed her as she lay dead. His act of necrophilia has stripped her, made her an animal, without protective human clothing. Often the dead ask for some favor from the living, but usually in the name of affection or filial piety. Melissa does not rely on piety in the case of Periander. She refuses him what he wants, the interest on his deposit, the lost or buried treasure, until he clothes her. He must undo the act of stripping, give her something as a countergift for the semen he deposited, cover her to protect her from further deposits.

Most interesting is her use of the word *marturion,* the "witness," the token that the messengers are to convey to Periander to prove that it is indeed Melissa who speaks to them at the oracle. She performs an act of exchange with Periander, giving the messenger a token that he, the messenger, will not understand but that will convey meaning to Periander. Like examples of writing to be discussed later, this message is neutral until it is deciphered by the receiver; it is like a *symbolon,* the broken bit of coin or bone that had no significance until its two halves were reunited. Periander must interpret the symbolic message that is opaque for the messenger.

She reminds him that he cast his loaves into a cold oven. It is as if she were reproaching him first for not loving her, then for producing children who will hate him (one of whom, his heir, does hate him), for murdering her and leaving her cold, for leaving her in the land of the dead naked—that is, humiliated and exposed and shivering—and for necrophilia. Her body is the oven, cold because dead, without even the meager heat of the female body. His seed is the bread, the loaves; just as he cuts down the highest sheaves of corn in the field, so he bakes in a cold oven. His acts of sowing and harvesting are all corrupt and defective, his reign a tyranny, his children disastrously ineffectual. This seed will not grow; the loaves will not bake. He violated her corpse or was so overcome with remorse or shock that he wanted to touch her again. Or he found a woman most desirable when most passive, cold, unable to resist or even respond to his desire.

This story recalls another anecdote, told of the Athenian tyrant Peisistratos. His wife was the daughter of a rival noble family, and their marriage was a dynastic matter, an attempt at healing a long series of battles

FIGURE 11. Hera and Zeus on a metope from Selinunte, 627–409 B.C. (Civic Museum, Palermo). Alinari / Art Resource, New York.

between rival houses. Not wanting to conceive an heir by this woman, not wanting, we assume, to mix his family line with hers or to create a child in her receptacle, he "lay with her unnaturally." This is remarkable in light of the law requiring that a man have sex with his wife a prescribed number of times per month. The woman's family was allowed to protest and demand a divorce if this requirement were not met. In fact, Peisistratos' wife returned to her mother, complaining of maltreatment, and it was only through extraordinary measures that he was able to reclaim her as his wife.[3]

Melissa then, according to Herodotus, describes her own dead body as a cold oven. Periander interprets the allegory correctly, knowing that he had sex (or mixed, mingled—*emigē*), with her when she was a *nekros* (a corpse). Herodotus calls her story a *sumbolaion* (a token, symbol; from *sumballō,* throw together). Periander, too faithful, perhaps, to the murdered Melissa, matches his knowledge of his necrophilia against the allegory and recognizes his truth. She is the cold oven, he the baker whose loaves will never cook. The word *sumbolaion* uses the same root, *ballō* (throw), as that in *epebale* (cast in), used here for the loaves, elsewhere for ejaculation.

Periander responds by subjecting all the women of Corinth to his desire. He orders them all to come to the Heraion, shrine of Hera, wife of Zeus, who is associated with the marital role of women (see figure 11). His stripping of all the wives makes cuckolds of all the citizens of his city, and it is this exposure that most strikes Herodotus. He introduces the anecdote with the stripping naked of the women, which is made equivalent to the slaughtering or leveling of all the male citizens who by their eminence threaten his position of superiority. The women, who lived inside their houses and were veiled, protected from the sight of any men not related to them, are thus exposed, given up to Periander's sight. He becomes the possessor of their hidden interiority. His transgression of other men's property, his invasion of the private, secret bodies of the women, as if he had entered and opened all the *gynaikeia* (the women's private rooms) of the city, is like his violation, after her death, of the hidden, private, cold, dead, interior recesses of Melissa, like his attempt to penetrate the buried world of the dead to learn the secret of the lost deposit from the buried recesses of the underworld.

His burning of all the women's clothes warms the earth, Melissa, and the oracle, so that when he sends again to the oracle, he learns the answer to the secret he sought. The heat warms the oven and produces the baked bread, the considered response he wanted.

Herodotus and Baking

Elsewhere in his *Histories,* Herodotus alludes to the analogy between the woman's body and the oven, between sexual intercourse and the practice of baking. Listing the gifts the wealthy Croesus sent to Delphi in honor of the oracle's correct answer to his riddle, he says:

> There were many other gifts of no great importance, including round silver basins; but I must not forget to mention a figure of a woman, in gold, four and a half feet high, said by the Delphians to represent the woman who baked Croesus' bread.
>
> *Histories* 1.51

The statue of the baker is mentioned in part to support the view of the Greeks that Croesus was the wealthiest of men and the most ostentatious. After mentioning the statue, extravagantly inappropriate for a baker, but perhaps appropriate to a sexual partner, Herodotus says that Croesus also sent his own wife's necklaces and girdles. The ornaments of the legally designated sexual partner, the girdle, the loosening of which signified marriage and intercourse, connect the woman baker with the role of sexual partner. Further evidence for this association is provided in Herodotus' account of the revolt of Babylon:

> . . . the Babylonians, in order to reduce the consumption of food, herded together and strangled all the women in the city—each man exempting only his mother, and one other woman whom he chose out of his household to bake his bread for him.
>
> *Histories* 3.151

Here the mother is spared and, rather than the wife, the woman who provides the essentials of life. Sex and bread are again assimilated; the mother is a forbidden sexual partner because of the taboo on incest. Although she might bake bread, another woman is designated as the man's partner, his "bread-baker."

Another passage suggesting the association of sexuality and baking occurs in the story of Perdiccas. This ancestor of Alexander of Macedon was singled out from among his brothers in the following manner. Perdiccas and his brothers, expelled from Argos, are at work in Lebaea in Macedonia:

> . . . in Lebaea the king's wife cooked the food. Now it happened that every time she baked, the loaf intended for the boy Perdiccas swelled to double its proper size. . . . it occurred to the king that it was a warning from heaven of some important event.
>
> *Histories* 8.137

Perdiccas' swollen loaf is a sign of his preeminence in the family; it is he who first wins sovereign power in Macedonia and is the father of the ruling family. His political power is represented phallically here, by the size of his loaf.[4]

Each of these episodes implicitly or explicitly associates sexual practices and power with the baking of bread. The provision of this necessity of life is connected with the exercise of political power; the woman, who is in the story of Melissa explicitly identified with the oven, is elsewhere the baker of bread, the partner in life of the sovereign, the guardian of the loaf.

Cannibalism

If the loaves of bread (*artous*) are not the semen of Periander, then they must stand for his penis, and the plural may indicate that he committed necrophilia more than once. Given the Aristophanic association between eating and sex—the association between the genitals and various kinds of cakes—this passage would suggest a sort of homophagia in Dionysiac terms, the eating of raw flesh as analogous to sexual activity. But if we see the loaves as potential children, the anecdote leads to the complex of myths concerning the devouring of children. If children are baked in the oven, which is the mother's womb, then, like loaves of bread, they are meant to be eaten, consumed by the baker.[5]

In the most important myths of cannibalism of the Greeks, the consumed are children. And they are usually cooked and served to their fathers. An exception is Kronos' swallowing of his children in the *Theogony:* here, significantly, the motive of the father is to stop time and the progression of generations, to avoid the supersession of the next generation. In the other myths we can perhaps see a similar motive. Certainly Hesiod's myth of the metals, positing different "races" of men, suggests anxiety in this culture about inheritance and the displacement of the old by the young. There is none of Homer's heroic resignation to the succession of generations, likened by Glaukos to the generations of leaves on a tree (*Iliad* 6.146).

If children are cooked in the oven of the mother's uterus, then they are cooked again in these myths of cannibalism. Sons are cooked and, most often, devoured by their unwitting fathers. An exception is the father of Pelops, Tantalos, who killed his son and cooked him, planning to serve him to the gods in order to test them, to see if they could tell the difference between human flesh and that of an animal. Tantalos, Niobe's father, committed various crimes against the gods; in another myth he abused the hospitality of the gods, among whom he had been admitted.

The myth of Kronos devouring his children, memorably depicted by Goya, connects also with the notion of stones as seeds or as offspring. According to the account in Hesiod's *Theogony:*

> Rheia succumbed to Kronos's love and bore him illustrious
> children. . . .
> But majestic Kronos kept on swallowing [*katepine*] each child
> as it moved from the holy womb toward the knees;
> his purpose was to prevent any other child of the Sky Dwellers
> from holding the kingly office among immortals.
>
> 453–62

According to Earth and Heaven, Gaia and Ouranos, Kronos was destined to be overcome by his own son. Rhea feeds Kronos a great stone wrapped in swaddling clothes in place of their son, Zeus. Earth tricks Kronos, and he vomits up his offspring: "The stone last swallowed was first to come out" [*prōton d'exemesen lithon, hon pumaton katepinen*]. Zeus sets the stone up at Delphi, where according to Pausanias it was daily anointed with oil (*Description of Greece* 10.24.6). This myth reveals a motive for consuming one's offspring: the avoidance of replacement by one's children. Only Zeus is able to interrupt the sequence of time by defeating all rivals and by refusing Thetis as a bride—Thetis who was to bear a son greater than his father.

Philomela, sister of Procne, was raped by her sister's husband Tereus, who then cut out her tongue to prevent her from accusing him. Philomela communicates his crime to Procne by weaving her story. Procne revenges herself by serving him their cooked son Itys at a meal. The gods change the characters of the story to birds.[6] Procne's motive, like that of the filicide Medea, is to destroy her husband's house by destroying his descendance, the prized possession of the Greek male. Sophocles' Electra compares herself to a mourner for Itys: "Suited rather to my heart / the bird of mourning / that 'Itys, Itys' ever does lament, / the bird of crazy sorrow, Zeus's messenger" (*Electra* 147–49).

The myth of Agamemnon's house contains another story of inadvertent cannibalism. Atreus, son of Pelops of the ivory shoulder, at odds with his brother Thyestes, fed him the flesh of his children because, in some versions of the myth, Atreus' wife had been Thyestes' mistress. She gave a divine portent—the lamb with golden fleece, which had appeared in Atreus' flocks as a sign that he should be king—to her lover Thyestes. (Euripides gives a version free from cannibalism in *Electra* [699ff.]. The cannibalism is referred to in Euripides' *Orestes* [1007–10].) The cannibalism in the story of Tantalos and Pelops thus continues, transformed into an unwitting act by the father. The only survivor of the feast among Thyestes' children is Aigisthos, who, becoming Clytemnestra's lover, helps her destroy Atreus' son Agamemnon.

The sacrifice of her daughter Iphigenia is another motive for Clytemnestra's murder of Agamemnon. Here the theme of sacrifice, implicit in other related myths of cannibalism, is explicit; the substitution of a deer, an animal that might be consumed after sacrifice, suggests the theme of cannibalism in the family's history. It is linked to any story of human sacrifice, since, except in the case of a holocaust in which the whole offering was burned for the gods, the worshippers ate the flesh of the sacrificed animal.

Herodotus tells another story of a father fed his son for revenge. Astyages, ruler of the Medes, wished to do away with his grandson because of his daughter's prophetic dream predicting that her child would rule in Astyages' place. He ordered a member of his household, Harpagos, to kill the child. Harpagos fails in his mission, and the child is later discovered living with the family of a cowherd. Astyages then invites Harpagos to send his own son to court, as he intends to celebrate his grandson's deliverance with a sacrifice to the gods (*Histories* 1.118). Harpagos is pleased that Astyages is not angry, and he sends his only son to the king:

> When Harpagus's son arrived at the palace, Astyages had him butchered, cut up into joints and cooked, roasting some, boiling the rest, and having the whole properly prepared for the table . . . To Harpagus was served the flesh of his son: all of it, except the head, the hands, and the feet, which had been put separately on a platter covered with a lid.
>
> When Harpagus thought he had eaten as much as he wanted, Astyages asked him if he had enjoyed his dinner. He answered that he had enjoyed it very much indeed, whereupon those whose business it was to do so brought in the boy's head, hands, and feet in the covered dish, stood by Harpagus's chair and told him to lift the lid and take what he fancied. Harpagus removed the cover and saw the fragments of his son's body.
>
> *Histories* 1.119

All these myths of cannibalism speak to the complex of metaphors connecting intercourse with baking, reproduction with cooking, the production of food with the reproduction of children. The generational conflicts in Greek culture that are stressed by these myths of paternal devouring of offspring suggest the difficulties of supersession, especially in this society undergoing rapid social change and questioning the traditional social arrangements and religious practices. Instead of yielding to their sons, the mythic Greek fathers, like Oedipus and Periander, destroy them; the mother, the receptacle in which those sons were produced, is merely a conduit in which the seeds are placed, the space in which the future conflict is generated.

Arkesilaos and the Corrupted Mother

Another Herodotean story refers to the image of the oven and to a hero's mother in a narrative where male misreading of the figure of the oven leads to destruction. The first Arkesilaos of Cyrene, on coming to power over the city, quarreled with his brothers, who left Cyrene and founded the neighboring city of Barca. Arkesilaos' grandson, also named Arkesilaos, exiled himself, because of civic strife, from Cyrene. When he consulted the oracle at Delphi about the possibilities of return to his city, he was told:

> . . . when you return to your country, be gentle. If you find the oven full of jars, do not bake them but send them away downwind. But if you do heat the oven, enter not the land surrounded by water, for otherwise you will die, and the best of the bulls with you.
>
> *Histories* 4.162–65

Arkesilaos "forgets" or misreads this oracle. When he returns to Cyrene and finds that some of his enemies have shut themselves up in a high tower, he stacks wood around their hiding place and burns them alive. Realizing too late that "this was what the oracle had meant when the Priestess warned him, if he should find the jars in the oven, not to bake them," he tried to avoid death but was killed by the people of Barca. The oven, a figure for reproduction and life, was perversely misused by Arkesilaos, who paid for his misuse with his own life in the city of his grandfather's brothers.

Arkesilaos' own mother, Pheretime, also represents a disturbed reading of the positions meant to be held by various members of the ancient family. In exile, Pheretime continually asked her host for an army to restore her family to power in Cyrene; her host, Euelthon, finally gave her a golden spindle and distaff with wool ready to work on it. When she objected, asking once again for an army, her host replied that "he had sent her a present which, unlike an army, he thought suitable to her sex" (*Histories* 4.162).

When Pheretime finally got her army, she showed how little she honored the traditional roles of weaving woman, the guardian of the hearth, and the passive mother-oven. When those who had killed her son were captured, she impaled them on stakes around the wall of the city. "She also cut off their wives' breasts, and stuck those up, too, in the same position." Her act of violence and revenge, so uncharacteristic of a Greek woman, seeks to protect the interior space of the city rather than the hollow which is the *oikos,* the household, the space set apart for the woman. She is punished for her violation of the cultural order, as Herodotus points out: "Pheretima's web of life was also not woven happily to the end. No sooner had she returned to Egypt after her revenge upon the people of Barca, than she died a horrible death, her body seething with worms while she was still alive" (*Histories* 4.205). The woman who might have been content with a woman's life, weaving and entreasuring the goods of the *oikos,* dies horribly through the spontaneous corruption of the living body, in a parodic inversion of the spontaneously reproductive female body.[7]

Ovens

The female body is sometimes perceived by the Greeks as dangerously self-sufficient, as enabling female autonomy; a stronger representation insists on male ownership of that body's fertility and its interiority, on the maintenance of its inviolability. The oven analogy alienates the processes of reproduction from the autonomy of the parthenogenetic earth. And it is thus an alternative to the self-sufficient earth and to the furrow. The possibility of ownership and the need for mediation become apparent with the oven analogy. Ovens are property more liable to exchange than fields of the earth, given the Greeks' ideas of ancestral land-holding. Ovens seem to produce things to eat, but they in fact contribute only a receptacle for the process of baking the father's loaves. Children, as the products of the male's labor, can be seen as the inevitable victims of the hungry father or of the traitorous father who is punished for his treachery by being forced to consume his own child's flesh.[8]

Aristophanes and Ovens

Aristophanes, the great comic poet of the later fifth century B.C., frequently used the metaphor of cooking to refer to sexual intercourse, referring to the female sexual organ as an oven. He connects the metaphor with sexual pleasure and the desirability of abundant reproduction.

Aristophanes' *Peace,* for example, was produced in 421, perhaps just before the "Peace of Nikias," which was meant to end the Peloponnesian War.[9] It abounds with culinary obscenity. It begins with a dung beetle dining voraciously on cakes made of dung. Its master plans to ride it to Zeus and to feed it on his own excrement. As Jeffrey Henderson points out, the obscenities of the first part of *The Peace* are scatological, and they put the discomforts of wartime in comic relief; in the second part, Aristophanes uses sexual imagery to celebrate the peace.[10] But the two contrasting worlds are bound together with culinary and gustatory imagery. For example, his use of *empureuein* means to "roast the phallus in coitus" (*The Peace* 1137). Henderson says:

> *optēsō* at *Aves* 1102, used by Dicaeopolis of his penis (he promises to "bake" it in the serving boy), has an obscene tone, like *optanion* at *Pax* 891 . . . The image in these two places is of the cunt or anus as an oven in which to bake the penis in coitus. It is worthy noting that the heating of the phallus, too, was said to be desirable; in *CA* 5.16 Dem. a woman remarks that dildoes lack the heat . . . of a real penis.[11]

The remark provides further evidence of the widespread belief in women's lower body temperature. It is interesting that Aristophanes refers to the process of baking and roasting not in relation to reproduction, to the maturation of the embryo, but rather to the act of intercourse itself. The woman is assumed to lack heat, if she finds the dildo insufficiently warm. But the act of congress generates heat, enough heat to cook the phallus.

In *The Peace,* the female's pubic hair is said to be black from the smoke of the councillors' pans:

> TRYGAEUS: Have a good look at all the delights I'm providing you with. You will be able without delay to lift her legs high in the air and then have yourself a feast of a time! You will observe her capacious oven.
>
> SLAVE: Whee-shew! It's gorgeous! Lovely and sooty too! I bet the Council stirred things up a bit in there before the war!

[touti d'horate touptanion hēmin kalon.
dia tauta kai kekapnike tar' entautha gar
pro tou polemou ta lasana tēi boulēi pot'ēn.]

The Peace 891–93

Henderson points out that in *The Wasps* (line 1374), *to melan* is used for pubic hair, indicating a black spot from smoke, and it "may have been a common slang term." He also notes that in *The Knights* (line 1286) "stirring up the coals" refers to cunnilingus.[12] (In *Thesmophoriazusae* [line 912], the arms of Helen become her coals.) Another reference to the female organs as baking hot coals includes "having a young girl and stoking the/her coals" (*ekhonth'hetairan kai skaleuont'anthrakas, The Peace* 440).

The images of peacetime contentment include sex and food in metaphorical exchange; eating is like intercourse, intercourse is like eating. The chorus describes the pleasures of peace:

Roast peas and acorns . . .
That's what I like to eat!

. . . And when I'm slightly tips-
y and the wife is in the bath,
I'll taste young Thratta's lips!
[*kanthrakidzōn tourebinthou,*
tēn te phēgon emporeuōn,
khama tēn thraittan kunōn,
tēs gunaikos loumenēs.]

The Peace 1136–39

Thratta is the Thracian slave-girl; *kunōn* means erotic kissing.

Trygaeus digs up Peace, who has been buried by the gods, and the result is sexual celebration. Fertility returns to the fields with the return of Eirene (lines 536, 706–8, 867ff., 1329–31). She and her attendants, Theoria and Opora, smell sweetly of harvest, perfumes, and wine. Trygaeus says in a double entendre: "Why, it makes me want to go home too and shove a mattock into the dear old earth again!" (*hōst'egōg'ēdē 'pithumō k 'autos elthein eis agron / kai triainoun tēi dikellēi dia khronou to gēdion,* 569–70). Opora is the harvest and Trygaeus the harvester; she is his prize. Peace is equated with sex, fertility, and plenty. Even the dung beetle will stay and eat Ganymede's ambrosia.

The imagery at the end of the play, a celebration of peace, focuses on harvesting the fruits of the earth, eating and cooking and enjoying her bounty, and on celebratory sex; the comedy ends with a hymn to Hymen, god of marriage:

What shall we do with Harvest so fair? . . .
We'll gather her in and lay her all bare!

[*trugēsomen autēn, trugēsomen autēn.*]

1338–39

Trugan means to gather fruit and crops; the bride is to be "harvested." Henderson calls this "a marvelous example of the thematic and symbolic use of obscene double entendre."[13] The play ends with the command for the crowd to eat *plakountas,* "flat-cakes," elsewhere used to refer to the female genitals (1357).

Throughout *The Peace,* Aristophanes takes up the analogy between intercourse and cooking. Women's bodies are not only the fields to be ploughed, sown, and harvested; they are also the plants growing in the fields, the ovens in which the loaves are placed, and the edible delicacies produced from that oven. Unlike the tragic discourse of Sophocles—which associates the plowed field of Jocasta's body with incest, catastrophe for the city, and suicide—Aristophanes' comic analogies suggest the fluidity of invention in the Athenian culture and its penchant for metaphorizing, as well as the centrality of the female body as a site for reproduction and for erotic pleasure.

Ancient Medicine

Aristophanes is not alone in using the analogy between intercourse and cooking, between the oven and the woman's body. Ancient medicine used the analogy between cooking, coction, *pepsis,* and processes in the body to account for the workings of disease, as well as to describe the growth of the embryo in the uterus. Coction and mixture (*krasis*) lead to a proper balance in the body and thus to health: "A man is in the best possible condition when there is complete coction [*hotan pan pessētai*] and rest" (*Ancient Medicine* 19).[14]

G. E. R. Lloyd discusses ancient medicine's views on the woman in "The Female Sex: Medical Treatment and Biological Theories in the Fifth and Fourth Centuries B.C."[15] He describes the debate in pre-Aristotelian medical texts concerning the issue of women's contribution to generation. Some ancient medical authors disputed the claim, expressed by Apollo in the *Eumenides,* among others, that women are simply receptacles for the male seed.

The author of *On Regimen* says: "The males of all species are warmer and drier, and the females moister and colder" (34). This writer is somewhat unusual in attributing to women a contribution to the embryo, although he shares the common view that the female is weaker than the male: "Male and female have the power to fuse into one solid, both because both are nourished in both and also because soul is the same thing in all living creatures, although the body of each is different" (*On Regimen* 28). Nonetheless, he sees the female as inevitably weaker than the male;

each parent "secretes" bodies: "Now if the bodies [*ta sōmata*] secreted from both happen to be male, they grow up to the limit of the available matter, and the babies become men [*andres*] brilliant in soul and strong in body. . . . If the secretion from the man be male and that of the woman female, should the male gain the mastery, the weaker soul combines with the stronger" (28). He continues, accounting for the production of three kinds of men and three kinds of women, and ends with this analogy:

> If anyone doubts that soul combines with soul, let him consider coals. Let him place lighted coals on lighted (or, according to Littré, "unlighted") coals, strong on weak, giving them nourishment [*trophēn*]. They will all present a like substance, and one will not be distinguished from another, but the whole will be like the body in which they are kindled. And when they have consumed the available nourishment, they dissolve into invisibility. So too it is with the soul of man [*anthrōpinē*].
>
> *On Regimen* 29

Here, as is customary, the process of generation is associated with heat, coction, and consumption; here, too, we see the alternative tradition to that adopted by Aristotle, one which argues for a contribution, albeit a weaker one, from the female to the embryo.

Baking the Embryo

In the Hippocratic treatise called "The Nature of the Child," we encounter the analogy between embryonic development and baking:

> As it inflates (in the womb), the seed forms a membrane around itself; for its surface, because of its viscosity, stretches around it without a break, in just the same way as a thin membrane is formed on the surface of bread when it is being baked; the bread rises as it grows warm and inflates, and as it is inflated, so the membraneous surface forms.
>
> The Nature of the Child, 12.325

It is important to situate these texts generically, as part of a body of medical texts produced in this period, which are involved in debates concerning contested matters of therapy and cause. It is also important *not* to maintain the scholarly tradition of isolating generically distinct discourses from one another, of considering such texts as the province only of historians of science. To read these medical texts in light of the Aristophanic play about baking and intercourse, and vice versa, is to see them as part of a cultural network, as the horizon of speculation about the female body reached through the process of analogy.

Aristotle and Cooking

The traditional oven metaphor allows for the image of a devouring mother, one fed through the vaginal mouth with grain, typical of the Greek city's diet, assimilable to the seed of the male. The impregnation of the woman is consumption of the seed by the woman. But the metaphors are often mixed. In other embryological accounts, the embryo itself is not devoured; it, in fact, consumes the substance of the mother and grows.

The trope of the body as oven is illuminated by the discussion of the Greeks' ideas on hot and cold in Marcel Detienne's *Gardens of Adonis.* There he gathers evidence to illuminate the Greek representation of women as naturally colder than men, a "thermal prejudice" as Giulia Sissa calls it, that supports some of Aristotle's ideas about the natural inferiority of women. Hesiod warns that men are feeblest in the Dog Days, the hottest days of summer; since women are warmer than usual, their extraordinary heat, combined with that of men, will overheat and dry out the male partner (Hesiod, *Works and Days* 586–88).

Although his work is later than that of the fifth-century writers, Aristotle's work on embryology provides valuable evidence for the Greek notions concerning the relative warmth of the male body, and for the analogy between embryological and culinary concoction. The cooking of food is what distinguishes animals from human beings. Aristotle argues that the body continues the process of cooking, of "coction," *pepsis,* after food is consumed. Semen is simply the final stage of that coction, the most digested, most "civilized" form of the body's blood and food. Menstrual fluid is less cooked, since the female body is naturally cooler than the male (*GA* 726b30).[16] Aristotle seems to describe fecundation at some points in his argument as a "curdling"; the masculine semen is warm and compensates for the colder nature of the woman's body, completing its cooking.

Giulia Sissa shows in detail how the pre-Socratic theory of residua, semen as a product of the whole body, as the source of the embryo, in fact allows for the logical possibility of female parthenogenesis, which Aristotle seeks to avoid. In his view, the male cannot be parthenogenetic, any more than can the female, since the semen is considered to be soul without body. The menstrual fluid is necessary, as material is to form. Aristotle seems to efface the danger implicit in having the child reside in the female's stomach.[17] It is she who is devoured; the milk she provides for the child is simply a mediate stage between the menstrual flow and that same substance transformed by the animating sperm into an embryo. When she has ceased lactating, her menstrual flow will resume.

How is the notion of the cold female body then reconcilable with the representation of that body as an oven? It is first conceivable in a model of reproduction as male parthenogenesis, a pre-Socratic, Hippocratic view of semen as residue. Thus the male's semen, like Periander's loaves, would be placed in the female receptacle, which, however, according to the traditional view, is not yet an oven, being cold. But the parthenogenetic male semen provides its own heat, and the female body is a container for the deposit and for the self-generating process of cooking. Aristotle discards the possibility of female parthenogenesis while preserving the dominance of the male principle of soul; his work perpetuates the metaphorical connection between the female body and the oven in that it conceives of the female body as cooler than the male and as the passive material from which the embryo grows. The great scientific work of Aristotle, read and accepted as truth for centuries, thus takes up the metaphorical system expressed both in Herodotus and in Aristophanes, that the female body is a container, like an oven, to be filled up with the semen, which provides soul and form to the material container.

Trophonios

Cultic evidence supports the comic, medical, and philosophical writers' analogy between cooking and generation. Pausanias was a travel writer who gave detailed descriptions of the ancient world in the second century A.D. Although his work is late and cannot be used to account reliably for the state of things in the fifth century B.C., his evidence is often useful for verifying the survival of monuments and objects known to have existed in the classical period.

Pausanias' evidence demonstrates the persistence of certain notions of cult; he describes the oracle of Trophonios, mentioned in Euripides' *Ion,* in terms that recall the ancient connection between the earth and ovens, between the processes of baking and of concoction of the embryo, between burial and placement in another kind of container, the oven. (Trophonios apparently means "the Feeder," from the verb *trephō.*) According to Pausanias, the preparation for consultation at the oracle of Trophonios was most elaborate. He first recounts the myth of Trophonios: Erginus consulted the oracle at Delphi concerning his childlessness; the Pythia said, alluding to the traditional analogy between ploughing and intercourse:

> Erginus, son of Cylmenus Presboniades,
> Late thou camest seeking offspring, but even now
> To the old plough tree put a new tip
> [*histoboēi geronti neēn potiballe korōnēn*].
>
> *Description of Greece* 9.37.4

Erginus gets a new wife, and she bears two children: Trophonios and Agamedes. Trophonios was supposed to have been Apollo's child. The two become famous builders of sanctuaries. They built the temple of Apollo at Delphi and a treasury for Hyrieus, which they systematically robbed until Agamedes was trapped inside. Trophonios cut off his brother's head so that he would not expose Trophonios when tortured. Then, "The earth opened and swallowed up Trophonius [*kai Trophōnion men entautha edexato hē gē diastasa*]" (9.37.7). Trophonios, son of Apollo, is taken up, consumed by the gaping earth.

Anyone who consulted the oracle of Trophonios at Lebadeia, near Delphi, first spent a certain number of days in a sacred building. During this time he abstained from hot baths and bathed in the river Hercyna; he made many sacrifices of animals whose entrails were examined to determine whether Trophonios would welcome him. If a sacrificed ram's entrails were propitious, he prepared for his descent. During the night he was bathed in the river by two thirteen-year-old boys; he drank from the fountains of Lethe (Forgetfulness) and Mnemosyne (Memory); and he then looked at an image said to have been made by Daedalus and went to the oracle dressed in linen.

> The oracle is on the mountain, beyond the grove. Beyond it is a circular basement of white marble, the circumference of which is about that of the smallest threshing floor [*periodos de tēs krēpidos kata halōn tēn elakhistēn estin*], while its height is just short of two cubits. On the basement stand spikes, which, like the cross-bars holding them together, are of bronze, while through them has been made a double door. Within the enclosure is a chasm in the earth [*khasma gēs*], not natural [*ouk automaton*], but artificially constructed after the most accurate masonry. The shape of this structure is like that of a bread-oven [*kribanōi*].
>
> *Description of Greece* 9.39.9–10

This is a very curious description that combines autochthonous and culinary metaphors. The basement is like a threshing floor on which the grain is spread. The consultant of the oracle, the son of earth, is like the grain to be threshed. The earth is the threshing floor, the door like the chasm which swallowed up Trophonios. And it is like an oven into which the grain, child of earth, descends. He holds barley cakes, kneaded with honey, and pushes his feet down into the hole in the earth, trying to insert his knees. "After his knees the rest of his body is at once swiftly drawn in, just as the largest and most rapid river will catch a man in its eddy and carry him under" (*Description of Greece* 9.39).

"After this those who have entered the shrine learn the future, not in one and the same way in all cases, but by sight sometimes and at other times by hearing. The return upwards is by the same mouth [*stomiou*], the feet darting out first" (*Description of Greece* 9.39). This description reveals the tenacity of the traditional metaphorical structures; the oracle is a threshing floor, spiked door, chasm, and oven. One entered it feet first, in a reverse birth, through a mouth, and came out the same way.

The word *halōs,* threshing floor, is the name of a circular "piazza" sanctuary at Delphi. The word *zōnai,* used of bronze cross-bars, is used for women's belts or girdles; to loosen the *zōnē* is to have sex (*Odyssey* 2.245) with a bride and later can refer to childbirth. The chasm is belted like a woman's body. It has a double door, like lips, like the gates of a city, like the door of a house, like the folds of a tablet. A *khasma . . . khthonos,* a chasm in the earth, is said by Creusa to have swallowed up her father Erechtheus in Euripides' *Ion* (line 281). The Homeric hero Agamemnon speaks of the earth gaping open for him: "let the wide earth open to take me" (*moi khanoi eureia khthōn, Iliad* 4.182). Death is the opening up, the swallowing by the earth. The consultation of this oracle is thus both a death and a rebirth.

The ambiguity of the descent is confirmed in Pausanias' use of the comparison with a bread oven, *kribanos.* Liddell, Scott, and Jones define it thus: "covered earthen vessel, wider at bottom than at top, wherein bread was baked by putting hot embers around it."[18] The word is used by Herodotus in describing the habits of the Egyptians: "Those who wish to use the byblus at its very best roast it before eating in a redhot oven (*en kribanōi*)" (*Histories* 2.92). The papyrus plant, then, that figures so prominently in the Aeschylean tragedy of the Danaïds, is prepared in this oven, like the body of Pandora. The term is also used for the potter's oven.

The language of Pausanias' description shows that this is a particular form of earth oracle. The earth that swallowed up Trophonios does not kill those who consult the oracle at Lebadeia; Pausanias says, "They say that no one who has made the descent has been killed, save only one of the bodyguard of Demetrius" (*Description of Greece* 9.39.12). This man did not perform the proper rites and "was not cast out of the sacred mouth [*stoma to hieron*]." There is a danger of death here, but this seems to be a place, like Cumae, where one may descend to the underworld and be allowed to emerge as one of the twice-dead. The imagery and language suggest that the shrine is a chasm, door, mouth, and, most of all, oven from which the consultant is reborn.[19]

The Trophonios shrine oven is particularly interesting (although the evidence is rather late), since this oven greatly resembles a vase, and it therefore has aspects of Pandora and of the container vases. In addition, it is the anteroom, as it were, to a chasm in the earth that leads first to Chaos—that is, the first entity in Hesiod's cosmogony—then to Earth, who is the second being who emerges out of the yawning and gaping Chaos. The consultant of the oracle thus passes into the earth, into a state of death and even of nonbeing, and then is born again. The ritual drinking from the streams of Forgetfulness and Memory recalls the myth of Er in Plato's *Republic* and other accounts of experiences after death.

The oven is a logically intermediate form between the earth, the furrow (different from the parthenogenetic, uncultivated Ge of Hesiod), and the blank tablet. The tablet is meaningless without inscription. Earth begins as autonomous, then comes to need planting, sowing, harvesting—that is, male agency. The oven needs always to be filled and heated. The representations of the female body as an oven are most consistent with its comparisons with the earth, even the unfurrowed, parthenogenetic earth. The oven need not be broken into; it is created with a mouth, filled up with the equivalent of grain, or (if it is seen as a site of cremation) with bones.[20]

The oven is a suggestive metaphor for the woman's body, one that may derive from neolithic times but that survives well into the postclassical period. It has pleasurable associations, as, for example, in the Aristophanic text. It continues the theme of the earth/body metaphor while furthering the process of alienation from the earth. The oven is not autonomous, needs fueling, is a possession—quite unlike the self-sufficient and bountiful earth of Hesiod's *Theogony*. It thus occupies an important logically mediate stage in the spectrum of metaphors for the female body, one which responds to the Athenians', and others', gradual sense of alienation from the traditional agricultural practices of their ancestors.

Seven

TABLET

> The Greek *pinax* or *deltos* consists of a framed board, the interior of which is filled with a mixture of wax, coloured by pitch, *maltha,* and is then written on with a pointed stylus. Several such boards can be held together by a leather thong.
>
> E. G. Turner
> *Athenian Books in the Fifth and Fourth Centuries B.C.*

> The wax tablet . . . comprised a wooden base, rebated with raised edges, and the hollow filled with a sheet of wax on which letters could be scratched with an iron or wooden stylus. The tablet could be erased by using the handle of the stylus to polish out the letters; the friction of rapid rubbing melts the wax slightly, and smooths the waxen surface for re-use.
>
> Donald Jackson
> *The Story of Writing*

The woman as field-to-be-ploughed is perhaps the most stereotypical analogy used throughout Greek culture, in the marriage ceremony, in ritual, and in lyric, tragic, and comic poetry. Another metaphor, rivaling that of the field and furrow, is woman's body as a tablet, as a writing surface. Although it coexists with the language of plowing and sowing, especially in the texts of tragedy, the metaphor represents a recoding, a transformation, of the language of agriculture associated with the archaic period, an acknowledgment of the new place of writing in fifth century culture. If Sophocles betrays an anxiety about abandoning the territory of Attica and the traditional practices of agriculture, if these practices are seen as deeply implicated in the religious life of the city and in the rituals that link human and agricultural productivity, then painters, poets, and writers of the sixth and fifth centuries begin to establish a new metaphorical nexus—a link between intercourse and writing. The body of woman, no longer the productive, parthenogenetic earth, is rather a blank surface, a *tabula rasa,* a field not for plowing but for inscription. The metaphor of inscription is less direct and less obvious. The woman is the *deltos,* the pubic triangle (like a delta) to be sowed/inscribed; she is the tablet folded up on itself, the papyrus that must be unfolded to be deciphered.

The metaphor of writing is more ambiguous than that of ploughing. The plough leaves its furrow, its mark, and then the sower leaves seeds that sprout new life. The stylus makes its mark and the marks themselves are the seeds. Marks on the tablet both inscribe possession and generate new marks. But the connection between writing and human reproduction is more attenuated than the connection with sowing seed. The myth of Kadmos contains both as a matrix; the metaphor of inscription is more alienated; it is the sign of a culture and economy more distant from primary production. Writing--the marks of commerce and literate culture—may produce income and the food and shelter necessary for life, but it does so in a more mediated way. The farmer sows seed and harvests grain; the merchant keeps his accounts, earns money, and with it buys bread. In this chapter I consider various examples of the analogy between the woman's body and a writing surface, from the rounded exterior of a ceramic vase to the wax tablet of a juror in the Athenian courts. The earlier examples rely on the analogy between various objects used as writing surfaces and the female body. In later texts, the connection between the female body and the writing tablet is made more explicit. The uses of this metaphorical complex echo the metaphors used of the ploughed earth, but the tablet, as a passive, receptive surface, is denied the power to generate new letters or new words. The metaphor of the tablet represents the analogue most logically distant from the metaphor of the autonomous, parthenogenetic, fertile earth.

Pindar and Phallic Inscription

Pindar addresses Aineas, "who trained the chorus" for the performance in Arcadia of the sixth *Olympian,* thus:

> for you're a trusty messenger, bearer [*skutala*]
> of the Muses' code, sweet bowl of thunderous songs.
>
> 90–91

A *skutala* is "at Sparta, staff or baton, used as a cypher for writing dispatches, a strip of leather being rolled slantwise around it, on which the dispatches were written lengthwise so that when unrolled they were unintelligible. . . . (C)ommanders abroad had a staff of like thickness, round which they rolled these strips, and so were able to read the dispatches" (Liddell, Scott, and Jones). This coding device, unique in the Greek world, may be contrasted with the tablet, the most commonly used surface for inscription in daily life.

Pindar's *skutala,* which also appears in the *Lysistrata,* is a fascinating object, a *fascinum* like the phallus itself. It is a coder, an instrument for making language incomprehensible to the uninitiated. The rod and its equivalent, the second rod, make the message legible after the strip of leather has been unrolled and lost its sense. The carrier of the message himself may not know the content of the coded strip, so that he is like the vehicle, the medium of the code; the *destinataire* and *destinateur* at each end of the communication share the same desire, or a mimesis of the same, each a copy of the other.[1]

Pindar's messenger is eminently phallic, and his Spartan metaphor is appropriate to his aristocratic, athletic, probably pederastic art. The chorus trainer, Aineas, is a phallic presence, wrapped up like a may pole, who unfurls the Muses' songs around his own body. He is the *logos* who animates Pindar's distant text, the mixing bowl in which the festive drinks are prepared. In the metaphor of the *deltos,* the writing tablet is folded up and must be spread open; but in that of the *skutala* the strip of leather is wrapped around the body of the baton, adorning it with signs that are made intelligible again through its presence. Writing is only for the initiated, those who can decode it through the presence of the interpreter, the messenger who is the phallic extension of Pindar himself.[2]

Creation and the Potter

As a counter to the phallic representation of the writing surface exhibited in the *skutala,* the most common representations of writing present analogies with the female body and its receptive interiority. Just as the working space, the field for labor, becomes more and more alienated from the earth, so the woman's body is instrumentalized, becoming a mere surface to be inscribed. The division of labor between mental and physical labor widens as the Athenian economy becomes more and more dependent on slavery. The writers of the fifth century come to see themselves more as writers than as citizens participating in the city's political life; the legends told of the alienated Euripides, who supposedly composed in a cave far from the city, may speak to a new self-consciousness about the literary artist within the ancient city.[3]

The metaphor of the woman as writing surface is the most abstracted form of the metaphorical system I have discussed. It may have developed from the representation of the female body as a ceramic vase. Hephaistos, as potter, makes the first woman from earth and water. Homer, too, says human beings are made of these elements. The analogy between the woman's body and the vase is especially significant here, because ceramic vases were important sites of "inscription" as well as of pictorial representation and narrative. Even earlier, however, we can see the analogy between bodies and vases and the ways in which abstract ornamentation illuminates the later metaphors of inscription in the body.

If the woman's body is like a jar, a *pithos,* as I argued in chapter 5, a vase molded from earth, then it is like those real *pithoi* used to store grains, oil, wine—to hold the goods of life; the vase thus resembles the earth itself. And vases were used at various epochs to contain the bones and ashes of the dead. As Donna C. Kurtz and John Boardman tell us in *Greek Burial Customs:*

> [In the Geometric Period] the most common ash urns were clay vases—neck and shoulder handled *amphorae,* the latter having replaced the belly handled *amphorae* early in the geometric period, although these continued to be made in a monumental form. . . . very small children and infants were buried in pots—*pithoi,* hydriai, amphorae and jugs of coarse ware with or without incised decoration, or of finer ware with . . . painted patterns. . . . The *pithoi* normally stood upright. . . . The mouth of the pot was closed by a smaller one, a shard, a stone slab, or a lump of clay.[4]

The modern scholar, like Hesiod, uses anthropomorphic terms to describe the clay jar. The *pithos* stands and has lips, neck, and shoulders. Some of them have "knobs" that evolve from earlier vases with nipples. Vases are like bodies, especially women's bodies; they are like the earth, the clay from which they are made; they hold grains, sustain life, and receive the dead. And like Pandora's body, they are decorated.

Geometry

In the Geometric Period the rounded body of the jar was covered with abstract signs, in a caressing of the surface that absorbs that surface. The most magnificent example of Geometric vase-painting occurs on the Dipylon vase, found in the cemetery area of Athens (see figure 12). It is a funerary vase that bears a representation of a funeral, the laying out of the corpse and mourners with extended arms (probably women), surrounded by elaborate patternings of abstract design. We can read the proliferating complexity and elaboration of shapes, the fertile genius of Geometric art, as both celebration and containment. The vase contained death, the remains of the deceased. The vase both depicts the body and is itself a body that contains the decay, the ashes of a body. The brilliance of the decoration—prolific and hard-edged, both linear and multiple—keeps at bay the chaos of bodily disintegration. As the earth contains corruption and gives forth new life, so the vase contains the dead and allows for the proliferation of new life, the generation of endless new forms and new shapes.

The vase is like the earth, the body of the mother, pregnant with signs, with the multiplicity of creation; it is she who gives and receives life. The swastika, the meander, stars, zigzags, lines—all suggest the variety of the forms of existence, the variety of creatures worked into Pandora's adornment; all are contained by the shape of the vase, inscribed upon its roundness.

The worship of the earth goddess and the making of figurines of ivory

FIGURE 12. Attic vase from the Dipylon cemetery (National Museum, Athens). Alinari / Art Resource, New York.

and other early materials were apparently important aspects of prehistoric cult. But we can see in the decoration of the vase an ambivalence, a desire to adorn but also to control its surface. There is a quality of fragmentation and colonization of the vase's fullness; a desire to win, through decoration, the assurance of the reproduction of the beasts and fishes of land and sea.[5]

The lines can also be read as *desmoi,* as bonds, as lines that cover and remain in the surface of the body as markers of possession, limiting and containing its movement. The colonizing, binding quality—the desire to control through inscription—is evident on a ceramic figurine of a woman from Boeotia made in the sixth century B.C. (see figure 3). The lines on the body of the figure ornament her, but they also constrict, imperialize, and map her as the territory of the maker of the work of art. She is rendered symmetrical, static, a thing to be regarded. Decoration is worship, but it is also bondage—the mark of possession, the appropriation of the surface of the body. The figurine is a thing, a commodity to be exchanged, traded, sold, or given as an offering, and, like a coin, it carries on it the signs of its maker and master.

The writing on later vases also speaks to the reader, the viewer of its rounded form. It is usually a claim to ownership or domination of the form, and it is often an appeal for admiration or desire. At writing's origin is the Geometric decoration, which colonizes as it keeps death at bay.[6] R. M. Cook gives a concise catalog of inscription on vases.[7] If the painted decoration on the Boeotian figurine indicates a desire for both decoration and control of the body, then the inscription of letters on painted pottery, an important feature of Greek ceramic art, has consequences for the metaphor between the body and the vase. Inscriptions on vases first appeared in the latter part of the eighth century, that is, probably contemporaneously with Homer and perhaps with Hesiod. These inscriptions become more numerous in the sixth century. Painted or incised, stamped or in ink, they could be placed on the vase before and after its baking in the kiln.

Some vases are signed by painter and/or potter. "The earliest certain signatures are of the second quarter or middle of the seventh century." In Attica, signatures were most common around 500 B.C. The vases themselves, like bodies with tongues, are made to speak and to designate their authors: "*Egrapse* and *epoiēse* are the two normal verbs of signature—'so and so painted me' and 'so and so made me.'" *Graphein* means both to paint and to write, so the reference is interestingly ambiguous; it is the inscription itself that is made to speak. "Making" may refer to the potter—the shaper of the clay—or to the master of the ceramic workshop. "The signatures of makers are more than twice as common as those of painters." "Mottoes" also appear on vases; for example, Cook mentions "*kalon eimi potērion*—'I am a good cup,'" where once again the vase is given a voice.

This is a phenomenon very distant from our alienated world, where the mass production of plastic dinnerware would seem to disallow this animistic practice of inscription in the first person. If the pot has a voice, then so do those objects fitted with heads, and still more the numerous ceramic figurines, especially the cult figures of women who seem to have some sort of buried life. Like Lévi-Strauss's speaking signs (i.e., women), these objects are both commodities for exchange and carriers of speech, when they have been so inscribed by their makers.

Homeric Writing

The creation myths connect the act of shaping a vase from earth and water with the creation of the first woman. In the *Iliad,* Menelaus curses those afraid to meet Hektor in battle, saying: "No, may all of you turn to water and earth . . ." (7.99). The suggestion is that men were formed of water and earth and will go back to these elements, without even the *sēma,* the sign, the hero's promised barrow.

Homer calls writing *sēmata*—signs—and interestingly uses the same noun for: the mark on a horse's forehead, an omen, a barrow that marks a grave, the token of identity (*Iliad* 6.176), and the mark on a lot (*Iliad* 7.189).[8] Glaukos tells the story of Bellerophon, who is sent on a Hamlet-like errand to be punished for his virtue in refusing Anteia, Proitos' deceiving wife. Anteia has lied to her husband about an attempt by Bellerophon to force himself on her:

> He shrank from killing him, since his heart was awed by such action,
> but sent him away to Lykia, and handed him murderous symbols
> [*sēmata lugra*],
> which he inscribed in a folding tablet, enough to destroy life,
> and told him to show it to his wife's father, that he might perish.
> *Iliad* 6.167–70

In the Iliadic passage, writing is connected with adultery, with women's treachery and deception.[9] It is made invisible to the bearer; Bellerophon carries the signs with him, not knowing what they are. They are *lugra,* baneful. In the *Odyssey,* there are *pharmaka lugra,* baneful drugs, that Helen says were given her by Polydamna:

> of Egypt, where the fertile earth [*zeidōros aroura*], produces the
> greatest number
> of medicines, many good in mixture, many malignant.
> *Odyssey* 4.229–30

Drugs, like the *sēmata lugra,* are associated with the deceits of women, those descendants of Pandora.[10] Through the Helen passage, which links the *delta* of Egypt with the grain-giving earth (perhaps suggesting the parthenogenetic production of drugs), we see again an association of women, body, earth. In the Bellerophon passage, the baneful signs are folded in the *pinax,* which is like the *deltos*—folded, therefore hidden and life-destroying, soul-destroying. Proitos' signs are secret and kill far away. Only by superhuman, heroic efforts is Bellerophon able to defeat the deadly machinations of the distant king and win his daughter's hand.

In another Bellerophontic legend (the hero is from Ephyra, source of baneful drugs, *Odyssey* 2.328), women lift their skirts over their heads and expose their genitals in an apotropaic gesture that succeeds in driving off besiegers of their city. Writing is bound up with these dangerous parts, the folded *deltos* of the woman, which when exposed can defeat the warriors, although both Hamlet and Bellerophon survive. This unveiling and opening up gesture reveals the unseen, which is deadly; just as Pandora's opening of the jar unleashes plagues, so the opening of the *pinax,* the lifting of the skirts, allows the text to be read, allows a deadly message to be uncoded.

Coins

Unlike the folded *pinaxes* or *deltoi,* the surfaces of vases and coins are immediately legible. The vase is a rounded body with lips, belly, and mouth, a container that stands on legs and bears utterances in the first person on its surface. These signs are decorations, bindings, promises of richness within, prayers for continued creation in the world, and signs of desire and admiration, of possession and offering. Coins do not contain anything. They are themselves objects of value, made of precious metals pulled out from the entrails of mother earth. And if, as is so often the case, the Greeks are structural anthropologists (like Lévi-Strauss) and see the exchange of women as a marker of culture, then the exchange of inscribed coins is something like the "marital dialogue." Some kinds of coins bore the figures of women (see figure 13)—for example, the famous Demareteion of Sicily.[11]

At first the writing on Greek coins was not extensive. "The initial letter of the community served to indicate the authority by which the coin was issued. . . . As with the spread of writing the legends become longer, it becomes necessary to arrange them decoratively so as to fill the vacant spaces of the field or form a border."[12] The representations on the coins begin with animal types, often monstrous, hybrid creatures. The human head is represented, as well as tortoises, gorgons, the gorgon's apotropaic face, and sphinxes. The female head at Syracuse, the Demareteion mentioned earlier, the portrait of a real woman, marked an especially important moment in the development of Greek coinage, although the goddess Athena and her owl appear on the coinage of Athens. The coin itself is like a body, which is then impressed, inscribed, with image and letters.

FIGURE 13. Decadrachms by Euainetos and Kimōn with the image of Arethusa, from Syracuse (National Museum, Syracuse, Italy). Alinari / Art Resource, New York.

A legend on an early coin says, "I am the mark of Phanes"; thus, like the vases, the inscribed coins are made to speak in their own voice. It was Peisistratos who, rejecting the family badges of the aristocracy, placed Athena and her owl on his coinage; according to Charles Seltman, Peisistratos' coinage was "almost the earliest coinage that depicted a human head, while the three initial letters of the city's name also marked a new departure in ancient mint practice."[13] The oligarchs, in times when Peisistratos was not in power and after his sons' reigns, continued to mint contesting images, for example, the bull's head of the Eteoboutad clan.[14] Under the so-called Cleisthenian democracy, the city returned to the sign used by the tyrant, and Athena's head appeared on the coinage. Special coins were issued to mark the victory of Marathon: tetradrachms with an olive-crowned Athena on one side and on the reverse an owl with a waning moon and olive twig.[15] (The Spartans had not appeared on the battlefield at Marathon, because they could not leave Sparta until after the full moon.)

Aristophanes suggests that the owls depicted on the coins have the power to reproduce in the parabasis of *The Birds:* ". . . owls from Laurion—an inexhaustible supply. They shall nest in your homes and breed in your purses hatching little coinlings, jingle jingle jingle."[16] Owls are feminine in Greek, and here they proliferate parthenogenetically. If we see the inscription on coins as a kind of writing, then here Aristophanes represents the proliferation, the reproduction, of writing as analogous to avian reproduction; the female is the coin, the thing that gives birth to the next generation—to the *tokos,* the interest, and the *tokos,* the offspring.[17]

Inscription on the Mind

In *Prometheus Bound,* Aeschylus has Prometheus describe how he gave writing to humankind: "And further I discovered to them numbering, preeminent among subtle devices, and the combining of letters as a means of remembering all things, the Muses' mother, skilled in craft" (lines 459–61). The *synthesis,* the combining, of letters is considered a mother, a matrix of the work of the female Muses. The Promethean myth of the culture-bringer is reworked by Sophocles in the *Antigone*'s ode to man, in which all these arts are no longer the gifts of a god but human beings' own achievements.

The metaphor of inscription on the *phrēn,* or mind, was a commonplace. For example, Prometheus boasts of his gifts to humankind: He is the father of the mother of the Muses; like Apollo who kills the dragon in the recesses, he leads humankind out of darkness, the female space, into the Muses' light.[18] Prometheus then prophesies to the passing Io and tells her to make note of his prophecy:

First to you, Io, I shall tell the tale
of your sad wanderings, rich in groans—inscribe [*eggraphou*]
the story in the tablets of your mind [*mnēmosin deltois phrenōn*].
Prometheus Bound 788–89

Like the visitor to any oracle, Io is to record the oracular pronouncement of Prometheus, but she is to engrave it *in her mind*. Her itinerary, describing the journey past the daughters of Phorkys (with a single tooth among them), the Gorgons, and the other monsters, and past the river Aithiops to her destination, is recorded in the text:

travel by his banks along
to a waterfall where from the Bibline hills
Nile pours his holy waters, pure to drink.
This river shall be your guide to the triangular
land of the Nile . . .

810–15

The mention of the *deltos* of the mind, associated above with the inscription of the woman by the man, is followed in the text by the Graiae, female monsters who share a tooth, like a letter. In the Cadmeian myth, the Gorgons are caught in art, in arrested motion, and they are capable of turning any living being into a stone, a dead letter.

Io is to go up to the base of the Bibline mountains, whose name recalls the *bublos* or *biblos* (papyrus). Biblinos means made of papyrus or papyrus rolls, that is, books. Egypt, source of papyrus, is the land of writing, of all inscription. The Nile finds its ancient source at this site. In this triangular land, triangular like the *delta,* like the *deltos* of Io's mind, she will be impregnated by Zeus' touch and breath and will bring forth his children.

Prometheus inscribes in Io's *deltoi* her itinerary and her reproductive fate in the land of the delta and the papyrus. He plays with the pun on *deltos* and *delta,* making them his. The Greek letter "delta" comes, possibly, from the Hebrew *daleth* or door; the woman's illiterate memory, her *phrēn,* is like the door into her body, like the door into the earth that is the Nile delta. She is triangle, delta, door; she is *deltos,* inscription, fold.[19] Zeus will impregnate her as Prometheus does with his words. (Later, he says a *pontios mukhos,* "a recess of the sea" (line 839), will bear her name.) Women cannot read, cannot write, but they can carry the inscription of culture in their memory and in the delta/*deltos* of their body.

Suppliants Inscribed

Although Aeschylus was a strong partisan of democracy, he seems to have considered the world of women—their kinship-oriented, familial loyalties and chthonic affinities—as threatening to the rational, legalistic institutions of the *polis.* Let us look at Aeschylus' *Suppliants,* a play about the

Danaids, who are extraordinarily vulnerable women fleeing Egyptian bridegrooms, all but one of whom are destined to kill their husbands on their wedding night.[20]

The power of writing to aid memory, to *be* memory, serves as the basis for several of Aeschylus' sustained metaphors in *The Suppliants;* he distinguishes among different kinds of writing. The Danaids and Egypt, their home, are associated with the ephemeral writing on papyrus and tablets, while the Greek city is bound by laws inscribed in stone or bronze. These durable materials mark the Greeks' difference from their neighbors. The Danaids have fled Egypt, the land of the *delta;* they mention Procne, the wife of Tereus, in their first appeal (lines 58–62). According to some versions of this myth, Procne read the story of her husband's rape of her sister, Philomela, who, tongueless, wove signs into a cloth. This story of reading and writing, briefly evoked, introduces the theme of inscription in the context of violence against relations.

The maidens' father, Danaus, uses the scriptural metaphor as he admonishes them: ". . . I advise your taking / Care to seal my words [*deltoumenas*] within your mind" (lines 178–79). Their memory is like an empty tablet, and the law of the father is to be inscribed there. They are like the delta of the Nile and like the *deltos,* the tablet. The Danaids speak of themselves as *sperma semnas mega matros,* "the mighty seed of our august mother" (lines 141, 151; cf. 275). The theme of autochthony and spontaneous generation, later associated with the Nile delta, is here invoked as Pelasgos describes his land, once polluted, then cleansed by Apis (lines 264–67). Like Pandora, Earth can let loose horrible disease upon the earth; autochthony and parthenogenesis are not always benevolent. The Danaids will inscribe the text of the father and refuse the marital ploughing, the breaking open of the furrow by the Egyptians. Their refusal is represented as a desire to remain daughters.

King Pelasgos uses the metaphor of impression as he rejects the Danaids' claim to be of Argive stock:

> . . . or the Nile may foster
> Such a likeness; or the images
> Of Cyprus, carved by native craftsmen.
>
> 280–82

He speaks of them as plants, *phuton,* and then perhaps as coins, using the word *kharaktēr,* which was used of the mark pressed, stamped into a coin, as well as the brand on a slave or animal. He is stressing their foreignness, and he goes on to compare them to nomads or Amazons, here called *anandrous kreoborous*—manless, mateless, and flesh eating. Not only are these women inscribed by the father; they are marked with a *kharaktēr* by male artificers, men whose maleness is emphasized by the last word *arsenōn.*

When Pelasgos seems unwilling to accept them as suppliants, unwilling to protect them against men of their own country, they threaten to hang themselves: "Statues with new tablets (*pinaxi*) to adorn" (line 463). The wooden images of the god will be decorated with their bodies, which they strangely call, following their father's imagery, *pinakes*—tablets, the writing surface like the *deltos*. Their remarks are a riddle (*ainigmatōdes*) to Pelasgos, a riddle whose meaning they unfold; Pelasgos says: "Speak simply" (line 464). The word he uses, *haplōs* (simply), comes from *haplous* (single), opposed to *diplous* (two-fold), and here connects its meaning of "simply," "plainly," with the sense of "singly," or "in one way." *Diplous* (double) is used of cloaks and articles of dress. The foldedness of the *pinax,* of the *deltos*—its doubleness and closure—refuses reading, and the man demands an opening of the text, the cloak, the body, the metaphor. They gloss their earlier riddle most explicitly by threatening to hang themselves.[21]

When the Egyptians appear and begin to drag the Danaids away, the king appears to drive off the rapists. As he does so, he expresses a curious disdain for ephemeral written texts, as he proudly describes the decree passed unanimously by his people to guarantee the Danaids' safety:[22]

> Joined, doweled, and bolted stays this law,
> That neither scratched on tablets [*pinaxin*], nor book-sealed
> [*en ptukhais biblon,* literally, "in the folds of papyrus"],
> You hear announced by the tongue of freedom's voice.
>
> 944–49

The first metaphor seems an allusion to inscription in stone or bronze. The "dowel" would refer to the fixing of an inscription, of a law, thus a more permanent kind of writing than the writing on a tablet or papyrus, which he often deprecates. In fact, the laws of Solon, for example, were long displayed on wooden *axones* (tablets fixed on a wheel) in the city of Athens.

The analogies between the women's minds and bodies made by Danaus and the Danaids are contrasted with this firmer resolve, either inscription in stone, wood, or bronze, or simply the absolute presence of the face, mouth, and tongue. The sense here too, as above, is that the tablets hide things in folds, while Pelasgos demands frankness, openness, and the audibility of the *logos,* the speaking voice, and of the publicly recorded decisions of the city.

Danaus says, "reeds cannot conquer wheat" (*bublou de karpos ou kratei stakhun,* line 761), that is, the lustful Egyptians, pursuing the Danaids, cannot overpower their protectors, the Argives. *Bublos,* papyrus, *deltos/delta*—all refer to Egypt. When Pelasgos describes the inscribed decree of the Argives, he is comparing the visible, open, public inscription on stone to the *logos,* the audible voice of the *demos,* the *polis.* And this visible, audible text is contrasted unfavorably with the closed, folded, secret language of the *pinax,* of the folds of papyrus. The women who would hang themselves would remain folded, papyric, Egyptian; they kill their husbands perhaps to avoid the exposure of this secrecy and closure. The wheat ear, the phallic stalk with its visible seeds, the phallus given by Demeter, is the source of the Argives' livelihood and pride. To become proper Greek brides, the Danaids must refuse the replication of their closed, Egyptoid, deltaic bodies, and accept other bridegrooms, open themselves to their new world.

The Danaids exhibit submissiveness to their father after the departure of their suitors' herald (lines 968ff.). He advises them: "Above my other counsels cut this wisdom: / Time becomes the touchstone of the alien" (991–93). Once again his advice to them is presented in scriptural, metaphorical language and must be set in contrast to the earlier remarks of the king against more ephemeral forms of writing. Is the writing in memory, which the Danaids are required to perform, like engraving in stone and more authentic? Is there a contrast being expressed between the Egyptians, who use scriptural metaphors repeatedly, and the Argive king Pelasgos, who dissociates himself from their forms and patriotically speaks for the *logos?*[23] The contrast is one consistent with the representation of Egypt in Herodotus' text in which Egypt is a land of greater antiquity than Greece, where the assembled mass of statues of priests has proved that the Greek heroes could not have descended so recently from the gods. Herodotus reports a story about Hekataios, who presented to the Egyptians a genealogy that connected him with a god in the sixth generation. The priests showed him, as they showed Herodotus, "wooden figures" (*kolossous xulinous*), "for every high priest sets there in his lifetime a statue of himself; counting and pointing to these, the priests showed me that each inherited from his father." There were 345 such figures. The Egyptians are thus established as a people of repetition, patrilineality, counting, mimesis, and representation—eminently civilized in part because they know themselves to be so far from divine generation (*Histories* 2.143). The Danaids, then, come from this distant and ancient land, hypercivilized, from a people claiming great distance from the gods. Writing and counting and repetition are the Egyptians' characteristically human skills. Egypt is the land of records, of the preservation of the past. Here in Aeschylus' text Egypt seems to be associated with darkness, with sexual violence, and perhaps with the *ainigmata* of writing—the folded, hidden space of the *deltos* that is like the ancient *delta.*

Danaus associates his daughters' desirability with that of summer fruit in a passage that recalls Sappho:

> I beg
> You not to bring me shame, you who have
> That bloom that draws men's eyes: there is no simple

Guard for fruit most delicate, that beasts
And men, both winged and footed, ravage.

994–99

Here too there is a sense of secrecy, of sweetness, *inside.* Like the closed folds of the *pinakes,* the tablets, the fruits protect themselves from harm, from consumption, from legibility. Here Danaus invokes the metaphor of plowing but speaks to the *sea,* which again and again is spoken of in Homer as *atrugetos,* unharvested, barren. Danaus says, as if he were refusing the metaphor of fertile furrow for his daughters:

Let no shame for us,
But pleasure for our enemies, be done,
For which, in great toil, great seas were ploughed.

1006–7

His daughters, who are like ripe fruit, are not to be ploughed by their suitors; there is a suggestion of incest and of the harem, and a refusal of the ploughing metaphor so commonly expressive of fruitful, legal marriage. The tragedy ends with no promise of security; the chorus says it will be content with something better than evil, "if ill / is one-third my lot" (1070).

The Danaids' sex is like the tablet, to be inscribed with their father's admonitions, but he sees it in this way because of his fear and desire for them. They are the ripe fruit with hidden sweetness, the rounded body with its goodness inside, like the fruit Sappho describes so poignantly. It is because he, too, is fascinated and attracted by their sweetness, by their fruit, that he wants to mark them with *his* signs, to make them vases decorated with his words, tablets closed in on his warnings. But they associate this imagery with suicide. They describe themselves as tablets, as *pinakes,* only when threatening to hang themselves. It is as if the paternal inscription is equal to death. They see accepting their father's law as deathly; yet equally they fear the violence of their suitors, the plowing, the reinscription that is the right of the husband. The father wants them to bear only his marks. They want to refuse inscription altogether; they are vulnerable, victims, to be touched only by a delicate breath like that of Zeus that impregnated their ancestor Io. There is a reversal of the place of women, a desire to remain doves, fruit, weak, needing the inscription of the father or the decree of the Argives. They want to hide, to refuse all sexuality.

The Danaids' sexuality is projected onto the violence of the marriage bed—the Greeks often imagined women to be secretly violent and enraged.[24] The notions of violence, of Clytemnestra the murderess, of the flesh-eating Amazons, and of the Amazonian Lemnian women go along dialectically with the view of them as fields, tablets, ripe fruit, doves: all these images of passivity are dialectically connected to the other, less often expressed, images of butchery and murder. The repression takes its toll in this way: The image of the field produces a counterimage of the poisonous earth sending up miasmas, disease, poison, monsters. The image of the tablet produces the deadly signs of Bellerophon and, of course, Phaedra—the words that kill are associated with the father's revenge and with the law's inscription.

In the legend, although the later plays are lost, the Danaids, perversely inscribed by their father, kill their husbands on their wedding night at the moment they might receive a new inscription, the name of the husband. Danaus is a powerful father, one who feels too intensely the desirability of his daughters. They are too much bound to him; he has inscribed them too deeply. Danaus reverses the myth of Io, the beast/maiden. He says beasts flying and walking will despoil his daughters and then, with the lines about ploughing the sea, expresses his real desire: that his daughters not be ploughed, that the sea (*pontos*) be sterile (*astrugeton*), that he hoard them.

As in the *Oresteia,* Aeschylus may want to show progress and the movement of history, and to end with the endogamously appropriate marriage of Lynceus and Hypermnestra, while showing the earlier stage, that of the unrepentant Danaids refusing endogamous marriage, as an archaic, transcended moment, one contaminated by the barbaric upbringing of the Danaids. The young maidens, fearful of marriage, hold close to the father in an overly endogamous bond. They act out the normal young girls' Amazonian, Artemisian resistance to marriage, to the hyperbolic extent of murdering their husbands like the bad women of legend, such as Clytemnestra and the Lemnian women. But they are reconciled to marriage and become the appropriate founders of the Greek Thesmophoria. They are emblematic of a process, the transformations of history and of personal maturation. The incestuous, endogamous family gives way to the appropriately heterogamous family. In *The Suppliants* the chorus represents an archaic stage, both historically and socially. They call on their father (Zeus/Danaus) not because they have a fantasy desire for Zeus but because they are young girls still living with their family of birth before being transferred to a family of marriage.

Much evidence suggests the difficulty of this transition, including the funerary image of the marriage rites and the myth of Demeter and Kore, so well analyzed by Marylin Arthur.[25] I would place *The Suppliants* in the same category; it is about the production of wives from the raw material of girls. Girls are wild animals, untamed, raw, almost undifferentiated sexually. And they are still their father's property, that is, *inscribed* by their father. The proper end of a "girl" is marriage and reproduction, that is, inscription by the husband.

R. S. Caldwell gives a psychoanalytic reading of *The Suppliants:*[26]

> As the pre-dominant imagery of the play, as well as mass murder which is the climactic action of the trilogy, demonstrates, the Danaids are not preoccupied with acquiring the male organ but with the wound they have suffered and its possible recurrence: not with becoming men themselves, but with reducing men to their own mutilated state.
>
> . . . The major patterns of imagery revolve around such metaphors as the picking of fruit, the shedding of blood, attacking snakes, walls threatened, and flowers which must be guarded. The sexual prospects of the Danaids threaten a reanimation of the original wound; when these future threats become present reality, the Danaids will be compelled to seek vengeance in a like manner, by beheading (i.e., castrating) their violators.
>
> Pp. 23, 49

According to Caldwell, the Danaids are neurotics, like Freud's female patients who supposedly fantasized about paternal seduction. Caldwell sees Hypermnestra, the only wife who spares her husband, as the heroine; she "frees herself from the collective neurosis," ambiguously desiring both children and her husband. She is "enabled to escape the illusions of the group."[27] This, too, is politically appropriate; just as the fifth-century Athenian feared bands of women—the Thesmophoriazusai, the Amazons, the Lemnian women—so the twentieth-century male psychoanalytic conservative values "individualism," the isolation of women in marriage, in servitude to one man.

Caldwell ends by showing how the trilogy describes a transformation from past to future. "This concept of the climactic struggle to be free of the burden of the past is clearly a dominant character of Aeschylean tragedy. . . . In a vision that went beyond morality, Aeschylus saw that on every level, from the psychic to the comic, the hope and shape of the future was contained in the effort to overcome the past." In the play, the transition is "centered on the transfer of love from father to husband."[28] He completely ignores the rapist tendencies of the Aiguptoi and assumes that overcoming the past by entering into heterogamy is the great *telos* of human female existence.

Caldwell reinscribes the Danaids with another version of an old discourse,[29] the old politics of identity that sees the female body as castrated, as a mutilated version of the male's. But it is not the Danaids who consider themselves mutilated; they are attempting to refuse what they see as mutilation, being broken into, consumed, and ruined by their suitors. The psychoanalytic reading crudely colonizes the ancient text from the point of view of modern phallocentrism.

The imagery of writing, of inscription, is not necessarily significant of castration. Some writing *is* removal, for example, writing in stone or writing on a tablet where one removes wax or incising a vase, but in fact writing was often done in ink and was marking, not removing; just as the *kharaktēr* on a coin was not cutting but raising the surface of the object. More significant than cutting is the mark of possession. Danaus wants to mark his daughters as his own, and here he is hieratic, Egyptian, static, and repetitious, as opposed to the spontaneity of the Argive *logos*. The women have to be processed—removed from the archaic, deadly, written world of Egypt—and made into Greek wives.

Inscription and the Body of the Mother

The Greeks see the sexes as profoundly different according to a more elaborate logic than our own. Each has what the other has not. The goal of the Greek male is to dominate the female and her body, to control its potentiality, to subdue it to his interests. This is done through elaborate ideological mechanisms. The fear of women's bodies comes not from its woundedness but from its power to wound. The dangers of women's bodies are always there along with their interior potentiality. The *pitch* of the *deltos* is like the sexual lubricants of women,[30] and the substances smeared on clothes by Deianeira and Medea, the *pharmaka* of women, are sexual liquids. Women can burn, devour (Skylla and Charybdis, Kalypso), transform (Circe), and murder (Clytemnestra, the Danaids). But they are not seen as castrated; rather, they often want to keep their bodies unopened, unbroken. It is the wife, the mature woman, who is broken into, opened up, not the girl. The girl is wild, untamed, like a horse, an unpainted jar, the unploughed earth; she must be converted into a furrow, a *pithos* with household goods inside, an oven cooking children.

Jocasta ends in Sophocles' *Oedipus Rex* as a silent furrow; she never speaks after the chorus speaks of her as such, and she is described as dead, hanging, all the more silent. Women were supposed to be silent, as Thucydides says in the funeral oration of Pericles:

> Perhaps I should say a word or two on the duties of women to those among you who are now widowed. I can say all I have to say in a short word of advice. Your great glory is not to be inferior to what god has made you, and the greatest glory of a woman is to be least talked about by men, whether they are praising you or criticizing you.
>
> *Peloponnesian War* 2.45

Women are to be "naturally" womanly and not to be spoken of. There is no sense of their speaking. Yet on the tragic stage, as Slater and others have remarked, women do speak and act—sometimes with violence.

Writing and Oedipus' Daughter

I have already mentioned how the theme of ploughing figures in Sophocles' *Antigone;* the tyrant speaks of women brutally as fields to be ploughed (line 569). A second metaphor, that of inscription, is not as explicit but informs the character of Antigone at several levels. First, the poet refers to his own art in the great ode on man, which expresses ambivalently the optimism of the fifth century, and which is ironically placed within this tragedy of terrible misunderstanding, inflexibility, and suicide. The chorus begins its celebration of human accomplishment:

> Many the wonders but nothing walks stranger than man
> [*anthrōpōn*].
> This thing crosses the sea in the winter's storm,
> making his path through the roaring waves.
> And she, the greatest of gods, the earth—
> ageless she is, and unwearied—he wears her away
> as the ploughs go up and down from year to year
> And his mules turn up the soil.
>
> 332–41

This magnificent ode begins with the expansion of a typical doublet, land/sea, which universalizes the claim; all is either land or sea. The sea is given a "back," is animated. Earth, its complement, is *highest,* greatest of the gods; in Hesiod's account, she was first. She is unperishing, unwearied (verbally, these adjectives prepare for the analogy already mentioned, between Antigone and the ploughed earth; she calls herself "without marriage bed, without bridal song" [*alektron anumenaion,* 917]).

The earth is worn away, *apotruetai,* like a coin, as the ploughs (syntactically, at least, free of human agency) wind, turn round, revolve. The mention of the "offspring" ("race," "kind") of horses evokes the theme of generation. Reproduction is linked to agricultural production. The earth here, unlike that of *Oedipus Rex,* is inexhaustible and promises not only the crops of the field but animals as well. The image is one of violence, but also of inexhaustibility. Can this image be connected with that of writing? The word *boustrophedon* (turning like oxen in ploughing) was used of writing from left to right and right to left alternately. The earth is inscribed, as is Antigone who is associated later with the ploughing of the earth.

In the great debate between Kreon and the heroine, Antigone associates herself with kin, blood, and family and refuses the secular law of the tyranny. She refuses to be assimilated into the new culture of human law, the written code:

> For me it was not Zeus who made that order.
> Nor did that Justice who lives with the gods below

mark out such laws to hold among mankind.
Nor did I think your orders were so strong
that you, a mortal man, could over-run
the gods' unwritten and unfailing laws.

450–55

She obeys the unwritten laws (*agrapta . . . nomisma*) and compares them with his mortal pronouncements. Like the majority of women in the culture of the audience, perhaps, illiterate, she goes by the old laws, which were unwritten, known to all. But because of their unwritten character, the old laws were associated particularly with the aristocracy, who administered them as they saw fit.

One of the innovations of the Athenian democracy, connected with the rise of literacy, was the inscription of the city's laws.[31] Sophocles alludes to the contemporary debates on the status of law. As Vernant and others have shown, for example, the debate between Kreon and Antigone echoes with the word *nomos* (law) and its derivatives; the two do not agree on its definition. Vernant says that "for Antigone, *nomos* denotes the opposite to what Kreon, in the particular position in which he is placed, also calls *nomos*. For the girl, the law means 'religious rule'; for Kreon it means 'an edict promulgated by the head of state'. . . . the ambiguity conveys the tension between certain meanings felt to be irreconcilable despite their homonymy. Instead of establishing communication and agreement between the characters, the words they exchange on the stage on the contrary underline the impermeability of their minds, the barrier between them."[32]

Especially in the case of Kreon and Antigone, the antagonism between the sexes makes it impossible to communicate; the archaic position, the female position, is the position of illiteracy. Illiteracy here means repetition, stasis, and indifferentiation. The religious rules by which Antigone means to act are known to all, always identical to themselves, without history; while Kreon's edicts, announced by heralds, are transitory, ad hoc, ephemeral, particularized. They are spontaneous and temporary; not written, but heralded.

Antigone believes in the unwritten law, but she is the one finally written by Kreon's law. She lives in a world that will not admit change. She compares herself, in her lyric dialogue with the chorus, to a creature of myth—Niobe, daughter of Tantalos (824–31). The chorus must remind Antigone in the next lines that Niobe was a goddess, and we mortals; but what matters is that Antigone does not recognize this. She lives in the world of legend and myth, not necessarily hubristically, not arrogantly assuming herself to be the equal of the goddess, but rather ahistorically. She does not know the passage of time. It is that which makes her the inhabitant of a different culture from Kreon; she lives without writing and without history, and so lives and dies as if she were Niobe, or, the chorus sings, as if she were Danaë. Both Danaë and Niobe were fertile, and the identification of Antigone with these women makes her virgin death more terrible. She is not a goddess, not the bride of Zeus, but a mortal who will die. The disjunction between her mythic reality and that of the city makes her tenacity more ironic and threatening to the survival of the city, which depends on marriage, on the metaphorical ploughing of women's fertile furrows. Her inscription, enclosure, entrapment in the past, with the dead, represents not just her own death but the potential threat to the city of women's archaic position within it. The chorus compares Antigone further to Lycurgus, who went mad when enclosed in a cave, and Cleopatra, whose sons were blinded by her husband's second wife, Eidothea, after Cleopatra was imprisoned. (Eidothea used a woman's instrument, the shuttle, to blind her stepsons.)

The blind Teiresias appears. He too cannot *read,* but he knows how to decipher the old signs, the birds' cries. What he hears is not their usual signs:

> I sat where every bird of heaven comes
> in my old place of augury, and heard
> bird-cries I'd never known [*agnot' . . . phthoggon*]. They screeched about
> goaded by madness, inarticulate [*bebarbaromenoi*].
>
> 1001–2

Like Antigone, he does not read; he hears. They know truths that are unwritten and unavailable to Kreon. He tells Kreon to change his mind so he will no longer be "foolish," "unfortunate" (*aboulos oud' anolbos,* 1026). But Kreon acts too late. Antigone, his son, and his wife all kill themselves.

The woman is inscribed in part because she is the space of labor—reproductive labor—in this culture, and writing is an act that is performed as labor. Also, because she is illiterate, she is the one "enacted," put into being by the act of inscription, particularly in the case of dramatic tragedy, where women spoke more publicly than they ever might in the *polis,* and where male actors played the parts of women. The woman here, on the tragic stage, can only exist through textualization. The fact of her textual existence reiterates the passivity of her cultural role.

Deadly Writing

Writing is associated with death here, but not in Derrida's sense nor in Plato's that it represents the dead letter, the voice or *logos* killed and mummified, incapable of speaking for itself or of engaging in dialectic. Perhaps the sense it has in the Greek texts, in Homer and beyond, is a literalization of that idea, an earlier stage in culture's relationship to writing. For the Greeks, it seems, writing can kill. This may be an archaizing feature of tragedy, since the *sēmata lugra* of the *Iliad* would be seen as belonging to the heroic age, to the age of the central figures of tragedy. In the dialectic between the *polis* and its past, the aura of menace around writing would be appropriate to the old, aristocratic, heroic characters. Even Pelasgos in *The Suppliants,* although a king, must consult his people on matters of state, and their *oral* vote is decisive.

The tragedians may be using the fear of writing to connote the world of heroes and legends. In that world, as in the world of the audience, women are illiterate, and they are seen as inscribed, therefore, as the objects of this suspect *technē*. Writing carries doom; it writes down death. It commands death for Bellerophon, suicide and murder for the Danaids, death for Herakles, suicide and death of Phaedra and Hippolytos, death by sacrifice for Iphigenia. It is as if writing communicates death, contaminating the receiver with its static quality. The bearer may be unaffected, but the receiver receives death. Thus, the medium, the woman, may be associated with death but not affected by it. Writing, which is dead, kills. It is a secret, hidden weapon. The wrapped writing of the *skutala* is animated by presence and the *logos* and ushers in celebration. The jar is decorated outside with signs, and inside is not writing but bones, ashes, diseases, as well as grains, oil, wine, the necessities of existence. The *deltos,* closed up like Pandora's *pithos,* when opened lets out death. The *deltos* has writing inside, which is concealed.

The Trachiniae

Sophocles' *Trachiniae* is a particularly rich source of metaphorical language concerning writing.[33] Its first word is *logos,* speech, and throughout there is a discourse on presence and absence, on the ways in which writing represents absence. Although I have discussed this tragedy elsewhere in connection with Greek views on closure and endogamy, with emphasis on the centaur's violation of Deianeira, I return to it here in order to look at the play of writing and speech, presence and absence.[34]

RAPE AND INSCRIPTION

Sophocles' *Trachiniae* presents the metaphor of inscription and associates it more directly with sexuality than does his *Antigone*. Writing is opposed to *logos;* Herakles' absence from his home has meant that Deianeira has been left with texts instead of her living husband. Like Antigone, Deianeira listens and hears. She speaks of Herakles as an absent farmer; she is the distant field, the ploughland out-of-place (*arouran ektopon,* line 32). Her metaphoric language here suggests that she has been sown and harvested, then abandoned; she is an apt surface for inscription as well. She worries, since she has been long without news from him (*akeruktos*):

> Yes, this tablet [*delton*] he left behind makes me think it must surely be some terrible trouble. Often I pray the gods I do not have it for my sorrow.
>
> 46–48

The tablet is like the field sowed, harvested, and abandoned. She is the surface ploughed and inscribed by the master.

Deianeira tells her son Hyllos that Herakles has left oracles (*manteia pista,* line 77), and if these are the inscriptions she mentions, once again writing is associated with death. He will either meet his death, or, having finished his labors, come to spend the rest of his life there with her. Deianeira reports:

> When King Heracles set off from home on his last journey, he left an old tablet [*palaian delton*], on which some signs had been inscribed. Never before could he bring himself to speak to me of this.
>
> 155–58

As R. C. Jebb points out, Deianeira's use of *xunthēmath'* here recalls the Homeric *sēmata lugra* (*Iliad* 6.168). Jebb says, "There is possibly a touch of designed archaism in the poet's phrase; he may have felt that it suited the heroic age to speak of writing as a mystery."[35] Is it not more likely to assume that Deianeira is meant to be illiterate, that it is she who might read these "tokens" as indecipherable, as requiring Herakles to explain (*phrasai*)? Like a fallow field, like a tablet with now incomprehensible signs, Deianeira waits. The tablet, according to Jebb, contained the oracle; Herakles thus faced with his last ordeal gave his will to Deianeira. The use of a phrase that echoes Homer's must also evoke the deadly connotations of the letter Bellerophon carried. Writing is messages of death, especially for one who cannot read. Here she fears the message, but it is already suggested that she is the inscription, just as she is the plowed field.

Deianeira sends "messages" (*logont'epistolas,* 493) with Lichas, but these are not, according to Jebb, written texts, but "mandates consisting in words," that is, her (verbal) messages to Herakles.[36] Much is made of the play of hearing—hearing the truth from the messenger, getting the truth from Lichas who at first deceived her. She resolves to win back her husband, who has sent a new bride ahead of him:

> I have had hidden in a copper urn
> for many years the gift of a centaur, long ago.
>
> 555–56

The gift has been hidden away in the interior of a *lebes,* a type of jar sometimes used as a cinerary urn. The place suggests again the analogy between the hidden interior spaces of the woman's body and the inside of the vase, both places that are associated with death.[37]

The gift of Nessos is stored in the deadly jar, and it recalls his act of violence against Deianeira. As he ferried her across a river, he touched her "with wanton hands" (line 565). Herakles shot him with an arrow tipped with Hydra's venom, and as he lay dying, he told Deianeira of a charm (*kēlētērion,* 575)—his blood, mixed with the venom, and in one version of the legend, with his semen—"so that he [Herakles] will never look / at another woman and love her more than you" (576–77). This "charm" will in fact kill Herakles. She speaks of his gift, the charm, as *writing*. It is a writing equivalent to rape; he has violated her with his mad hands and gives a deadly gift in exchange.

DEIANEIRA AS DELTOS

Deianeira continues to speak of Nessos' message as something hidden in the interior of the house, in the jar, in her self (578–90). Like Medea, but unknowing, Deianeira steeps the garments of her victim in the substance that will kill; the theme of the poisoned robe suggests an alternation between inside and outside. The poison is brought from deepest inside, and when used on the garment, which is like a second skin, it burns and destroys. It is as if the proper place for this substance were in the interior of the body, the jar, the house. The centaur's blood, the Hydra's venom, even perhaps the centaur's semen, all belong within; when they are out of place, brought out of the body's recesses, they wreak havoc. Deianeira's body too has its hidden interior spaces that the sexually violent centaur threatened, and it is their externalization, their visibility to Nessos, which sets in motion the action of the poison. She paradoxically wants to keep her actions hidden, in darkness, while the cloak she gives her husband will be unmistakably revealed in the light of the sun. "Only be discreet. In darkness one may be / ashamed of what one does [*hos skotōi / k'an aiskhra prassēs*] without the shame of disgrace," says Deianeira to the chorus (596–97).

The alternation of dark and light, interiority and exteriority, is associated with male and female realms. The centaur has penetrated her darkness; she will bring his precious bodily fluids to the light. When she delivers the cloak to Lichas, she tells him to be sure to keep it in darkness until the last moment (604 ff.):

> . . . you shall carry a token [*sēma*] of this vow which he
> will understand from the familiar encircled print
> of my seal [*sphragidos*].
>
> 614–15

The cloak is within a casket. Like Deianeira herself, carried from her father by Herakles, it bears the seal of its possessor. The inscription of the possessor is the seal, like the *sphragis* of Theognis' verse.[38] She has sealed her signet into the wax that closes and protects the container. The mark of the owner is the impression on the outside, the *kharaktēr* that guarantees the source and the purity of the contents. The centaur's violation of Deianeira extends to the contamination of this casket and its burden; Deianeira's seal cannot protect Herakles because she herself has had her seal broken. The motif of inscription and impression then partakes of the general themes of boundaries and endogamy in this tragedy.

The seal itself is said to have a fence, *herkos,* suggesting the enceinte of a fortress and of the body, the *herkos odontōn,* the fence of the teeth mentioned often by Homer (e.g., *Iliad* 4.350). The body's interiority is protected by the teeth (which are seeds and letters elsewhere). He will recognize the mark, the fence, the outside, the mimesis impressed by the signet and will remain misinformed about what lies inside. She speaks earlier of the site of Herakles' "sacrifice" as *herkos hieron,* a sacred *temenos;* it is as if her seal will cut into him as the centaur violated her, as sacred space is set apart or "cut out" from the secular. *Herkos* is a fence, enclosure, the place enclosed, courtyard, a wall for defence, the wall of the teeth. It is also used of a net for birds (*Odyssey* 22.469); it is the safe inside, but it is also an inside that can enclose and therefore threaten. Herakles will not be safe at the sacrificial enclosure, nor is Deianeira a safe interior space for the hero. And *sēma,* we will remember, means a sign not only of the sender but also of the grave—a barrow, a tomb. Thus the *sēmata lugra,* the deadly signs, of the *Iliad* doubly transmit a message of death. There is a play, too, on the sense of folding and unfolding. Deianeira says to Lichas that his thanks, which from her is single (*haplēs*) will be made double, that is, folded (*diplē*), by Herakles (619). The unfolding of the cloak will open up her foldedness, her poisonousness, to the light.

Deianeira begins to realize her accidental crime when the tuft of wool with which she spread the potion destroys itself. Deianeira describes how conscientiously she followed the instructions of Nessos:

> I neglected none of the instructions that beast
> the centaur explained to me, lying in agony
> with the sharp arrowhead in his side. I kept them
> like an inscription on bronze that cannot be washed away.
> 680–84

The barb that stabs the centaur is like a stylus, or a brush, drawing the ink which is his blood from his side. She speaks of his words almost as if he spoke some official language. She treasures his words, saves them, even though he has proven himself her enemy by breaking into her, engraving her. His words are unwashably (*dusnipton*), irremovably engraved in her; she has been inscribed, her seal broken, not by her husband but by this horse/man. Jebb says that "laws, rituals, oracles etc. were often engraved on bronze tablets."[39] Bronze also recalls the *lebes;* she is the funeral vessel of bronze and the *deltos,* the writing tablet, of bronze. She is the *deltos,* the surface ready to be engraved or inscribed by the master, like every virgin, and she has been marked.

The centaur told Deianeira to keep the unguent in a secret place, always remote from fire and from the sun's warm rays (685–86). The unguent, *pharmakon,* is both poison and cure.[40] *Mukhois,* the secret places, might refer metaphorically to the recesses of the body as well as to those of the house. As the woman's cave has *mukhoi* (*Odyssey* 5.226), so the woman's part of the house is its innermost part. She is to keep herself fireless, away from the sun, untouchable, in the women's quarters, chaste in the memory of Nessos.

The woman is at the center of the house, at the hearth; exposed to the light of the sun, to the outside, she is out of place. The tuft of wool Deianeira used, thrown into the sun's light, causes the earth to go mad like a Maenad:

> . . . But from the earth
> on which it rests, clotted foam [*aphroi*] boils up
> like the rich liquid of the blue-green fruit
> from the vines of Dionysus, poured on the earth.
>
> 701–4

The female, the aphrodisiac one, displaced, rages out of control on the mountain tops. Herakles, like the wool, is destroyed by the *pharmakon.* Before he dies, he kills Lichas, for whom the gratitude was to be doubled, folded, two-fold. Herakles throws him against a rock into the sea:

> It pressed the pale brains out through his hair,
> and, split full on, skull and blood mixed and spread
> [*diasparentos haimatos*].
>
> 781–82

The word *diasparentos,* "is scattered into fragments," comes from *diaspeirō,* "scatter or sow about," with the same root as *sperma.* The fragments of Lichas' brain are vainly sown. The unfolding, like a sowing, is this time deadly. And when Deianeira learns of Herakles' sufferings she kills herself on her marriage bed.

Herakles, as he lies dying, recalls that he was meant to be killed not by a living being but by someone living in Hades. The dead centaur killed the living man, using writing, the instrument of death; the woman was merely the vehicle of inscription. The oracles recorded by Herakles himself (*eisegrapsamen,* 1167) predicted his fate (157).

Deianeira begins the *Trachiniae* speaking of herself as a field left behind after being ploughed, sowed, and harvested. The playwright uses the metaphor of inscription to recode this conventional imagery, to represent the heroine not only as an abandoned field, left fallow, but as a tablet inscribed by her absent husband, inscribed as well by his enemy, the centaur whom he killed but whose dead words, engraved in Deianeira as in bronze, remain to destroy him. The dominant sense of writing in this play is a reinscription of the imagery of ploughing and sowing; writing is suspending meaning, preventing actualization. The letters, once written, are like seeds that have been planted but rest in dormancy, seeds that have not yet borne fruit; but when brought into the light, they poison and destroy the hero Herakles.

Comic Inscription

THE PIG

Like Sophocles, the comic playwright Aristophanes recodes the imagery of ploughing and sowing—the canonical, almost sacred language of the city-state for the description of the act of marital intercourse—and represents that act in scriptural metaphors. In *The Wasps* (422 B.C.), which is about the Athenians' obsession with the law courts, Aristophanes plays with the analogy between ploughing and writing. The slaves' master, Philocleon, is so devoted to serving on juries in the numerous trials of the city (labor paid for by the city), that he has wax under his fingernails from scratching a long line, for a heavy fine, in the voting tablet. In a mock trial, where the railing for a pig pen, the *khoirokomeion,* is used to simulate the law court, the mention of pig begins to be obscene. *Khoiron* means the female genitals; *khoirokomeion* (844) means a pen for keeping swine in, but also (Liddell, Scott, and Jones) "bandage [sic] used by females."[41]

Then Philocleon complains impatiently, saying:

> O these delays! You weary and wear me out.
> I've long been dying to commence my furrows.
>
> 849–50

The Greek is *alokidzein . . . to khorion. Alokidzein* is from *aulax, alox,* furrow. He wants to furrow his *pinakion,* to plough into the tablet that sets the fine, but here the image of marking, of writing, is associated both with ploughing and with sex. *Khorion*—place, land, spot—puns on *khoirion,* piglet; in *The Acharnians,* little girls are called *khoirion* (740); and later in *The Wasps,* Philocleon addresses the flute girl, saying *o khoirion* (1353, cf. 1364).[42] To plough a furrow in the land is to plow the piglet, is to write in the tablet.

Henderson discusses *delta* (not *deltos*), as a word used of the female genitalia, citing *Lysistrata* (151): "the pubic region is naturally delta-shaped"; and, "*delta* is used elsewhere in literature for its shape as the female pubis . . . and in cults in the form of triangular clay votive-offerings shaped to resemble the female parts."[43] Lysistrata refers to women's pubic area as a depilated *delta* in her description of how the women will arouse men's desire and then refuse to satisfy them (*Lysistrata* 151). Is her delta to be compared to the delta of the Nile, the island around which the rivers ran? The Nile *delta* was carved, inscribed down the center with the furrow of the river, as the woman's delta, depilated, is inscribed with her furrow. She is stamped, then, with the letter *delta*.

THE MESSAGE

In Aristophanes' *Thesmophoriazusae,* there is a parody of Euripides' *Palamedes,* a play about one of the inventors of writing. Euripides' kinsman, besieged in the secret women's festival, begins to call for help by parodying Euripidean tragedy. In the legend, Palamedes was killed at Troy by the Greeks, who suspected him of treachery because Odysseus had planted gold in his tent and written a forged letter from Priam to Palamedes. His brother Oeax apparently wrote the news of Palamedes' death on oar blades and threw them into the sea to inform their father. In Aristophanes' comedy, the kinsman sends out a cry for help to Euripides; he has no oars, so he writes on votive tablets:

> Why not send
> these votive slabs [*agalmat'*] instead [of oar-blades]? The very thing.
> Oar-blades are wood, and slabs are wood. I'll try.
> Now for the trick; fingers be quick;
> Do what you can for my notable plan.
> Slab, have the grace to permit me to trace
> Grooves with my knife on your beautiful face.
> The tale of my woe it is yours for to show.
> O, o, what a furrow! I never did see
> Such a horrible "R" as I've made it to be.
> Well, that must do; so fly away you,
> Hither and thither, off, off, and away.
> Do not delay for a moment, I pray.
>
> 773–84

The *agalmata* on which the kinsman writes may be tablets with votive inscriptions, to which he adds his message begging help. However, they may also be images of the goddesses in whose honor the festival was held. In that case, the inscription on the body of the image, perhaps an ancient *xoanon* made of wood, mimics the act of possession, and here the use of the word *aulaka,* furrow, links the act of inscription with that of ploughing. The letter *rho,* connoting "motion" according to Plato, may also resemble the *phallos*. He writes a phallus, part of the name of Euripides, into the body of the *deltos* or into the *delta,* perhaps, of the goddesses' image. (Immediately after, the chorus sings of women's woes.) The act of writing is made analogous to that of ploughing, and both are acts of sexual violence.

This passage is particularly significant because it uses the language of ploughing, the traditional sign for marriage and for the act of legitimate intercourse with the purpose of producing offspring. Here the imagery is overlaid with a new set of allusions, the connection made between the act of inscription, of carving a message into wood, and the act of reproduction. The fields of the *polis,* endangered, lost, property rather than the sacred analogue of the mother's body, the source of the autochthonous citizens' life, are transformed into portable tablets, the surfaces for inscription of merchants and poets. The violence of inscription, like the violence of the act of ploughing, is enacted in the body of the woman, who is represented as material—field, wood, a space for the labor of agriculture and, even more, of graphic incision.

Secret Writing

THE TATTOOED SLAVE

There are various kinds of writing associated with secrecy and with the female body, which contains a hidden interiority, a foldedness like that of the writing tablet. Deianeira keeps secret the text of the centaur's charm. The *skutala,* the encoded military message, is the phallus, the erection, in Aristophanes' *Lysistrata,* the bearer of the Muses' code, the performed text for Pindar. There is also the message unknown to the bearer. Herodotus associates writing with the passive receptivity of the body of a slave or a woman. He describes, for example, a message sent by Histiaios of Miletus to Aristagoras:

> He shaved the head of his most trustworthy slave, pricked the message on his scalp, and waited for hair to grow again. Then, as soon as it had grown, he sent the man to Miletus with instructions to do nothing when he arrived except to tell Aristagoras to shave his hair off and look at his head. The message found there was . . . an order to revolt.
>
> *Histories* 5.35

The message on the slave is tattooed and therefore permanent. But it cannot be seen by the bearer, the vehicle. He carries the signs, embodies them, but cannot decipher them himself. It is as if he were branded, appropriately for a slave, marked with his master's meaning. The head carries the signs, evocative of the curves inside the brain. The head must be shaved, as were the female genitalia in depilation, cleared for inscription. The surface must be visible, uncovered, and then covered again. The sharp instrument for pricking the signs is like the phallus. The slave is pricked (*estixe*), then his message is covered up again, then he moves. He is the mobile text, like the *pinax* or *deltos,* but also like the *skutala.* The problem is to avoid both the garrulity of the slave, who might be tortured, and the promiscuity of the text, which will communicate with anyone. Of course the slave, bought off or tortured, could simply reveal the message he had received, the command to shave his head. The device does not protect the tattoo from being read, but it puts the process of reading one step further from the interaction between two human beings, slave and guard. It is especially interesting that the message is one of revolt, since Greek slaves almost never revolted. Some ran away, but there were never massive slave revolts like those of Rome. This slave carries a message that he could never see and perhaps could not read anyway, if he were illiterate like most slaves, a message that he could never act on. Aristagoras can and does read the message and revolts.

Another secret message (*bublion*) is sent, Herodotus recounts, sewn up in the belly of a hare (*Histories* 1.123). Demaratus sends word to the Spartans that Xerxes is to invade Greece, but he fears his message will be read:

> There was only one way . . . to get the message through: this was by scraping the wax off a pair of wooden folding tablets [*deltion diptukhon*], writing on the wood underneath what Xerxes intended to do, and then covering the message over with wax again. In this way the tablets, being apparently blank, would cause no trouble with the guards along the road.
>
> *Histories* 7.239

This trick recapitulates the gesture of uncovering and recovering of Histiaios; here the wax, like the hair, is removed and replaced in an action parallel to depilation and reforestation. The message is folded into a diptych, a little *deltos,* and it looks blank (like Deianeira, who has already been inscribed, broken into). The tablet, which appears to be virgin, is illegible (*oukh eikhon sumbalesthai hoi Lakedaimonioi*). It is Gorgo (a significant name, certainly, as the Gorgon is the one who sees and whose sight turns men to stone), the daughter of Kleomenes, wife of Leonidas, who discovers the trick and tells them to scrape away the wax and find the letters (*grammata*) on the wood.

I have discussed the analogy made between women and foreigners in *Centaurs and Amazons.* Women are others, like slaves and animals; in the Herodotean anecdote, the slave is inscribed with the tattooed message, as women are seen to be inscribed by fathers and husbands. Their illiteracy, like that of slaves, kept them in a passive, subordinate position without access to texts or to history. The Herodotean accounts of writing do not present the same aspect of menace as some others, but they do associate writing with a sense of secrecy, coveredness, interiority, hiddenness. What is written should not be available to all; it should be disguised, covered, not open. The folded tablet must reach its proper destination.

IPHIGENEIA

Euripides' *Iphigeneia in Tauris* (414–12 B.C.), although composed before the worst despair of Athenian defeat in the Peloponnesian War, was written in the mood of the loss of the Sicilian expedition. Its plot points to the double nature of the letter, its different status in men's and women's worlds. Orestes comes to steal an *agalma,* the image of Artemis; Iphigeneia serves as her priestess; the Taurians sacrifice Greeks to this Artemis. Not recognizing her brother, Iphigeneia offers to save him from sacrifice so he can deliver to Argos a letter (*delton,* 584) written for her by a captive who has subsequently been sacrificed. Orestes says he himself will die instead of Pylades, who will take the letter. As she, the illiterate, hands Pylades the letter, she says: "Here is my letter, safe within these folds" (*deltou men haide polythuros diaptukhai,* 727). She will sprinkle water on the victim and he will be killed by the priests inside. Interiority is important in this play; the tablet has many doors, no clear path. The characters are inside the Dark Rocks (746). The text has become a hall of mirrors. Iphigeneia fears that the bearer of her message will fail her, and they go through a legalistic exchange about the binding circumstances of respective oaths to deliver: one the letter, the other Pylades' life.

Iphigeneia repeats her letter aloud: "I will tell you, slowly, line by line, / The contents of my letter," that is, what is written in the tablet's folds (*tanonta kaggegrammen'en deltou ptukhais logōi phrasō,* 760–61). Although she cannot write, she can tell him its contents, repeating, reciting it by rote: "For either you will place it in his hand / And the written words will speak to him or else, / If they are lost, your voice will be their echo" (*to sōma sōsas tous logous sōseis emoi,* 765). The message is doubled by this ostentatiously clumsy plot device, which permits the brother and sister to recognize one another. It is as if there were one system of communication for women, one for men. Women are locked into the oral form, into repetition, while men can carry the message that is written and therefore can be read but not repeated verbally. In fact, if Pylades died at sea, the letter would be lost too; if he were not lost, he would have no need of writing since he knows her message. The written text is rendered completely superfluous by this device. As Orestes hears the message immediately, when Pylades jokingly hands him the *deltos* and its folds (793), he has no need of the writing. He proves himself her brother with a cloth she had woven long before and by other proofs of memory. The cloth belongs to the women's world, to the preliteracy of women's work, and recalls the woven tapestry of the story of Tereus and Philomela.

Women belong to the preliterate world because they are uneducated, because they have the domestic skills so essential to the maintenance of the household, skills that do not require the skills of writing and reading, of enumeration, of history. Iphigeneia is rescued by her brother not by the text written by another but by the works of her own hand, the weaving women had always performed. Just as Penelope waited to be rescued from her suitors, as Procne suffered from the rape of her brother-in-law, so Iphigeneia is set in a world without the extension given by writing, the extension in time and space that the text allows.

Lies

In the Herodotean descriptions of writing, emphasis is placed on secrecy and deception. In Sophocles' *Trachiniae,* the message Deianeira bears is a lie in a way, but Nessos speaks the truth when he tells her how to employ the charm and when he says that Herakles will never love another woman. The message has the ambiguity of an oracle, available always for misinterpretation. In Sophocles' texts writing can be deceiving, but it is the interpretation, not creation, that fails to deliver the truth. In *Iphigeneia in Tauris,* men use writing while women depend on other forms of communication.

In other Euripidean tragedies, people write down untruth, and women's interiority is capable of delivering up not true children, but death by the word. Men write women's fate in the *deltos,* which becomes emblematic of their bodies, of the interiority that is inscribed by their masters. Writing may be a promise of fertility and propagation; Euripides turns it into a false promise. Phaedra's words poison and kill: she commits suicide, Hippolytus dies, and Theseus is destroyed by her lie. The emphasis in the image of the *skutala* is on protecting the text; with Euripides it becomes protecting oneself against the text, as it was in the Iliadic beginning with Bellerophon, although the text there written by Proitos was not itself a lie, but a murderous command. All these texts represent danger—for the sender, the bearer, or the receiver. Whereas the field can be fertile and productive as well as full of plagues and disease, there is very little praise of writing. Almost no one speaks of its value, of the ways in which it enables communication over long distance. The emphasis is on the way it can harm the ignorant carrier, the rebellious sender, the betrayed receiver. Is this an antidemocratic sentiment? Only Aeschylus, when Prometheus speaks of writing as a gift to humankind, sees writing as a positive *tekhnē,* and Aeschylus is the most democratic, although also perhaps the most misogynist, of tragedians.

Euripides extends the power of writing to the lie. Women's interiority is hidden and deceptive; they, like writing, can be false. Instead of communicating, the text can deceive, as can the woman, and, of course, as can the most sophisticated of tragic poets. Froma Zeitlin has discussed the matter of Phaedra's *deltos* in the *Hippolytus;* it is a text that destroys from inside.[44]

In *Iphigeneia at Aulis,* it is Agamemnon who writes a lying message to Clytemnestra; his servant finds him writing, erasing, sealing, and unsealing a *deltos:*

> You still have it in your hand—
> With those same words you've
> Been putting together. You seal
> The letter up—and then tear
> The seal open. You've been doing it
> Over and over again.
>
> 34–40

Sugkheō (37) means pour together, or commingle, thus to destroy or obliterate, thus to blur or confuse; as Agamemnon "pours together" his letters, so he pours down his tears. The language might suggest the link between seeds and letters. Agamemnon has planted his child Iphigeneia and will destroy her. He holds her still in his hands (*basiazdeis,* 36), and the feminine gender of *deltos,* with the relative pronoun distant from it, encourages this personification. He has sealed up her virginity, breaks it with the promise of marriage, but seals it up again as she is sacrificed a virgin. He throws the pine, the wooden writing tablet, to the ground, as he throws away his child, casting tears the while, tears that are *thaleron*—stout, sturdy, blooming, fresh, a word used often of youth (*Odyssey* 6.66). This man cries like a Homeric hero, but he does not have Homeric stature. Iphigeneia is the daughter he sowed (*hēn espeir'egō,* 90), and she must die before the fleet can sail to Troy. His brother, wanting Helen back, persuaded him, he says, to write.

"Then I wrote a letter, folded and sealed it (i.e., in the folds of the tablet: *en deltou ptukhais*), dispatched it to my wife asking her to send our daughter to be married to Achilles" (98–105). The folds of the *deltos* are made to contain his message, the lie. He uses the word *damar* for wife, a usage with the connotation of taming, subjecting, forcing, from *damazō,* overpower. An ironic usage, since in the end she will kill, taming him in her net like an animal. He takes on himself responsibility for the lies, joining them together; the word order suggests first that the lies are joined together around the maiden herself. She is the folded *deltos;* she is to be enfolded in her father's lies.

In the dark, Agamemnon sits, trying to write and send the truth: "Now in this letter I rewrite the message and put down the truth. This I was doing when you saw me in the dark unsealing the letter and sealing it again" (108–13). He loosens the folds of the *deltos,* as the bridegroom loosens the *zonē,* the maiden's belt, in a sign of taking possession of her (*Odyssey* 11.245). All the language associated with this *deltos* is sexually charged. The father's writing in the *deltos* would protect her virginity and her life, seal her up in safety. But he breaks open the *deltos,* which tells of his deception; he loosens, then binds it up again; he fastens it, but with the sense of closing, joining, like the lips of the vaginal opening. If he keeps the *deltos* intact, bound, the virginity and life of his daughter will be preserved. The tablet says that the new message must be added to the old, that his wife must not send her to Aulis' lap (*kolpode,* 120). He sends the messenger off with the seal, which also marks his letter: "This seal [*sphragida*]. Keep it. It is / The same as the seal on the letter [*deltoi*]" (156–57). The seal marks the closure, the guarantee of virginity.

And it is seized from the messenger by Menelaus; the messenger tells him, "It is not for you to 'loosen the *deltos*' (307), unseal the scroll" (307). But Menelaus has "lifted the seal," opened it (*anoixas,* 321, 325). Agamemnon is outraged by Menelaus' presumption, his opening of the closed text. Menelaus denounces Agamemnon, accusing him of dishonesty, of pretending not to want to rule, of promising to keep open doors to the people (*thuras . . . akleistous,* 340). When he gained power, he closed his doors and became "inaccessible and seldom found at home" (345). And he sent gladly for his daughter (361); now he changes his mind, sends a different message, what the text calls "other writing" (*allas graphas,* 364). Agamemnon defends himself by accusing Menelaus of desiring his worthless wife; he will not kill his child for vile Helen. But Iphigeneia arrives with her mother; she is bathing in a pool in a meadow, emblematic of virginity (422), with the horses, also associated with young girls and desire for them. And, although Menelaus is now, after seeing the girl, willing to forgo her sacrifice, Agamemnon insists that the mob, led by Odysseus, will force them to it. The meeting between daughter and father plays ironically, heavily, on the ritual association between funeral and marriage (e.g., 669). Iphigeneia is to be cut off from mother and father but not in marriage to Achilles, as she believes. He sends her inside. There is much emphasis on the place of women; girls, especially, must remain inside, in safety (739, 740).

The chorus sings of the fate of Troy and of her women's lamentations. They will sing of Helen and doubt that Zeus really came as a swan to Leda:

> But perhaps this is a fable
> from the book of the Muses [*en deltois Pierisin*]

Borne to me out of season,
A senseless tale.

798–800

These Pierian *deltoi* are the Muses', in which are recorded the *muthoi,* tales that are badly timed, even useless. Like the narrative on which the tragedy is based, like the tragedy, like Agamemnon's letter, like the worthless prize Helen, inscription can be false. The Muses can lie, just as Agamemnon and the poet can. Achilles makes much of the fact that he, the hero, will not lie (1005–6). When Clytemnestra accuses him of plotting Iphigeneia's murder, Agamemnon says: "I am destroyed—my secret is betrayed" (1140). The things he had hidden, his *krupta,* are exposed, given away, and betrayed; Clytemnestra says she will uncover all: "I shall give you open speech" (*anakalupsō . . . logous,* 1146). She says she was a good wife:

Witness that I, as your wife, have been
Blameless, modest in passion, and in honor
Seeking to increase your house so that
Your coming-in had gladness and
Your going-out joy.

1159–61

Her body is like his house, chaste, closed to strangers, increasing both with children and stores; he entered and left her and his house with pleasure. She gave him three daughters and a son, and now he will deprive her, kill her daughter, to pay for Helen. She threatens to become an evil wife herself. Agamemnon adduces patriotic argument (1271–72), and Iphigeneia herself resolves to die gloriously (*eukleē,* 1376) to ensure safety for Greek women from barbarians, to win for herself a glorious name (*kleos,* 1383), freeing Greece. Her life means nothing: "Rather in war is it far better that / Many women go to their death, if this / Keep one man only facing the light and alive" (1394, cf. *Iphigeneia in Tauris* 1005–6). She continues, giving her body to Greece, speaking the patriotic language of the Marathonomachoi: "They are bondsmen and slaves [*doulon*], and we, / Mother, are Greeks and free" (*eleutheroi,* 1401). Achilles is persuaded. She goes to meet her death in Artemis' meadow (1463), but the messenger reports, in a disputed passage, that at the altar a deer was sacrificed, a substitute for Iphigeneia (1544). Clytemnestra's last words are:

How know
That this is not a story merely told
That I may have relief from bitter pain?

1616–18

The story may be a lie; the narrative of the tragedy may be a lie; all stories may be lies to stop pain. So Euripides puts his own text into question.

Open or closed, hidden or revealed, the *deltos,* the *mythos* can be lies. The girl goes to her death for a lie; her salvation may well be a lie; the play itself a lie; and the political myth of Hellas a lie. Any text, any tablet, open or closed, can say the lie, and anything between truth and lie as well. There is total exhaustion of traditional narrative, genre, metaphor. Euripides looks back and mocks his own tragedy, *Iphigeneia in Tauris.* The pleasure of the Aristophanic text, which associates the act of writing with sex and with ploughing, has given way to a representation of the treachery of the written text. The lie is hidden in the *deltos,* inscribed by the father, by the fathers, by the tradition of stories, of the very legends of Hellenic glory that end by destroying the girl Iphigeneia, who is herself written to death.

The metaphor of the writing tablet coexists with other metaphors describing the female body. It represents that body as a space for scriptural labor. The space of graphic incision may be a vase, a coin, a material text like the wooden oar of the *Thesmophoriazusae,* or the tablet used for writing and erasure by the Greeks. This metaphor is embedded in a network of similar metaphors—the representation of the body as a field, a furrow, an oven, a stone, or space demarcated by stone. Although it is a commonplace for descriptions of mind, it seems to have special affinities for the description of the marking of the female body. The connotations of the tattooing of the slave only reinforce this notion that the object of inscription is a possession, a thing, a space defined by the law of property.

As the earth, once thought of as the autonomous source of all life, flowering and burgeoning without human labor, gives way to a notion of land possessed, marked, worked, and transferable, so too the metaphor of the female body as the source of life is overlaid with a representation of that body as a space of reproductive labor. And further, as the ancient city of Athens abandons its dependence on agriculture, even, in moments of crisis, abandoning the very land it once cultivated in an act of worship and piety, so the metaphors used to describe the reproductive labor of the family change.

The metaphors for the female body exist in a complex set; they seem interchangeable, but they also signify different attitudes toward the reproductive role of the female. There is an assumption of an ever more alienated set of metaphors for describing the female body. From being the autonomous earth, it is represented as a furrow that must be plowed by the husband, as an oven that must be filled and heated by the husband, as stone that is labored over, set in place, and constructed, which guards the property and chastity of the home. The metaphor of the tablet is the final logical moment in this process, a metaphor that emphasizes the passivity and receptivity of female interiority, that assumes that the mover of the stylus, the inscriber, the literate male who carves and marks the passive medium, alone has the power to generate the marks of the text, which will proliferate not on the tablet itself, but in the mind of the reader, who will again, himself alone, inscribe a new text on a tablet that has been erased, scraped clean. The process of alienation, of making the female body into property, alienable, portable, and absolutely passive, is challenged obliquely by Euripides, who sees the power of the lie, the capacity of the tablet to misrepresent the truth. The tablet becomes the space of literate labor, of ambiguous messages of death and of closure. Plato reworks this language and establishes a new logic of sexual difference.

III

THE WOMAN OF PHILOSOPHY

Eight

THE PLATONIC APPROPRIATION OF REPRODUCTION

The metaphorical system I have described, mapping only a part of a larger network that situates the female in ancient Greek culture, focuses on the female body as a space of reproduction and of thesaurization. It locates the female as a potential for producing goods or for protecting them. She becomes the locus of inscription, the folded papyrus that signifies the potential for deception. This potential is alienated from the earth and made dependent on the male Athenian citizen. The very fact of the network's metaphoricity links it with the practices of Athenian democracy, which described itself in relation to various others in terms of opposition.

After the political, social, and economic crisis of the Athenian defe in the Peloponnesian War, Athens abandoned some of the most radic features of democratic practice. Forced at first into a new and repressive oligarchy by the Spartans, it subsequently developed into a restored democracy, which, like that of the fifth century, in our terms would be called an oligarchy. Many writers of the late fifth and early fourth centuries joined in condemning democracy and its ideology of equality; the texts of the fourth century establish new terms for the location of the female.

Of particular interest in the fourth century, among the works of new comedy, legal orations, histories, and philosophical texts, are the dialogues of Plato, which create not only a new genre but establish the terms of philosophical intercourse for centuries to come. Plato's texts are at the origin of the tradition of Western metaphysics. Perhaps due to violent misreadings, failure to recognize the ironic aspects of his works or the subtleties of the interactions of his dialecticians, a particular representation of his views—an advocacy of idealism and of metaphysics—has marked philosophical discourse since the fourth century.[1]

I am interested here in a particular aspect of the Platonic text and in certain dialogues. I am interested in the ways in which Plato participates in or produces a change in the situation of the female in the world. This may seem to be a minor aspect of Platonic philosophy, especially since women are never present in the Platonic setting. Yet, I believe that Plato's appropriation of the reproductive metaphors of Greek culture used to describe the place of women and his use of this metaphorical network to authorize the male philosopher are linked to a metaphorical project—to the task of monistic metaphysics, the positing of a one—father, sun, god—who is the source and origin of the good. In certain dialogues—especially in the *Theaetetus*, the *Symposium*, and the *Phaedrus*—Plato uses the metaphorical language formerly employed to locate the female and makes a new philosopher of it.

The *Phaedrus,* as a text of seduction aimed at drawing the reader toward erotic life and therefore toward philosophy, plays on the Greek definitions of male and female, using the vocabulary of sexual difference in Greek culture to establish a new portrait of the philosopher as lover, inseminator, and fertile field.

My reading of the *Phaedrus* is concerned with the presence and appropriation of the female in the dialogue; Jacques Derrida's "La pharmacie de Platon" and his reading of this dialogue have influenced my understanding of Plato and of the place of his work in the philosophical tradition. Derrida's essay discusses the *Phaedrus* as a text establishing what he elsewhere calls a metaphysics of "presence."[2] He describes Plato's work as "logocentric," focusing on presence as opposed to absence, the living voice as opposed to writing, life opposed to death, soul opposed to body. The stronger term of various dualist oppositions is in Plato's work valorized through the use of what Derrida calls a "supplement"—here, writing, called a *pharmakon,* both poison and cure. Writing is an exemplary supplement, the not valorized side of an opposition used to establish the centrality and the value of speaking. Derrida describes the project of Platonic writing as the production of the son after the father's death: ". . . the disappearance of the good-father-capital-sun is . . . the precondition of discourse. . . . The disappearance of truth as presence, the withdrawal of the present origin of presence, is the condition of all (manifestation of) truth."[3] Derrida regards Plato, in his emphasis on truth, presence, and speaking, as aware of, yet caught in, the same contradiction as all thinkers who follow him. He insists on the truth of the living voice, yet writes; insists on the living presence of Socrates, yet writes only after Socrates' death. Furthermore, and wrongly, I think, Derrida describes what he sees as the exclusively masculine Platonic lineage of philosophy, a phallocentric model of philosophical discourse where the inheritance of dialectic passes patrilineally, from father to son. Derrida says:

> It is all about fathers and sons, about bastards unaided by any public assistance, about glorious, legitimate sons, about inheritance, sperm, sterility. Nothing is said of the mother, but this will not be held against us. And if one looks hard enough as at those pictures in which a second picture faintly can be made out, one might be able to discern her unstable form, drawn upside-down in the foliage, at the back of the garden. In the gardon of Adonis, *eis Adonidos kepous* (276b).
>
> P. 143

Although Derrida's reading is brilliant and illuminating, it is, I think, blind to its own phallocentrism to the extent that it fails to acknowledge Plato's desire to appropriate maternity to the male philosopher, to incorporate into the portrait of the philosopher the very metaphors traditionally used to represent the female in classical culture.

An analysis of the historical shape of logocentrism and of phallocentrism is necessary for real understanding of the text and of its relationship, first to Greek society, then to the lineage of philosophy to which Derrida refers. Derrida "misreads" the *Phaedrus,* at least at the level of sexual difference. The particular shape of Greek misogyny, because Greek society excluded women so radically from participation in intellectual life, made the form of Plato's sexual politics different from that of those who follow him. In the *Phaedrus,* there is, I will argue, as there is in the *Theaetetus* and the *Symposium,* a *mimesis* of the female, so that in the homoerotic movement of the dialogue, the female is perhaps more present than she is in later texts of the tradition where the less absolute social oppression of women leaves space for philosophy to be more radically phallocentric, to abandon the reproductive metaphors used of the female, and to describe her entirely in terms of lack.

The homoerotics of the *Phaedrus,* explicit and implicit, seem to center on relations between men. The result appears to be the exclusion of women from true *eros,* and therefore from philosophy, from access to the truth. Plato's misogyny can be demonstrated polemically from a variety of sources; it is possible to find many passages such as this one from the *Timaeus,* where the character Timaeus includes in his account of creation, almost as an afterthought, a discussion of the creation of women that is expressive of contempt and mistrust:

> According to the probable account, all those creatures generated as men who proved themselves cowardly and spent their lives in wrong-doing were transformed, at their second incarnation, into women. And it was for this reason that the gods at that time contrived the love of sexual intercourse by constructing an animate creature of one kind in us men, and of another kind in women. . . . in men the nature of the genital organs is disobedient and self-willed, like a creature that is deaf to reason, and it attempts to dominate all because of its frenzied lusts. And in women, again, owing to the same causes, whenever the matrix or womb, which is an indwelling creature desirous of child-bearing—remains without fruit long beyond the due season, it is vexed and takes it ill; and by straying all ways through the body and blocking up the passages of the breath and preventing respiration it casts the body in the uttermost

> distress, and causes, moreover, all kinds of maladies, until the desire and love of the two sexes unite them. . . .
>
> In this fashion, then, women and the whole female sex have come into existence.
>
> *Timaeus* 91a–d

Thus, at least according to Timaeus, the necessity for women and the torments of sexual desire came about originally because of the failure of men to live bravely and justly. As Pandora was sent to punish Prometheus for his deception of Zeus, so women are the result of men's inability to behave philosophically.[4]

The fantasy of masculine *autarkeia,* self-sufficiency, was a persistent theme in Greek culture. In Hesiod's myth of the time before the division between men and gods—before work, cooking, and sacrifice—women had no place. Men were contented and sufficient unto themselves. In the fifth century, the fantasy of single-sex, masculine culture appeared in the vehement wishes of Euripides' Jason and Hippolytus.[5]

The desire to "abject" the female, to use Julia Kristeva's term, to see her as pollution, to cast her outside, is part of the character of the obsessively chaste, Artemisian Hippolytus.[6] But it is a traditional strain of Greek social relations as well. Women were normally hidden away inside their houses, but they were also often, in ritual, "cast out" of normal social life. While their reproductive powers were necessary, women's bodies could be seen to endanger the city through their *miasma.*

Plato has seemed to some to share the fantasy of an exclusively male world. Philosophy, in the Platonic description (with the possible rare exception of an Aspasia or a Diotima, though never represented directly in the text), is a masculine endeavor. Women, whose wombs wander, who are dominated by the unphilosophical parts of their souls, do not appear. The dominant literary genres of the fifth century, tragedy, comedy, and history, in which individual women are portrayed, are in the fourth century joined, perhaps dominated, by legal orations in which only men speak and by the dialogues—accounts of men talking to each other.

Although in *The Republic* Plato says women are to be created of every class, to reproduce, to be the companions of men at every level of the state, they are nonetheless consistently described as by nature weaker, more abandoned, and less philosophical than men.[7] The implicit desire of masculine *autarkeia* is present also, perhaps especially in the *Phaedrus,* where seduction is an issue between man and man, where philosophy and the approach toward the good are the business of male lovers. Reproduction is there ascribed exclusively to men; they will inseminate each other with philosophy in a sexual act in which women have no place.

One can read a misogynist, phallocentric Plato who has a vision, especially in the *Phaedrus,* of a homoerotics based on absolute rejection of women from intercourse with men and based on the practice of philosophy that exiles women. Yet I want to identify a countercurrent in the *Phaedrus,* an undertext of dialectical movement between the sexes, a recognition that a definition of sexual identity in terms of contradictories, although argued for in the Platonic corpus, is not satisfactory. In the *Phaedrus,* Plato employs the fluid boundary between the sexes with great seductive power, especially in his portrait of Socrates. And he appropriates traditional metaphors—the descriptions of the female as defined by inner potentiality, by reproductive interiority—to the person of the male philosopher.

The female in the *Phaedrus,* although not characterized individually, is more than an "unstable form . . . at the back of the garden." She may be seen as another supplement that Plato delicately tries to control and appropriate in order to center on the male and thus on a homoerotic model for philosophy. Rather than enacting a rigid *diaeresis* between the sexes, Plato's text plays erotically with boundaries, with edges, with the space between one thing and its opposite, moving through separation to collection and back again. Plato uses the tension between the sexes in Greek culture to assert the authority of the male at the scene of philosophy, but also and more importantly, his own desire to appropriate the powers of the female makes that authority a very provisional one and marks the Platonic text as the threshold of a new description of sexual difference. If Plato appropriates the female powers of reproduction to the male philosopher, the philosophical tradition after him stresses the autonomy of that male, his self-sufficiency, his privileged access to the divine and the one, and that tradition describes the female as a defective male, a creature distanced from the absolute presence and union with the divine.

The *Phaedrus* is a text of seduction. It acts to allure the imaginary *erōmenos* whom Lysias desires to seduce with the first discourse.[8] Socrates offers two speeches designed at least in part to seduce his companion Phaedrus. The *Phaedrus'* movements of alternation and exchange make it a drama of sexual encounter between two men and between the reader and the text. Phaedrus comes with a gift from Lysias, shares it with Socrates, who remarks frequently and admiringly on Phaedrus' beauty and enthusiasm; they share in this conversation outside the boundaries of the city a seductive moment of intimacy. The themes of *diaeresis* and *synagogē,* central for the character Socrates in this dialogue, offer a model of erotic contact and separation. Socrates says, "I myself am a *lover* of these processes of division and bringing together" (*egōge autos te erastēs . . . to diaireseōn kai synagagōn,* 266b). The alternation between collection, the *synousia* of intercourse, and division, the *diaeresis,* glosses the comic myth of the *Symposium* (189d–193a), where Aristophanes tells of the original unity of the human body and its cutting, its division, into male/male, male/female, and female/female halves.[9] The act of intercourse is for Aristophanes an attempt to "re-collect," to reform the fragmented body in which we live.

The description of the logical method Socrates advocates has a polymorphously erotic dimension. The possibility of "collection," *synagogē, synousia,* between the two characters, between reader and writer, is at the heart of the dialogue. Spectator and reader are swept up in Socrates' ecstatic vision of the winged soul in a scene of great metaphysical resonance. And at the end of the drama there is a reassertion of difference, of separation, as Phaedrus promises to return to Lysias. The problematic mention of Isocrates, called Socrates' *paidika* (his "darling," 270b), seems on one level an attempt to establish a symmetry and distance between Phaedrus and Socrates. Isocrates is to Socrates as Lysias is to Phaedrus; the two older lovers return to their younger *erōmenoi* after playing with the possibility of connection between them on this sunny afternoon.

The logic of collection and division is not restricted to relations between men, however. If there is often in Plato's text a compulsive identification of the male as A and the female as not-A—an attempt to establish boundaries with an excluded middle, an obsessive movement of separation, of *diaeresis* between female and male—there is also in the *Phaedrus* an implicit and subversive argument for collection, for movement between contradictories as well. It is the tension between these movements that provides much of the erotic pleasure of reading the *Phaedrus*. And this is what makes this an important moment in the narrative I am making: the moment of the appropriation and eventual "metonymizing" of the female body.

Plato's text itself engages in an erotic metamorphosis that appears to obscure the evident misogyny in Greek culture, but it in fact reinscribes the female by locating her powers within the male. In the *Phaedrus* this reinscription occurs through a sort of Socratic transvestism, through a shifting between the opposites of male and female.[10] The language of the *Phaedrus* enacts this androgyny, this dialogue between sexual identities, in Socrates as he speaks. Socrates, for example, several times evokes the Bacchantes. In speaking of the lovers inspired by Zeus, drawing their liquid from Zeus, he says, using the feminine article and the masculine participle, that "if they draw the waters of their inspiration from Zeus, like the Bacchantes, they pour it out upon the beloved and make him, so far as possible, like their god" (*k'an ek Dios arutōsin, hōsper hai bakkhai, epi tēn tou erōmenou psuchēn epantlountes poiousin hōs dunaton homoiotaton tōi spheterōi theōi,* 253a). The simile mixes the female sexual identity of the Bacchantes with the action of irrigation in the passage where Socrates describes the moistening of the soul's wings. There he plays with the connection between erection and the growth of wings: "and as the nourishment streams upon him, the quills of the feathers swell and begin to grow from the roots over all the form of the soul" (251bc). The *trophē,* like mother's milk, is implicitly compared to an ejaculatory stream that meets a corresponding erection in the beloved, causing the buds of his wings to sprout. Both male and female are present in the insemination and nurturing of the wings; the Zeus-inspired Bacchantes are emblematic of the crossing of the sexes.

Socrates says, after hearing Phaedrus' discourse, that he *synebakkheusa* with Phaedrus, that he joined him in Bacchic frenzy (234d). DeVries in his commentary compares this with *ton synkorubantionta* (228b), pointing out the irony of this response to Lysias' precious discourse.[11] The later mention of the Bacchae is also ironic, yet it suggests a connection between the characters in the dialogue and the worshippers of Dionysos, probably most often women, who left their cities for anarchic celebration in the mountains, living outside the boundaries not only of the *polis* but of their sexual identity. They resemble Socrates, who is, in the *Phaedrus, exō teichous,* "outside the (city) walls," wandering through the liquid stream of the Ilissos, which threatens to dissolve his nature (229a). He says: "I investigate . . . myself, to know whether I am a monster (*thērion*) more complicated and more furious than Typhon, or a gentler and simpler creature" (230a). The mocking description of his self-examination is a prelude to his playing a hybrid of another sort.

Socrates speaks his first discourse *egkalupsamenos* (237a), veiled as one near death, or as a woman. He plays on the ambiguity of the veil, as does Socrates at the end of the *Trachiniae* (1071–80), where Herakles, veiled and dying, calls himself female, *thēlus,* in his weakness. Michael Nagler has elucidated the relation between the veil and female chastity in the Homeric text:

> . . . in the epic tradition, one encounters the veil as projector of sexual *charis* (note its visual epithets *liparos, sigaloeis,* "shiny, bright"), as hider of these attractive qualities for purposes of modesty (*kalumma, kaluptre,* etc.), and in various combinations and syntheses of these polar opposites.[12]

Veiled, Socrates is a woman, both seductive and chaste; with head bared, he is both a violated woman and a man.

In the tradition of poets from Homer and Hesiod on, Socrates speaks in the *Phaedrus* of being inspired by the Muses and by the Nymphs. The state of "enthusiasm," having the god or goddess in one, can connote a shifting of sexual identity. Cassandra, after having been possessed physically by Apollo and refusing him a child, is possessed once again, inhabited by the male god as she speaks his prophecy in the *Agamemnon* (1200–1210). The chorus calls her arts *tekhnaisin entheois;* the god, breathing delight (*pneōn kharin*), inspired her and entered her as the Muses and the Nymphs can enter and inspire and blur the identity of the poet. Socrates speaks ironically of the danger of being himself possessed by the Nymphs (*hupo tōn*

Nymphōn . . . enthousiasō, 241e). He recites a catalogue of cross-sex "enthusiasm," of the priestesses at Dodona who prophesy in their madness, of the Sibyl and others who, using "possessed prophecy" (*mantikēi entheōi*), foretell many things. These forms of ecstasy blur sexual contradictories; they suggest that double-sexed creature imagined by Aristophanes in the *Symposium.* Cross-sexed possession by the gods both erases the boundaries of sexual identity and, by crossing the edges of sexual difference, enacts a mimesis of intercourse.

Socrates' allusions to possession by divine figures are echoed in the text by a version of Socratic transvestism or ventriloquism, realized literarily. In the myth of the charioteer and his two horses (246a ff.), Socrates allusively mimes a character from another drama: Atossa, queen of Aeschylus' *Persians.* The image of the chariot probably alludes to Parmenides (28b1) and to representations in art, but the image of two horses, one docile, one anarchic, suggests the dream of Atossa as well (*The Persians* 181–99). Atossa says of the women of Xerxes' chariot: "One . . . towers / proud, her mouth obedient to the reins" (192–93). Socrates' good horse "needs no whip, but is guided only by the word of command and by reason" (*Phaedrus* 253a). In the Persian queen's dream, "the other stamps, annoyed, and rends apart / Her trappings in her hands; unbridled, seizes / The car and snaps its yoke in two" (*xunarpazei bia / aneu khalinōn kai zugon thrauei meson, The Persians* 194–96). Socrates' dark horse, at the sight of the beloved, "struggling (*biazomenos*) . . . and pulling, he forces them . . . he lowers his head, raises his tail, takes the bit in his teeth (*endakōn ton khalinon*) and pulls shamelessly" (*Phaedrus* 254d). Socrates, in his description of the charioteer, as *hupokritēs,* expounder and actor, puts himself in the place of Atossa. The intertextuality allows as well for an allusive identification between the internal parts of the soul, the horses, and the females yoked to Xerxes' chariot in Atossa's dream.

The ritual drama of Athens, tragedy and comedy, was just one occasion of sacred transvestism in the religious life of the city. Cross-dressing seems to have been especially prominent in rituals of puberty and adolescence. During the Oschophoria, a festival celebrated during the month of Pyanepsion, two well-born young men wearing female robes headed a procession from Athens to Phaleron, supposedly in memory of a trick the hero Theseus played on Minos.[13] Jean-Pierre Vernant interprets the ritual exchange of dress as a temporary participation in the other sex that preceded the distinct separation of the sexes in adulthood. I would argue further that in Greek culture, so repressive to women, where women were the paradigmatic "others," the temptation to play the other must have been a suppressed but enduring and powerful motive. Pentheus, in the *Bacchae,* is seduced into transvestism by his fascination with women's secrets.[14] The mantic powers of Teiresias himself were perhaps derived from the years he lived in the body of a woman.

One further mask that Socrates assumes in the *Phaedrus* is that of Sappho. His mention of the poets Sappho and Anacreon prepares the way for a later assumption of her lyric voice (235c). He says that he has heard something better than Lysias' discourse from Anacreon or from Sappho—called *kalēs,* perhaps to prepare for the unlovely Socrates who will assume her place. Then after his first, impious *logos* (251b), he offers a description of the effects of *erōs,* shadowed with allusion to Sappho 31 (*phainetai moi* . . .). Sappho there speaks of trembling, *tromos,* of cold sweat, *idrōs psuchros,* of the gaze at her lover, of a flame beneath the flesh. Socrates says:

> And as he looks upon him a reaction from his shuddering [*phrikēs*] comes over him, with sweat [*hidrōs*] and unwonted heat; for as the effluence of beauty enters him through the eyes he is warmed.

Sappho's was perhaps the canonical description of desire, with its brilliant evocation of heat, cold, trembling. To echo her response so deftly is to be possessed by her, to become the lyric poet possessed by the lyric poetess, to blur once again the line between the sexes by dressing oneself in the words and images of the other. In Sappho's poem, another homoerotic text, there is the curious phenomenon of desire suggesting a change of sexual identity. The gaze at her lover and at her lover's companion—the other, the male—makes Sappho set herself in his place. She undergoes a transforming identification that involved the physical metamorphosis described in the poem. The situation of homoerotic desire ensures the mimetic presence of the other sex in the *erastēs,* the lover.[15]

Socrates' transvestism, delicate and allusive as it is, is consistent with a pattern of the Greek male's fascination with and gradual appropriation of the socially suppressed female other. The mimesis of the female in the *Phaedrus* is perhaps a way of implicitly suggesting the theme of intercourse between Socrates and Phaedrus, by establishing a difference between them, one displaced from the *erastēs/erōmenos* (lover/beloved) difference, since both presumably are *erastai,* lovers (236b, 257b). But this taking on a female identity also plays with the possibility of the woman's presence at the scene of philosophy, a presence that is allusively represented in a strategy devoted to stabilizing the practice of philosophy around the central figure of the male.

A passage at the end of the dialogue (after the discussion of the *pharmakon,* writing) illuminates the movement of the appropriation of the female and shows how the traditional metaphors of description are transformed in the Platonic text. The field, the furrow—the dominant metaphors used for reproductive intercourse from the time of Homer—are here assimilated to a situation of pederasty and philosophy. Socrates transforms the commonplaces of poetry, marriage, and social practice and converts them to his own ends, a seduction of the soul of the lover toward beauty and philosophy.

After pointing out the futility of sowing one's seeds in a garden of Adonis (276b), Socrates describes a proper garden, one where words, like seeds, will flourish:

> . . . serious discourse about them [justice, etc., 276e] is far nobler, when one employs the dialectic method and plants and sows in a fitting soul intelligent words which are able to help themselves and him who planted them, which are not fruitless, but yield seed [*sperma*] from which there spring up in other minds other words capable of continuing the process forever.
> 276e–277a

The themes of the garden of Adonis and of the citizen-woman as a field for reproduction of the citizen-male's family have been brilliantly analyzed by Marcel Detienne in *Les jardins d'Adonis.* Here in answer to Phaedrus, whom Socrates jokingly calls *murrinousiou* (244a, perhaps referring punningly to Myrrha, Adonis' mother), Socrates alters the botanical code that opposed Adonis' gardening and Demeter's agriculture. He uses the imagery associated with Demeter, goddess of grain, of cereals, of fruitful human increase, of the furrow, the woman's sexual organs to be ploughed by her husband. Here the imagery of the fruitful field, characteristically used of women, crosses the sexes once again. This field yields not human children, a new generation to populate the *polis,* but *sperma,* seed. The philosopher who erotically implants his seed, his words, in the soul of the beloved will begin an endless process of purely masculine reproduction, where the produce is more words, more seeds.[16]

This passage demonstrates the gesture of appropriation of the network of metaphors associated with women and with their role in the city. The metaphor of the fertile field, of the furrow ploughed by the husband, used by Sophocles to describe Jocasta and, in the fifth century, connected with the myth of Thebes, is here reinscribed into the relationship of pederasty. The older philosopher, erotically bound to his beloved, plants not the seeds of the family, but the words of philosophy. He transfers the power of reproduction to the art of philosophy. The metaphor of inscription, also connected in the fifth century with the mind and body of the female, is linked here to the practices of pederasty and of philosophy. The female body is no longer the site of ploughing and sowing, of inscription and marking; it has been replaced by the soul of the male philosopher.

In other texts, Plato employs metaphors elsewhere associated with the act of heterosexual intercourse, or the metaphor of stones described in chapter 5. In the *Theaetetus,* Socrates repeatedly refers to himself as a midwife (149a ff.). This dialogue's narrative frame is a conversation between Euclides and Terpsion, who took notes on a Socratic report of a conversation he once had with Theodorus and Theaetetus. It is an aporetic dialogue that considers what knowledge is and ends without an answer. The whole text resonates with the metaphors described earlier as "locating" the woman and her body. In a consideration of the Protagorean utterance, "man is the measure of all things," Socrates describes how a theory of knowledge consistent with this view might evolve. He uses the language of reproduction to account for perception:

> Their [those who follow Protagoras] first principle, on which all that we said just now depends, is that the universe really is motion and nothing else. And there are two kinds of motion. Of each kind there are any number of instances, but they differ in that the one kind has the power of acting, the other of being acted upon. From the intercourse and friction of these with one another arise offspring, endless in number, but in pairs of twins.
>
> 156a

The model of generation is abstracted from a gendered, reproductive act to describe the process of perception; gender is here erased.

Later in the text, in an attempt to account for false judgment, Socrates develops the analogy between the mind and a wax tablet:

> Imagine, then, for the sake of argument, that our minds contain a block of wax. . . . Let us call it the gift of the Muses' mother, Memory, and say that whenever we wish to remember something we see or hear or conceive in our own minds, we hold this wax under the perceptions or ideas and imprint them on it as we might stamp the impression of a seal ring.
>
> 191cd

The rich and suggestive metaphor of the tablet, used in the fifth century for the mind but also frequently employed by such authors as Sophocles and Aristophanes to stand for the woman's body, has here been enlisted once again to describe a universal process, a gift of the Muses' mother, memory.

Socrates accounts for the differences in judgment by *evaluating* different minds' wax; of course, the philosopher's wax would be of excellent quality:

> When a man has in his mind a good thick slab of wax, smooth and kneaded to the right consistency, and the impressions that come through the senses are stamped on these tables of the

> "heart" [*Iliad* 2.851; 16.554]—Homer's word hints at the mind's likeness to wax—then the imprints are clear and deep enough to last a long time.
>
> 194c

Others, less fortunate, have muddy, impure, oversoft, or hard wax, and therefore judge falsely. Socrates finds the analogy with imprinting more satisfactory than the description of intercourse between the perceived and the perceiving.

Throughout this dialogue, Socrates refers to himself as a midwife who is bringing Theaetetus to give birth to ideas—some worthy of death by exposure, some more valuable. He says he is like a barren woman, beyond the age of childbirth, who can help others to reproduce: "How absurd of you, never to have heard that I am the son of a midwife, a fine buxom woman called Phaenarete!" (149a). This section is usually cited as an example of Socratic humility and irony; I would rather connect it with a subtext in this dialogue and elsewhere that allies the philosopher with the woman. Socrates continues, associating the skills of the midwife with those of husbandry:

> Consider the knowledge of the sort of plant or seed that should be sown in any given soil. Does not that go together with skill in tending and harvesting the fruits of the earth? . . . And so with a woman; skill in the sowing is not to be separated from skill in the harvesting?
>
> 149e

The woman, the midwife, can be a matchmaker because, like the farmer, she knows the right seed for a particular plot of ground. Socrates claims that his skills are like his mother's:

> My art of midwifery is in general like theirs; the only difference is that my patients are men, not women, and my concern is not with the body but with the soul that is in travail of birth.
>
> 150b

Not only is Socrates himself a midwife, a woman, although one past childbirth, but the young men who converse with him are feminized by their conversation with him:

> And in yet another way those who seek my company have the same experience as a woman with child; they suffer the pains of labor and, by night and day, are full of distress far greater than a woman's, and my art has power to bring on these pangs or to allay them.
>
> 151ab

This is appropriation of female experience, of the female body; it recalls Medea's cry:

> What they say of us is that we have a peaceful time
> Living at home, while they do the fighting in war.
> How wrong they are! I would very much rather stand
> Three times in the front of battle than bear one child.
>
> *Medea* 248–51

Socrates, no longer contrasting men's life in war with women's role at home of reproducing, reinscribes the act of generation, of reproduction, and transfers it to the philosopher, whose experience in labor and birth is idealized and made to transcend that of women.

At the end of the *Theaetetus,* Socrates returns to the description of himself as midwife. Just before referring to the indictment brought up by Meletus, which will bring about his death, he says:

> . . . this midwife's art is a gift from heaven; my mother had it for women, and I for young men of a generous spirit and for all in whom beauty dwells.
>
> 210c

This dialogue is of particular interest in part because it contains an elaborate description of the philosopher's difference from and superiority to all other mortals; for example:

> . . . from their youth up they [the leaders in philosophy] have never known the way to market place or law court or Council Chamber or any other place of public assembly; they never hear a decree read out or look at the text of a law. To take any interest in the rivalries of political cliques, in meetings, dinners, and merrymakings with flute girls, never occurs to them even in dreams.
>
> 173d

Thus the philosopher, the very exemplar used by Foucault to typify the Greek in his "history of sexuality," has contempt for politics, for the workings of democracy, even for ordinary heterosexual pleasure. A place above triviality and frivolity is established as the scene of philosophy; the female is both excluded and assimilated to a theory of monistic homoerotics.

In the *Symposium,* too, Plato uses the vocabulary associated with sexual difference in his description of Socrates. In his reaction to the discourse of Agathon, Socrates evokes the myth of Medusa, mocking Agathon's excess of rhetoric:

> . . . his speech reminded me so strongly of that master of rhetoric, Gorgias, that I couldn't help thinking of Odysseus,

> and his fear that Medusa would rise from the lower world among the ghosts, and I was afraid that when Agathon got near the end he would arm his speech against mine with the Gorgon's head of Gorgias' eloquence, and strike me as dumb as a stone.
>
> 198bc

The dialogue returns again to the theme of the stone image.

In this conversation within conversation, in a highly elaborate rhetorical frame of reportage, Socrates speaks the words of a woman, takes her place, acts her part in this dialogue that replaces the embodiment of the voice of the woman in the theater, which engaged in another form of transvestism with the male actor playing the part of the woman. In ancient Athens, in the theater, in ritual, in the philosophical dialogue, male actors played out the role of female in varieties of costume. And their exchange of identities, the transgression and movement across the boundary between the sexes, constituted an erotic pleasure. Plato uses that movement to play, to seduce, and finally to contain the female other. Here it is the philosopher who echoes the words of Diotima, "a Mantinean woman . . . who was deeply versed in this and many other fields of knowledge" (201d). Diotima instructs Socrates about love, and he repeats her discourse: "All men are pregnant (*kuousi*), Socrates, both in body and in soul" (206c);

> . . . those whose procreancy is of the body turn to woman as the object of their love, and raise a family. . . . But those whose procreancy is of the spirit rather than of the flesh—and they are not unknown, Socrates—conceive and bear the things of the spirit.
>
> 208e–209a

Socrates is made privy to the secrets of reproduction, and he shares his knowledge by engaging in a literary mimesis of this wisest of women. She teaches him that the philosophical intercourse, conception, pregnancy, and delivery of male lovers are superior to the corporeal acts of human women:

> . . . he and his friend will help each other rear the issue of their friendship—and so the bond between them will be more binding, and their communion even more complete, than that which comes of bringing children up, because they have created something lovelier and less mortal than human seed.
>
> 209c

Socrates repeats at length the words of his teacher Diotima; her words are contained, enclosed, locked within his own discourse as a "Mantinean," mantic, secret truth. Socrates' assumption of the place of the prophetess lies at the heart of his doctrine.

In the speech of Alcibiades, spoken not in praise of love but in praise of

Socrates himself, who thus "is" love, the association between the philosopher and the woman recurs. Alcibiades compares the effect Socrates has on him to the effects visible in a Corybant, a worshipper of the great mother: "For the moment I hear him speak I am smitten with a kind of sacred rage, worse than any Corybant" (215d); he compares Socrates to a Siren.

In an elaborate simile, an example of the "likening" game played by the Athenians, Alcibiades compares Socrates to a statue. His words suggest an analogy between this simile and the place of Diotima enclosed within the earlier discourse of Socrates:

> What he reminds me of more than anything is one of those little sileni that you see on the statuaries' stalls; you know the ones I mean—they're modeled with pipes or flutes in their hands, and when you open them down the middle there are little figures of the gods inside.
>
> 215ab

He returns to this simile later:

> I don't know whether anybody else has ever opened him up when he's been being serious, and seen the little images inside, but I saw them once, and they looked so godlike, so golden, so beautiful, and so utterly amazing that there was nothing for it but to do exactly what he told me.
>
> 216e–217a

The imagery echoes the pregnancy motif in Diotima's speech and again appropriates the vocabulary of female reproductive powers to the philosopher. He is masculine, most masculine, a silenus, a satyr, with an Apollo inside; these are figures associated with libidinality, with heterosexual and homosexual eros. But the notion of male pregnancy draws on the representation of the female; as Diotima is enclosed within Socrates' speech, as he is pregnant with her, with her teachings, so Alcibiades sees Socrates as pregnant, as entreasuring, as stone enclosing the riches of the gods.

The reinscriptions of the Platonic text convert the metaphorical network of the fifth century to a new prominence for the male, the philosopher, the figure whom Michel Foucault sees as the figure of mastery, the center of philosophical and erotic practices from this moment on. And they establish a space for a new inscription, the metonymic placing of the female in relation to her superior and inferior. This occurs in the text of Aristotle and defines her place for centuries. The male philosopher becomes the site of metaphorical reproduction, the subject of philosophical generation; the female, stripped of her metaphorical otherness, becomes a defective male, defined by lack.

Nine

CONCLUSION: THE DEFECTIVE FEMALE BODY

Aristotle says:

> . . . the female is as it were a deformed male (*pepērōmenōn*); and the menstrual discharge is semen, though in an impure condition; *i.e.,* it lacks one constituent, and one only, the principle of soul.
>
> *Generation of Animals* 737a25

Aristotle furthers the process of establishing a logical, systematic instrument for thinking about the world, the process which Plato had begun. For example, even though coined money had existed for centuries before the time of Aristotle, it is he who conceptualizes it, who sees how it functions within a logic of abstract value. Similarly, although women had long been subordinated to men in Greek culture, Aristotle rationalizes and explains their status in terms of abstract principles. Value can be measured in terms of the abstract entity, money; women are seen as human beings, not things, but beings deficient in value. They are no longer metaphorical equivalents to the fertile field, the productive earth; they are measured against the one, the male, and discovered to be lacking in value, deficient, estranged metonymically, as a mere part for the whole and perfected being, who is male.

If Plato appropriates the reproductive powers of the female for the male, and if he makes his philosopher an androgynous, a transvestite being with the extraordinary vision of a Teiresias, Aristotle goes beyond him. Plato sees the good, the sun, the father, the son, as metaphorically substitutable one for the other, and the assimilation of female power to the philosopher who resembles all of these is perhaps an attempt to represent the wholeness, the absolute sufficiency of the good. Aristotle abandons this attempt to integrate male and female. He instead relies on a metonymic strategy, not by representing the female as a fertile field, as the space of reproduction to be integrated into the male, but rather by claiming and accounting for the defective and partial nature of the female body. The male body is whole and complete, having come to its *telos,* having achieved perfection; the female body is a part for the whole, a thing lacking completion, lacking heat, lacking soul.

The reinscription of the woman's lack takes many forms in the subsequent tradition, leaving traces even within feminist theory. Lacan alludes in his mysterious way to Plato's *Symposium* in an essay called "The Subversion of the Subject and the Dialectic of Desire in the Freudian Unconscious."[1] His reference to the Platonic text is consistent with the metaphysical tradition, with the post-Platonic representation of the woman as defined by lack, by her metonymic relationship to the man. The male philosopher who lives a philosophical life is close to the divine, is rewarded with the sight of the good. He is whole; she is like him but incomplete.

Lacan's allusions to the *Symposium,* for example, contribute to a repetition of the ancient metonymy:

> Included in the *objet* a is the *agalma,* the inestimable treasure that Alcibiades declares is contained in the rustic box that for him Socrates's face [*figure*] represents. But let us observe that it bears the sign (−). It is because he has not seen Socrates's prick [*queue*], if I may be permitted to follow Plato, who does not spare us the details, that Alcibiades the seducer exalts in him the *agalma,* the marvel that he would like Socrates to cede to him in avowing his desire: the division of the subject that he bears within himself being admitted with great clarity on this occasion.
>
> Such is the woman concealed behind her veil: it is the absence of the penis that turns her into the phallus, the object of desire.[2]

Lacan identifies the female position with the metonymic; the woman is trapped in metonymy, a part standing for a whole.

I will look here at the feminist "appropriation" of Lacan, especially in its Anglo-American forms, since it is the practice of Lacanian feminists that concerns me most. But, of course, there are other tendencies in current feminist work that contribute to the same structures of phallocentrism, reinscribing an ancient and vestigial division of labor, which persists because it is reinscribed again and again in the new terms of new discourses, in new political and social and economic circumstances. In a typical reading, for example, Eva Keuls in *The Reign of the Phallus* sees Plato and Socrates from the place of modern phallocentrism: "The most influential thinker of late-fifth-century Athens, Socrates, was a friend of women. . . . What is more, Socrates' adoring disciple Plato developed into the Western world's first feminist."[3] This view is consistent with the rest of Keuls's book, which finally is an act of phallus worship, a writing of ancient history that sees only the phallus and is trapped in a relationship of antagonism with the object she constructs for herself. Her work seems to me merely to replicate the structures of our own culture, especially the position of the female metonymically deprived of the penis.

Our feminist work will be limited if we cannot learn to historicize our own theories of subjectivity and those theories' construction. Feminists interested in transforming gender, class, and race relations must take account of subjectivity, of the ways in which the myth of the ego, the isolated self, is produced psychically. Many feminists embrace psychoanalysis uncritically, become Lacanians uncritically, attempt to reorient their practice within the so-called imaginary, within the pre-Oedipal; others refuse the power of psychoanalytic theory altogether, condemning it as another of the power mechanisms of male culture, as an instrument of domination. I think these positions are mistaken. I think that we, as feminists, can learn from psychoanalytic theory while historicizing it. We can refuse psychoanalysis' claims to describe all culture, including a revolutionary future, while accepting its value for describing our desire, our socialization into capitalism. To try to will away the cultural experience of a gendered subjectivity without understanding its production is to court failure by appealing always to the rational, to the adult ego, a fiction that resists being acknowledged as a fiction.

I will mention in particular the work of Juliet Mitchell and Jane Gallop, because I think they are writers and thinkers of great authority, who have situated themselves within the Lacanian paradigm and who will have great influence on the course of feminist thinking about society, language, sexuality.

Juliet Mitchell, failing to historicize, says:

> To be human is to be subjected to a law which decenters and divides: sexuality is created in a division, the subject is split; but an ideological world conceals this from the conscious subject who is supposed to feel whole and certain of a sexual identity.[4]

We are made now to choose a gender, a relationship to the symbolic phallus; our desire is born from our alienation, from our psychic mutilation. But by not historicizing this concept of gender, Mitchell represents our historical experience of gender now as the destiny of "being human." We cannot equate our experience with "being human" everywhere, always, and forever. I have argued that to historicize the representation of difference, as I have done in my examination of the metaphors used by the ancient Greeks, might free us from the fascinated gaze at the phallus, which risks paralyzing feminist theory.

In *The Daughter's Seduction*, Jane Gallop acknowledges that the phallus is inseparable from the penis:

> Certainly the signifier "phallus" functions in distinction from "penis," but it must also always refer to "penis." Lacanians seem repeatedly to try to clear up that distinction as if it could be done once and for all. . . . Lacanians would perhaps wish to polarize the two terms into an opposition. . . . Such attempts to remake language to one's own theoretical needs, as

> if language were merely a tool one could wield, is a very naive, un-Lacanian view of language.[5]

The penis is of course implicated in the signifier phallus; without the sight of the boy's penis, without the sight of the girl's lack, there would be no castration complex, no resolution of the Oedipus complex, no language, no gender, no culture. Although she questions the attempt to keep separate the phallus from the penis, Gallop nonetheless is herself a Lacanian, and she seems to accept a view of civilization as depending on, depending from, this metaphysical phallus, this physical penis. She focuses on the difficulty of thinking their difference but not on the historical specificity of that particular double and transcendental signifier.

In a chapter called "Of Phallic Proportions: Lacanian Conceit," in *The Daughter's Seduction,* Jane Gallop betrays the extent to which she is caught up in the gaze at the phallus, that transcendental signifier. Her point of view shifts between being critical of the Freudian Ernest Jones and accepting his observations about the representations of the phallus. She says, for example, that Jones "did not expect to find that symbolism is disproportionately phallic."[6] The "is" of this statement establishes it as her view of symbolism as well; if she had written "*was* disproportionately phallic," one might assume that she was dissociating herself from his description. Then she writes: "The symbolic pre-eminence of the male organ runs counter to the civilized liberal tradition of balance between the sexes."[7] In this passage, she is ironic about Jones's arguments about a "harmonious relation" between the sexes, about "successful marriage," but not about his "theorist's" eye, his gaze at the phallus.

My argument has been that the erection of the phallus as a privileged symbol, as the transcendental signifier—the establishment of the male subject as the figure for wholeness to which the female and her body are compared—is not a universal fact of culture. It rather occurs in the philosophical tradition at the moment when women's humanity is conceded, when they are named as defective, partial men. The "symbolic pre-eminence of the male organ" is a historical fact, not a universal description of culture. To historicize it is to see differently.

Accepting uncritically the pre-eminence of the phallus leads Gallop in a later book, *Reading Lacan,* to a fascinating examination of the consequences of Lacanian thought for feminists.[8] There she argues:

> Lacan's major statement of ethical purpose, as far as I am concerned, is that one must assume one's castration. Women have always been considered "castrated" in psychoanalytic thinking. But castration for Lacan is not only sexual; more important, it is also linguistic: we are inevitably bereft of any mas-

> terful understanding of language, and can only signify ourselves in a symbolic system that we do not command, that, rather, commands us. For women, Lacan's message that everyone, regardless of his or her organs, is "castrated," represents not a loss but a gain. Only this realization, I believe, can release us from "phallocentrism."[9]

I disagree very much with this view, as must be apparent by now. To continue to consider the phallus as the transcendental signifier, to accept the inevitability of the "idea" of transcendence, to accept the fantasy of the subject who is supposed to know, to believe that the phallus, and language, control us but that somehow our escape lies in knowing that male privilege is an imposture, even though based on an acceptance of the centrality of the phallus—all this seems to me only to perpetuate a metaphysics of wholeness, presence, deism, and worship of the symbolic father. On the other hand, to see how such an ideology supports relations of male dominance, class and racial hierarchy, and the humility of the universally castrated might perhaps allow us to imagine democracy.

We need to create dialogic and historical texts, to imagine human possibilities beyond the restrictive, commodified terms in which we have come to understand sexual difference. Like Sappho, we want to subvert the logical categories of our culture. They support gender, race, class domination. I stand outside psychoanalysis, even as I acknowledge its power, in order to refuse its claims to describe both ancient culture and a future of equality. I remind myself that efforts of subversion, like Sappho's, are conceived within culture, within the languages which speak us, which we must turn to our own purposes. But if theory is a gaze, feminist theory must be more than a gaze at the same object, more than finding a new sameness, the preeminence of the phallus, the same castrated woman's body everywhere. We cannot *will* our way past gender or past individual subjectivity, but we can theorize, historicize, and imagine a future beyond domination.

NOTES

Introduction

1. Friedrich Nietzsche, *The Use and Abuse of History,* trans. Adrian Collins, 2d rev. ed. (New York: Liberal Arts Press, 1957), 4.

2. On feminism, see Toril Moi, *Textual/Sexual Politics* (London: Methuen, 1985); Elaine Showalter, ed., *The New Feminist Criticism* (New York: Pantheon, 1985). On psychoanalysis and feminism, see, for example, Janine Chasseguet-Smirgel, ed., *Female Sexuality: New Psychoanalytic Views* (Ann Arbor: University of Michigan Press, 1970); Juliet Mitchell, *Psychoanalysis and Feminism* (New York: Random House, 1974); Juliet Mitchell and Jacqueline Rose, eds., *Feminine Sexuality: Jacques Lacan and the école freudienne,* trans. J. Rose (New York: Norton, 1982); Jane Gallop, *The Daughter's Seduction: Feminism and Psychoanalysis* (Ithaca: Cornell University Press, 1982); idem, *Reading Lacan* (Ithaca: Cornell University Press, 1985); Shirley Nelson Garner, Claire Kahane, and Madelon Sprengnether, eds., *The (M)other Tongue: Essays in Feminist Psychoanalytic Interpretation* (Ithaca: Cornell University Press, 1985). On psychoanalysis and classical antiquity, see, for example, Marylin Arthur, "Politics and Pomegranates: An Interpretation of the Homeric Hymn to Demeter," *Arethusa* 10, no. 1 (1977): 7–47; George Devereux, *Dreams in Greek Tragedy* (Berkeley: University of California Press, 1976); W. Thomas MacCary, *Childlike Achilles: Ontogeny and Phylogeny in the "Iliad"* (New York: Columbia University Press, 1982). On women in antiquity, see the fundamental works of Sarah Pomeroy: *Goddesses, Whores, Wives, and Slaves: Women in Classical Antiquity* (New York: Schocken, 1975); and *Women in Hellenistic Egypt: From Alexander to Cleopatra* (New York: Schocken, 1984). See also the following works by Marylin Arthur: "Liberated Women: The Classical Era," in *Becoming Visible: Women in European History,* ed. Renate Bridenthal and Claudia Koonz (Boston: Houghton Mifflin, 1977); "The Dream of a World without Women: Poetics and the Circles of Order in the *Theogony* Prooemium," *Arethusa* 16 (1983): 97–116; "Cultural Strategies in Hesiod's *Theogony:* Law, Family, Society," *Arethusa* 15 (1982): 63–82; "Early Greece: The Origins of the Western Attitude toward Women," *Arethusa* 6, no. 1 (1973): 7–58. See also Ann L. T. Bergren, "Language and the Female in Early Greek Thought," *Arethusa* 16 (1983): 69–95; Averil Cameron and Amelie Kuhrt, *Images of Women in Antiquity* (Detroit: Wayne State University Press, 1983); Helen Foley, ed., *Reflections of Women in Antiquity* (London: Gordon & Breach, 1982); John Peradotto and J. P. Sullivan, eds., *Women in the Ancient World: The Arethusa Papers* (Albany: State University of New York Press, 1984).

3. See Michel Foucault, *Histoire de la sexualité,* vol. 2, *L'Usage des plaisirs* (Paris: Gallimard, 1984).

This first volume of Foucault's "recentering" on "la généalogie de l'homme de désir" (p. 18) is focused on antiquity and is limited to a male perspective. As Foucault says (p. 29):

> C'est une morale d'hommes: une morale pensée, écrite, enseignée par les hommes et adressée à des hommes, évidemment libres. Morale virile, par consequent, où les femmes n'apparaissent qu'à titre d'objets ou tout au plus de partenaires qu'il convient de former, d'éduquer, et

> de surveiller, quand on les a sous son pouvoir, et dont il faut s'abstenir en revanche quand elles sont sous le pouvoir d'un autre (père, mari, tuteur). . . . [C]ette reflexion morale . . . est une élaboration de la conduite masculine faite du point de vue des hommes et pour donner forme à leur conduite.

His discussion of the phenomenon in question, this "thématique de l'austerité sexuelle" (p. 30), is conducted in terms of four great domains of experience. "Pourquoi est-ce là, à propos du corps, à propos de l'épouse, à propos des garçons et de la vérité, que la pratique des plaisirs a fait question?" It seems appropriate to note that Foucault begins at the point where my discussion ends, with the description of the philosophic man. As he points out, the population involved in the practices he describes—important for his history of sexuality as a precursor of Christian sexual morality, the "techniques of the self," ("techniques de soi" [p. 17])—was a relatively limited one:

> Dans la pensée antique . . . les exigences d'austerité n'étaient pas organisées en une morale unifiée, cohérente, autoritaire et imposée de la même façon à tous: elles étaient plutôt un supplément, et comme un "luxe" par rapport à la morale couramment admise.
>
> (p. 2).

The practices he delineates form part of the denigration of woman, the assimilation of her role into the single transcendental philosophical self.

Foucault concludes his discussion of marriage by arguing that the rules of an exclusively conjugal sexual practice for males as well as females existed within classical culture, in certain texts, although it was surrounded by a society where law and customs made no such demands. But, he insists, the existence of this call for reciprocal sexual fidelity must not be confused with a first sketch of the ethic dominant later. The temperance demanded of the male is different from that demanded of the female; the male *chooses* temperance as a refinement: "cette austérité se présente . . . comme un raffinement dont la valeur exemplaire ne prend pas la forme d'un principe universel" (p. 201). And the man's fidelity is not owed to his wife; his *sōphrosunē* is owed to himself. As the following quotations show, the man's temperance and the woman's virtue are two simultaneous *exigences;* they are not reciprocal forms:

> le comportement sexuel des deux époux n'était pas interrogé dans la pensée grecque classique à partir de leur relation personnelle
>
> (p. 203);
>
> le point de la problématisation était dans la tempérance dont avait à faire preuve, pour des raisons et dans les formes correspondantes à son sexe et à son statut, chacun des deux conjoints
>
> (p. 203);
>
> La vertu de la femme constituait le corrélatif et la garantie d'une conduite de soumission; l'austérité masculine relevait d'une éthique de la domination qui se limite
>
> (p. 203).

In fact, Foucault's work adds more evidence to the view that in Greek society women were seen almost as another species from that of men.

See also the third volume of *Histoire de la sexualité, Le Souci de soi* (Paris: Gallimard, 1984), which considers the fate of the subject in later antiquity, from the second century B.C. to the second century A.D.:

> c'est le développement d'un art de l'existence qui gravite autour de la question du soi, de sa dépendance et de son indépendance, de sa forme

universelle et du lien qu'il peut de doit établir aux autres, des procédures par lesquelles il exerce son contrôle sur lui-même et de la manière dont il peut établir la pleine souveraineté sur soi

(p. 273).

4. All translations of Greek tragedies are from *The Complete Greek Tragedies,* ed. David Grene and Richmond Lattimore (Chicago: University of Chicago Press, 1959).

5. There are other important traditions in psychoanalytic work, particularly that of the object-relations school, which have had a major influence on some American feminist tendencies; see, for example, Nancy Chodorow, *The Reproduction of Mothering: Psychoanalysis and the Sociology of Gender* (Berkeley: University of California Press, 1978); Margaret Mahler, *The Psychological Birth of the Human Infant* (New York: Basic Books, 1975); and D. W. Winnicott, *Playing and Reality* (New York: Basic Books, 1971). Although these works have been important in American feminist social scientific work, I am concerned here with the Freudian-Lacanian model which has dominated literary studies and the humanities in general. In addition, I believe that although feminists within the object-relations school have sought to correct the male bias of traditional psychoanalytic work by focusing on mother-child relations and on the preoedipal, as Jacqueline Rose points out, they must often fall back on a notion of "imprinting" to account for gender difference (Mitchell and Rose, *Feminine Sexuality,* 37). And in focusing on the "preoedipal" phase, they necessarily accept the traditional paradigm of the crucial oedipal phase even as they seek to undermine the androcentrism of other schools of psychoanalysis. I should mention here that I am not concerned with the Jungian school of psychoanalysis, for it seems to me that the Jungian school, even more absolutely than traditional Freudian psychoanalysis, ahistorically reifies and universalizes culturally specific patterns of gender difference.

6. See, for example, Arthur, "Politics and Pomegranates"; Pietro Pucci, *Hesiod and the Language of Poetry* (Baltimore: Johns Hopkins University Press, 1977); Charles Segal, *Tragedy and Civilization: An Interpretation of Sophocles* (Cambridge, Mass.: Harvard University Press, 1981); and Froma Zeitlin, *Under the Sign of the Shield: Semiotics and Aeschylus' "Seven against Thebes"* (Rome: Ateneo, 1982).

For a powerful and courageous statement on the issue of theory in classical studies, see John Peradotto, "Texts and Unrefracted Facts: Philology, Hermeneutics, and Semiotics," in *Semiotics and Classical Studies,* ed. Nancy Rubin, special issue of *Arethusa* 16, nos. 1, 2 (1983): 15–33.

Chapter 1. To Historicize Psychoanalysis

1. Victor Shklovsky, "Art as Technique," in *Russian Formalist Criticism: Four Essays,* trans. and ed. Lee T. Lemon and Marion J. Reis (Lincoln, Neb.: University of Nebraska Press, 1965), 12.

2. See Nicole Loraux, "Sur la race des femmes et quelques'unes de ses tribus," in *Women in the Ancient World,* special issue of *Arethusa* 11, nos. 1, 2 (1978): 43–87.

3. Michel Foucault, *An Introduction,* vol. 1 of *The History of Sexuality,* trans. Robert Hurley (New York: Random House, 1978).

4. Gilles Deleuze and Félix Guattari, *Anti-Oedipus: Capitalism and Schizophrenia,* trans. Robert Hurley, Mark Seem, and Helen R. Lane (New York: Viking Press, 1977). See also the important work of Alice A. Jardine, *Gynesis: Configurations of Women and Modernity* (Ithaca: Cornell University Press, 1985).

5. See, among Jacques Derrida's many works: *Dissemination,* trans. Barbara

Johnson (Chicago: University of Chicago Press, 1981); *Of Grammatology,* trans. Gayatri Spivak (Baltimore: Johns Hopkins University Press, 1976); *Writing and Difference,* trans. Alan Bass (Chicago: University of Chicago Press, 1978); *Positions,* trans. Alan Bass (Chicago: University of Chicago Press, 1981); and *The Post Card: From Socrates to Freud and Beyond,* trans. Alan Bass (Chicago: University of Chicago Press, 1987).

6. E. Ann Kaplan, "Is the Gaze Male?" in *Powers of Desire,* ed. Ann Snitow, Christine Stansell, and Sharon Thompson (New York: Monthly Review, 1983), 309–27.

7. H. G. Liddell and Robert Scott, *Greek-English Lexicon,* rev. ed. (Oxford: Oxford University Press, 1888).

8. Sigmund Freud, *The Standard Edition of the Complete Psychological Works of Sigmund Freud,* translated from the German under the general editorship of James Strachey, in collaboration with Anna Freud, assisted by Alix Strachey and Alan Tyson, 24 vols. (London: Hogarth Press, 1953–74), 19:252. (All future citations from Freud's work will be from this edition, hereinafter referred to as *SE*.)

In *The Interpretation of Dreams,* Freud discusses the symbolism of the genitalia, establishing fixed equivalencies between parts of the body and objects represented in dreams:

> All elongated objects, such as sticks, tree-trunks, and umbrellas (the opening of these last being comparable to an erection) may stand for the male organ—as well as all long, sharp weapons, such as knives, daggers, and pikes. Another frequent though not entirely intelligible symbol of the same thing is a nail-file—possibly on account of the rubbing up and down.—Boxes, cases, chests, cupboards and ovens represent the uterus, and also hollow objects, ships and vessels of all kinds.—Rooms in dreams are usually women.
>
> (*SE* 6:389)
>
> Tables, tables laid for a meal, and boards also stand for women—no doubt by antithesis, since the contents of their bodies are eliminated in the symbols. "Wood" seems, from its linguistic connections, to stand in general for female "material."
>
> (6:390–91)
>
> . . . all weapons and tools are used as symbols for the male organ: e.g., ploughs, hammers, rifles, revolvers, daggers, sabres, etc.
>
> (6:391)

He interprets the dream of an agoraphobic:

> the . . . dream alluded to the infantile sexual theory according to which girls are boys who have been castrated (cf. "On Sexual Theories of Children"). When I suggested to her that she had had this childish belief, she at once confirmed the fact by telling me that she had heard the anecdote of the child's saying to the little girl: "Cut off?" and of the little girl's replying: "No, always been like that."
>
> (6:399)

The joke suggests that the dreamer in fact does not share Freud's view on the infantile castration theory; little boys and psychoanalysts may see the female body as cut, while little girls and women may see their bodies otherwise, as having "always been like that."

Certainly, Freud acknowledges the importance of the symbolism of the mature female body as well; most often it is represented as a container, as a hollow, in his view. He mentions some dreams in which the female body is seen as a landscape; for example, he describes "the dream of an uneducated woman whose husband was a policeman" under the heading "The Male Organ Represented by Persons and the Female Organ by a Landscape" (6:401).

He also states:

> . . . it is a fact that the imagination does not admit of long, stiff objects and weapons being used as symbols of the female genitals, or of hollow objects, such as chests, cases, boxes, etc., being used as symbols for the male ones. It is true that the tendency of dreams and of unconscious phantasies to employ sexual symbols bisexually betrays an archaic characteristic; for in childhood the distinction between the two sexes is unknown and the same kind of genitalia are attributed to both of them. But it is possible, too, to be misled into wrongly supposing that a sexual symbol is bisexual, if one forgets that in some dreams there is a general inversion of sex, so that what is male is represented as female and *vice versa*. Dreams of this kind may, for instance, express a woman's wish to be a man.
>
> (6:394)

This is a typical no-exit statement. Only two positions, male and female, are interchangeable; the attribution of sameness to genitalia that are ascribed to children is clearly understood only from the position of the male child, and the argument ends with the reminder that (some) women want to be men.

What is most interesting to me is not that Freud claims that the female body is defined by castration, although this is implicit in his mention of the female's desire to be male. Rather, in contrast to the symbols or metaphors of antiquity, his vocabulary seems reduced, reduced to one like that of Apollo in Aeschylus' *Oresteia*. The female body is seen by the infant as castrated, by the adult as a receptacle. One ancient view, of the parthenogenic, self-sufficient, all-giving earth is gone. Although Freud alludes to ancient topoi such as the dream of sex with one's mother, he misinterprets them to confirm his hypothesis which is based on castration, on presence and absence. He cites Otto Rank on Julius Caesar's dream of sex with his mother "which was explained by the dream augurers as a favourable augury for his taking possession of the earth (Mother Earth)" (6:434, n.1). Freud interprets Hippias' dream also, saying, "These myths and interpretations reveal a true psychological insight. I have found that people who know that they are preferred or favoured by their mother give evidence in their lives of a peculiar self-reliance and an unshakable optimism which often seem like heroic attributes and bring actual success to their possessors" (6:434, n.1; this was written, or added, in 1911). Freud misreads the ancient accounts in his own interest; they reinterpret the familial or kinship symbolism in light of the political. What matters to Hippias is not fear of incest but desire for the land, for power; the possession of and power over the earth have to do not with sex but with production, with consumption. He who owns the earth has power and wealth. The earth, once autonomous, self-generating, and productive, is like a mother who needs a master, a husband. The fear is of her autonomy and unmastered power.

Freud is much further along, in a purely commodity economy, when he sees the female body as a receptacle and the phallus-penis, the presence of which determines the male body, as that meant to be contained by that receptacle. There is no longer any danger of self-sufficiency, because the phallus-penis fills up (controls) the hollow space of the container.

9. Jacques Lacan, *Ecrits* (Paris: Seuil, 1966): "le plus saillant de ce qu'on peut

attraper dans le réel de la copulation sexuelle" (p. 692). Alan Sheridan translates this phrase as "the most tangible (element) in the real of sexual copulation" (*Ecrits: A Selection* [London: Tavistock, 1977], 287); Jacqueline Rose renders it: "what stands out as most easily seized upon in the real of sexual copulation" (Mitchell and Rose, *Feminine Sexuality,* 82).

10. Karl Marx, *Capital,* trans. Eden Paul and Cedar Paul, 2 vols. (London: Dent, 1930), 1:45–46. Georg Lukács, in his discussion of commodities in "Reification and the Consciousness of the Proletariat," says that the problem of commodities must be considered as the central structural problem of capitalist society: "The transformation of the commodity relation into a thing of 'ghostly objectivity' . . . stamps its imprint upon the whole consciousness of man; his qualities and abilities are no longer an organic part of his personality, they are things which he can 'own' or 'dispose of' like the various objects of the external world" (Georg Lukács, *History and Class Consciousness: Studies in Marxist Dialectics,* trans. Rodney Livingstone [London: Merlin, 1971], 100).

11. Lacan, *Ecrits,* trans. Sheridan, 287. (Unless otherwise indicated, future citations from Lacan's work will be from this edition.)

12. See the work of Jean Baudrillard: for example, *For a Critique of the Political Economy of the Sign,* trans. Charles Levin (St. Louis: Telos, 1981), and *The Mirror of Production,* trans. Mark Poster (St. Louis: Telos, 1975). See also Mark Poster, *Foucault, Marxism, and History: Mode of Production versus Mode of Information* (Cambridge: Polity Press, 1984). For a ground-breaking discussion of the equivalence between the phallus and the money form, see Jean-Joseph Goux, "Numismatiques," in *Economie et symbolique* (Paris: Seuil, 1973), 53–113.

13. Lacan, *Ecrits,* 287.

14. Eva C. Keuls, *The Reign of the Phallus: Sexual Politics in Ancient Athens* (New York: Harper and Row, 1985). See also Jane Gallop, "Phallus/Penis: Same Difference," in *Men by Women,* ed. Janet Todd, special issue of *Women and Literature,* n.s. 2 (1981): 243–51.

15. Luce Irigaray, *Speculum: Of the Other Woman,* trans. G. Gill (Ithaca: Cornell University Press, 1985), and idem, *This Sex Which Is Not One,* trans. Catherine Porter with Carolyn Burke (Ithaca: Cornell University Press, 1985).

16. Jacques Derrida, "The Purveyor of Truth," trans. W. Domingo, J. Hulbert, M. Ron, and M.-R. Logan, *Yale French Studies* 52 (1975): 97.

Chapter 2. Desiring the Greeks

1. See also "Psychopathic Characters on the Stage," *SE* 7:306–8.

2. On cryptomnesia, see *SE* 19:261, 263n.

3. Karl Marx and Friederich Engels, *The German Ideology, Part One* (New York: International Press, 1970).

4. See G. E. M. de Sainte-Croix, *The Class Struggle in the Ancient Greek World: From the Archaic Age to the Arab Conquests* (Ithaca: Cornell University Press, 1981), for a discussion of Marx's views on antiquity and for a ground-breaking Marxist study of Greek culture. See also Ellen Meiksins Wood and Neal Wood, *Class Ideology and Ancient Political Theory: Socrates, Plato, and Aristotle in Social Context* (Oxford: Blackwell, 1978).

5. For such references, see R. S. Caldwell, "Selected Bibliography on Psychoanalytic and Classical Studies," *Arethusa* 7, no. 1 (1974): 115–34.

6. See MacCary, *Childlike Achilles.*

7. See, for example, Philip Slater, *The Glory of Hera* (Boston: Beacon Press, 1968).

8. Arthur, "Politics and Pomegranates."

9. MacCary's work takes Lacan into account and is a valuable contribution to both psychoanalytic studies of the classics and work on the *Iliad*. He tends to accept the Lacanian paradigm for the history of subject, without great attention to the Lacanian emphasis on language and the unconscious, and also to follow Lacan's emphasis on male subjectivity.

10. For a survey of this work and a valuable analysis of it, see James Clifford, "On Ethnographic Authority" *Representations* 2 (1983): 118–46. See also George E. Marcus and Dick Cushman, "Ethnographies as Texts," *Annual Review of Anthropology* 11 (1982): 25–69.

11. Marjorie Shostak, *Nisa: The Life and Words of a !Kung Woman* (New York: Random House, 1981).

12. Jeanne Favret-Saada, *Deadly Words: Witchcraft in the Bocage,* trans. C. Cullen (Cambridge: Cambridge University Press, 1980).

13. See Roy Wagner, *The Invention of Culture,* rev. ed. (Chicago: University of Chicago Press, 1981).

14. *Greek Lyrics,* trans. Richmond Lattimore, rev. ed. (Chicago: University of Chicago Press, 1960), 41.

15. Denys Page, *Sappho and Alcaeus* (Oxford: Oxford University Press, 1955), 95.

16. On Sappho, see Jack Winkler, "Gardens of Nymphs: Public and Private in Sappho's Lyrics," *Women's Studies* 8, nos. 1, 2 (1981): 65–91; John D. Marry, "Sappho and the Heroic Ideal: *erōtos aretē*," *Arethusa* 12, no. 1 (1979): 71–92; Anne Giacomelli, "The Justice of Aphrodite in Sappho Fr. 1," *Transactions of the American Philological Association* 110 (1980): 135–42; and Page duBois, "Sappho and Helen," in *Women in the Ancient World: The Arethusa Papers,* ed. J. Peradotto and J. P. Sullivan (Albany: State University of New York Press, 1984), 95–105.

17. On this issue, see Marcel Detienne, *The Gardens of Adonis: Spices in Greek Mythology,* trans. Janet Lloyd (Atlantic Highlands, N.J.: Humanities Press, 1977). This book has profoundly influenced my study.

18. See, for example, Hélène Cixous, *Portrait de Dora* (Paris: des Femmes, 1976).

19. *Greek Lyrics,* trans. Lattimore. 34.

20. See Roman Jakobson, "Two Types of Language and Two Types of Aphasic Disturbances," in *Fundamentals of Language,* ed. R. Jakobson and M. Halle (The Hague: Mouton, 1956). Contiguity disorder is described in the following terms by Jakobson: "This contexture-deficient aphasia . . . diminishes the extent and variety of sentences. The syntactical rules organizing words into a higher unit are lost; this loss, called agrammatism, causes the degeneration of the sentence into a mere 'word heap'" (p. 71). He associates this collapse of syntax with a failure "to combine simpler linguistic entities into more complex units." Thus metonymy is alien to the contiguity disorder, and metaphoric substitution becomes the only possible utterance. Metaphor, isolated, operates on the level of substitution, analogous to a vertical, paradigmatic axis of language. The opposite of this feature of language is metonymy, the combination of units into syntactical order. Jakobson describes aphasics who have a "similarity disorder," who are trapped in the metonymic. "Such an aphasic can neither switch from a word to its synonyms and circumlocutions, nor to its heteronyms, *i.e.,* equivalent expression in other languages. Loss of a polyglot ability and confinement to a single dialectal variety of a single language is a symptomatic manifestation of this disorder. . . . (F)or an aphasic who has lost

the capacity of code switching, his 'idiolect' becomes the sole linguistic reality" (p. 68). Metaphor is alien to the similarity disorder.

21. On metaphor and metonymy, see Lacan, "The Agency of the Letter in the Unconscious or Reason Since Freud," in *Ecrits,* 146–78; Jean-Luc Nancy and Philippe Lacoue-Labarthe, *Le Titre de la lettre: Une Lecture de Lacan* (Paris: Galilée, 1973); Jacques Derrida, "White Mythology," in *Margins of Philosophy,* trans. Alan Bass (Chicago: University of Chicago Press, 1982), 207–71; and Gallop, "Metaphor and Metonymy," in *Reading Lacan,* 114–32.

22. Martin Heidegger, *An Introduction to Metaphysics,* trans. R. Manheim (Garden City, N.Y.: Anchor Press, 1961), 154.

23. Keuls, *The Reign of the Phallus.*

24. Page duBois, *Centaurs and Amazons: Women and the Prehistory of the Great Chain of Being* (Ann Arbor: University of Michigan Press, 1982).

25. Aristophanes, *The Frogs,* trans. R. Lattimore (New York: New American Library, 1962).

26. Marsh H. MacCall, *Ancient Rhetorical Theories of Simile and Comparison* (Cambridge, Mass.: Harvard University Press, 1969).

27. Plato, *The Collected Dialogues,* ed. Edith Hamilton and Huntington Cairns (Princeton: Bollingen, and Princeton University Press, 1961).

28. See Loraux, "Sur la race des femmes"; Linda S. Sussman, "Workers and Drones: Labor, Idleness, and Gender Definition in Hesiod's Beehive," *Arethusa* 11, nos. 1, 2 (1978): 27–41; and Claude Calame, *Les Choeurs de jeunes filles en Grèce archaïque,* 2 vols. (Rome: Ateneo e Bizzarri, 1977).

29. See Pomeroy, *Goddesses.*

30. Keith Hopkins, *Conquerors and Slaves: Sociological Studies in Roman History,* vol. 1 (Cambridge: Cambridge University Press, 1978); see also W. W. Tarn, *Alexander the Great* (Boston: Beacon Press, 1956).

Chapter 3. Field

1. For a discussion of the metaphor in the field in the Vedic tradition, see Wendy Doniger O'Flaherty's *Women, Androgynes, and Other Mythical Beasts* (Chicago: University of Chicago Press, 1980), with which classicists unfortunately have little familiarity:

> The image of the woman as an insignificant receptacle for the unilaterally effective male fluid persists. . . . The woman is the mere "field" in which the seed is sown, not an active partner in the process. . . . [S]emen is regarded as more powerful than uterine blood. . . . The "field" metaphor is a natural development from the Vedic premise of unilateral creation (already somewhat androcentric) supported by the Upaniṣadic tendency toward misogyny. The early expressions of this idea are often coupled with aggressive and competitive feelings, not only toward the woman but toward the rival seed-sower.
>
> (p. 29)

See also "The Myth of the Mare" (Ibid., 166–202).

2. On Homer, see Seth Schein, *The Mortal Hero: An Introduction to Homer's "Iliad"* (Berkeley: University of California Press, 1985), for a valuable synthesis of recent scholarship. See also Gregory Nagy, *The Best of the Achaeans: Concepts of the Hero in Archaic Greek Poetry* (Baltimore: Johns Hopkins University Press, 1979); James Redfield, *Nature and Culture in the Iliad: The Tragedy of Hector* (Chicago: University of Chicago Press, 1975); Michael N. Nagler, *Spontaneity and Tradition: A Study in the Oral Art of Homer* (Berkeley: University of California Press, 1974);

Charles Segal, *The Theme of the Mutilation of the Corpse in the Iliad* (Leiden: Brill, 1975); and Page duBois, *History, Rhetorical Description, and the Epic: From Homer to Spenser* (Cambridge: D. S. Brewer, 1982).

3. On the epithets, see Paolo Vivante, *The Epithets in Homer: A Study in Poetic Values* (New Haven: Yale University Press, 1982).

4. *The Iliad of Homer,* trans. Richmond Lattimore (Chicago: University of Chicago Press, 1951). (All future citations from the *Iliad* will be from this edition.)

5. On the *hieros gamos,* see Walter Burkert, *Greek Religion,* trans. John Raffan (Cambridge, Mass.: Harvard University Press, 1985), 108–9; see also H. W. Parke, *Festivals of the Athenians* (London: Thames and Hudson, 1977), 112; Aristotle, *Athenian Constitution* 3.5.

6. See duBois, *History,* 9–11. Plutarch says, in the *Quaestiones Romanae* (102.288c), that the seventh day after birth is a dangerous one for the child, since that is the day the umbilical cord usually comes away: "but until it comes off, the child is more like a plant than an animal." (Cf. Aulus Gellius 16.16.2–3, where, citing Varro, he says, "he likens the branches of a tree to the feet and the legs [of the child], and the stock and trunk to the head.")

7. Burkert, *Greek Religion,* 175. Farnell says that the Gaia cult was "aboriginal" in Attica; see Lewis Richard Farnell, *The Cults of the Greek States,* vol. 3 (Oxford: Clarendon, 1906), 15.

"In gathering a certain medicinal herb, a careful Athenian would put into the hole a honeyed cake as an expiatory offering to Ge, a sacrificial gift of common use in her ritual; and in the search for hidden treasure, a man would pray to her as the guardian of wealth" (Hesiod, *Theogony, Works and Days, Shield,* trans. Apostolos N. Athanassakis [Baltimore: Johns Hopkins University Press, 1983]). (All future citations from Hesiod's work will be from this edition.)

8. Earth is the mother of all, and it is her son Kronos' castration of his father that fertilizes Gaia: "Gaia took in all the bloody drops that spattered off, / and as the seasons of the year turned round / she bore the potent Furies and the Giants" (*Theogony* 183–85). For an important reading of the *Theogony* that uses the notions of metaphor and metonymy, see Marylin Arthur, "Cultural Strategies." It is Gaia's primacy that must be dispersed by the textual labor of Hesiod's poem.

One of the most interesting aspects of the cult of Earth will be treated later, in chapter 6, which discusses cooking metaphors. Earth was also often associated with the practice of incubation (ritual sleep and dreaming), since dreams were thought by some to arise from the earth (Farnell, *The Cults,* 3 : 8). Plutarch says her temple at Delphi was near the fountain of Castalia; Apollo slew the dragon Python and usurped her (daughter's) power; see Joseph Fontenrose, *Python: A Study of Delphic Myth and Its Origins* (Berkeley: University of California Press, 1959). The snake or dragon was often associated with the earth goddess.

9. On the name "Hellenes," see Thucydides *History* 1.32.

10. Nicole Loraux, *Les Enfants d'Athéna: Idées athéniennes sur la citoyenneté et la division des sexes* (Paris: Maspero, 1981); John Peradotto, "Oedipus and Erichthonius: Some Observations on Paradigmatic and Syntagmatic Order," *Arethusa* 10, no. 1 (1977): 85–101.

11. See Deborah Boedeker, *Descent from Heaven: Images of Dew in Greek Poetry and Religion* (Chico, Calif.: Scholars Press, 1984).

12. The connection of wool and dew, discussed by Zeitlin in reference to the ritual of the Arrēphoria, is implicated in the name of Erichthonios (Froma Zeitlin, "Cultic Models of the Female: Rites of Dionysus and Demeter," *Arethusa* 15 [1982]: 129–57). The name Erichthonios is said to come from *khthōn* (earth) and

from either *eris* (strife) or *erion* (wool). The wool, like the golden fleece, may refer to pubic hair, and the dew to semen. Dew is also sometimes associated with young animals. Also, in the *Odyssey,* the dew is called female and is said to be threatening to Odysseus as he prepares for sleep (*thēlus eersē*); *The Odyssey of Homer,* trans. Richmond Lattimore (New York: Harper and Row, 1967), 5.467. (All future citations from the *Odyssey* will be from this edition.) See also Boedeker, *Descent,* passim. Odysseus covers himself "like the seed of fire" (*sperma puros,* 5.490); the liquid dew here is not semen but its opposite, a female liquid that will quench the male fire. In the *Theogony,* the Muses pour sweet honey (i.e., dew [*plukerēn eersēn*]) on the tongue of the good prince (*Theogony* 83).

13. See Zeitlin, "Cultic Models"; Boedeker, *Descent;* and Burkert, *Greek Religion,* 228–33.

14. See Loraux, "Sur la race des femmes"; Pucci, *Hesiod,* 82–126; and Marcel Detienne, "Le Travail agricole comme pratique religieuse," in *Crise agaire et attitude religieuse chez Hésiode,* Latomus Collection, no. 68 (Brussels: Berchem, 1963), 32 ff.; and Jean-Pierre Vernant, "Le Travail et la pensée technique," in *Mythe et pensée chez les Grecs,* 2d ed. (Paris: Maspero, 1966), 199.

15. DuBois, *History,* 19–21.

16. Pucci, *Hesiod,* 88.

17. But see Loraux, *Les Enfants d'Athéna,* 89.

18. Pucci, *Hesiod,* 89.

19. Burkert says of this passage: "Here, perhaps from ancient Neolithic tradition, we find the association between ploughing/sowing and procreation, and between harvest and birth" (*Greek Religion,* 108).

20. Detienne, *Crise agraire.*

21. See Detienne, *Gardens of Adonis;* Burkert, *Greek Religion,* 242–46; and Zeitlin, "Cultic Models."

22. See N. J. Richardson, *The Homeric Hymn to Demeter* (Oxford: Oxford University Press, 1974), 11; and Arthur, "Politics and Pomegranates."

23. See also *Odyssey* 5.490.

24. See R. B. Onians, *The Origins of European Thought* (Cambridge: Cambridge University Press, 1951).

25. See Richardson, *Homeric Hymn;* George E. Mylonas, *Eleusis and the Eleusinian Mysteries* (Princeton: Princeton University Press, 1961); and Burkert, *Greek Religion,* 276–78, 285–90.

26. Pucci, *Hesiod,* 115.

27. Parke, *Festivals,* 107; and Burkert, *Greek Religion,* 109, 237–42.

28. Parke, *Festivals,* 108.

29. Burkert, *Greek Religion,* 238.

30. Parke, *Festivals,* 116.

31. Ibid., 117.

32. Freud says that in some tribes the act of defloration is performed not by the husband but by a priest, or by an instrument to protect the husband from dangers, either from the opening of this closed space or from the anger of the woman whose body is thus broken into. "The Taboo on Virginity," *SE* 11: 192–208.

33. Zeitlin, "Cultic Models," 141. Chirassi-Colombo discusses the difference between male and female in the ritual example of Pyanepsion: "Le donne possono agire solo 'ritualmente', cioè nel tempo controllato e limitato della azione sacrale mentre ogni possibilità di intervento immediata, temporale, storica, è concentrata nella cerchia ristretta dei maschi iniziati (adulti) in finzione di *polîtai*" (I. Chirassi-

Colombo, "*Paides* e *gynaikes:* note per una tassonomia del comportamento rituale nella cultura attica," *Quaderni Urbinati di Cultura Classica,* n.s. 1 [1979]: 58).

34. Zeitlin, "Cultic Models," 141.

35. Parke, *Festivals,* 86.

36. Ibid., 87.

37. On this period, see John V. A. Fine, *The Ancient Greeks: A Critical History* (Cambridge, Mass.: Harvard University Press, 1983); A. French, *The Growth of the Athenian Economy* (London: Routledge and Kegan Paul, 1964); and *Cambridge Ancient History,* ed. John Boardman and N. G. L. Hammond, 2d ed. (Cambridge: Cambridge University Press, 1982), vol. 3, pt. 3.

38. A. Andrewes, "The Growth of the Athenian State," in *Cambridge Ancient History,* vol. 3, pt. 3, p. 382. For an earlier and now disputed view, see W. J. Woodhouse, *Solon the Liberator: A Study of the Agrarian Problem in Attica in the Seventh Century* (London: Oxford University Press, 1938). Also see John V. A. Fine, "Horoi," *Hesperia,* suppl. 9 (1951): 167–208; and French, *Growth,* 20ff.

39. M. I. Finley, "Land, Debt, and the Man of Property in Classical Athens," in *Economy and Society in Ancient Greece,* ed. B. D. Shaw and R. P. Saller (London: Chatto and Windus, 1981), 63.

40. French, *Growth,* 18.

41. Ibid., 108.

42. Ibid., 26.

43. See G. E. M. de Sainte-Croix, *The Origins of the Peloponnesian War* (Ithaca, New York: Cornell University Press, 1972).

Chapter 4. Furrow

1. Nonnus, a late Greek poet, speaks of the castrated organs of Ouranos as *arotra* (ploughs; *Dionysiaca* 12.46), and he plays on the words *arsena . . . arotra . . . ērōsen . . . hudōr/speirōn aspora* [*nōta thalassēs*] (12.46–47; see epigraph).

The Socrates of Plato's *Cratylus,* explaining the names of the gods, etymologizes that Artemis got her name "*hōs ton aroton misēsasēs ton andros en gunaiki,*" that is, because "she hates sexual intercourse (i.e., "plouging," *aroton*) of the man in the woman" (*Cratylus* 406b).

See also the rich body of iambic poetry, with its explicit, though frequently metaphorized, descriptions of sexual acts. For the comic metaphors linking agriculture and sex, see Jeffrey Henderson, *The Maculate Muse: Obscene Language in Attic Comedy* (New Haven: Yale University Press, 1975): "As in all agricultural metaphors for the female genitals, a strong underlying idea is always the taming of the land and the consumption of its products by the males and their phallic tools" (p. 47). Henderson further says, "Freud's observation [in *The Three Essays*] that although the genitals most strongly arouse us, we do not consider them attractive has to be rejected in the case of the Greeks. That the female genitals were, in fact, considered especially attractive by the Greeks is indicated not only by the nature of the practice of cunnilingus, but by the frequent references . . . to the many types of genital depilation practiced by Greek women and to the many kinds of perfumes used to enhance lovemaking" (p. 152) (or to disguise women's real body smells).

As examples of agricultural metaphors for sexual acts, Henderson lists, among others: *alōan* (to thresh); *bolokopein* (to break up clods before the sowing); *georgein* (farm, plough[?]); *trugān* (gather fruit and crops); *oruttein* (dig). He also lists sexual metaphors from sport, like hitting and piercing, especially verbs from *ballein* (p. 170). Here there are verbs with the sense of wounding or penetration: *ana-*

peirein (spit; *Acharnians* 1007); also *anapegnunai* (fix on spit; *Ecclesiazusae* 843); *balaunein* (penetrate; *Lysistrata* 337); but they may usually refer to male homosexual intercourse.

Metaphors, other than ploughing, that Plutarch used to describe the marital relation include: bee stings (m masculine), household vessels, fire, fishing with poison (f feminine), horses, riding (m), moon (f), sun (m), music, mirror (f), ropes, wine and water, shoe (f), cats (f), bees (f), elephants, bulls, tigers (m), bee with philosophy (m). He begins his homily on marriage by comparing the male's attentions to bee stings and urging the wife not to be annoyed but to wait for the honeycomb; he ends by urging the husband to collect philosophy like a bee and then, "carrying it within your own self, impart it to her" ("De coniugalia praecepta" 145b). He adds that women have parthenogenetically produced "misshapen, fleshlike uterine growths," called moles, without men's cooperation; the same thing can happen in their minds if they do not receive "the seed of good doctrines" (*logōn khrēstōn spermata,* 145d).

Does ploughing the furrow mean opening up a space in which to plant a seed, a seed that needs no contribution from the earth? If so, it is an ideologically persuasive gesture, transforming the all-bountiful earth into an empty, lifeless container. Is there a shift from earth as autochthonous to earth as container? Certainly one can see field, tablet, stone, and oven as empty containers waiting for seed, letters, statues, and food to be inserted and kept safe. The female space may be seen as full and potential, but it is rather simply seen as a necessary receptacle. There is a spectrum of possibilities here, from the autarkic, parthenogenetic earth, to the field that, once opened and seeded, gives life, to a field empty and dead, which must contain the male principle of life, the seed of fire (e.g., Odysseus is likened to the seed of fire in a distant field *Odyssey* 5.490). But even the stories of autochthonous birth require the equivalent of seed—the stones of Deukalion and Pyrrha, the dragon's teeth in the Kadmos myth, and the semen of Hephaistos in the myth of Erichthonios. So perhaps from the beginning there is an argument for bisexual reproduction, but a desire for male single-sex reproduction (see, e.g., Euripides' *Hippolytus,* 616–24). The earth is never seen as spontaneously giving birth or producing goods, except in the very beginning of Hesiod's account of the *Theogony* and in his references to a time before labor.

2. *Pindar's Victory Songs,* trans. Frank J. Nisetich (Baltimore: Johns Hopkins University Press, 1980).

3. See Jean-Pierre Vernant, "Le mariage," in *Mythe et société en Grèce ancienne* (Paris: Maspero, 1974), 62–63.

4. Zeitlin, "Cultic Models."

5. On this play, see Helene P. Foley, *Ritual Irony: Poetry and Sacrifice in Euripides* (Ithaca: Cornell University Press, 1985), 205–58; Charles Segal, *Dionysiac Poetics and Euripides' "Bacchae"* (Princeton: Princeton University Press, 1982); and Marylin Arthur, "The Choral Odes of the *Bacchae* of Euripides," *Yale Classical Studies* 22 (1972): 145–79.

6. Ileana Chirassi-Colombo, "*Paides* e *gynaikes:* note per una tassonomia del comportamento rituale nella cultura attica," *Quaderni Urbinati di Cultura Classica,* n.s. 1 (1979): 25–58.

7. Jean-Pierre Vernant, "The Historical Moment of Tragedy in Greece: Some of the Social and Psychological Conditions," in Jean-Pierre Vernant and Pierre Vidal-Naquet, *Tragedy and Myth in Ancient Greece,* trans. Janet Lloyd (Atlantic Highlands, N.J.: Humanities Press, 1981), 1–5. See also, in the same volume, also by J.-P. Vernant, "Tensions and Ambiguities in Greek Tragedy," 6–27.

8. See Zeitlin, *Under the Sign.*

9. Herodotus, *The Histories,* trans. Aubrey de Sélincourt, rev. A. R. Burn (Harmondsworth: Penguin, 1972).

10. Herodotus also tells the story of the Boeotian Thebes. The Thebans aided Peisistratos, Athens' tyrant, and were thus politically associated with tyranny (*Histories* 2.61). Herodotus connects the worship of Dionysos in Greece with Kadmos (2.49). But the Gephyraean clan, among them Harmodius and Aristogeiton, who according to Herodotus were of Phoenician descent and expelled from Boeotia, were the slayers of the tyrant's son Hipparchus in 513 B.C. (5.57). The Phoenicians, among them Kadmos, are said to have brought the alphabet to Greece (5.58). The Thebans sent earth and water, signs of submission, to the Persian invader, Xerxes (7.132), and later advised Mardonius on how best to conquer Greece (9.2), although he later laid waste their lands and made a refuge for his army there (9.15). Nonetheless, the Thebans fought with the Persian Artabazus and his army against the Athenians at Phocis (9.67). The other Greeks, after their victory at Plataea, marched to Thebes, wasted the city's lands, and assaulted its walls until the Thebans surrendered their leaders (9.86–88). Thus the Thebans ideologically represent tyranny in all its forms by association with Peisistratos and with Dionysos the god in whose honor Peisistratos established Athenian tragic performances. They expelled the family of the tyrannicides, who ended up in Athens and were seen as great liberators in the fifth century. The alphabet can be connected, perhaps, with the tyrant and with the recension of the Homeric text. The accessibility of written texts would serve to break the power of the aristocracy's unwritten laws, but of course it is also a crucial feature of the democratic *polis.* Most important of all was the "medizing," the Theban support for the Medes during the Persian Wars, which was support for tyranny and enslavement, against every sort of freedom the Athenian democrats loved. One of the great oppositions the Athenians used to define their identity was that of Greek versus barbarians (see duBois, *Centaurs and Amazons*). The Thebans had allied themselves, through their adherence to the Persian cause, perhaps irrefutably to the side of the barbarians; their antidemocratic views, long held (cf. Pindar and Alexander's respect for him), made them a source of ideologically dangerous, oligarchic, as well as barbarian, tendencies. Amphitryon, husband of Alkmene, mother of Herakles, lived in Thebes and was welcomed by the Spartoi (Pindar *Pythian* 9.79f); Herakles was the iconographic sign of Peisistratos and his family.

11. Jean-Pierre Vernant, "Oedipus without the Complex," in Vernant and Vidal-Naquet, *Tragedy and Myth,* 63–86.

12. In his essay on space and movement in Greek religion, Jean-Pierre Vernant establishes the crucial importance of the opposition he describes for gender categorization in ancient Greek culture. My argument throughout this book owes a great deal to this essay. Vernant discusses the important emblematic function of the virgin goddess Hestia in "Hestia-Hermès: Sur l'expression religieuse de l'espace et du mouvement chez les Grecs," in *Mythe et pensée,* 97–143. She is goddess of the hearth, at the center of the *oikos:* "au milieu du *megaron* quadrangulaire, le foyer mycénien, de forme ronde, marque le centre de l'habitat humain" (p. 98). She also "roots" the house in the earth; the circular hearth signifies immutability and permanence: "Point fixe, centre à partir duquel l'espace humain s'oriente et s'organise, Hestia, pour les poètes et les philosophes, pourra s'identifier avec la terre, immobile au centre du cosmos" (p. 99). She exists in a relationship of opposition to Hermes: "A Hestia, le dedans, le clos, le fixe, le repli du groupe humain sur luimeme, à Hermes, le dehors, l'ouverture, la mobilité, le contact avec l'autre que soi"

(p. 101). The archaic representation of space demands a center, a fixed point; in relation to this privileged spot, direction is established.

Paradoxically, the woman must be both an element of commerce, a mobile entity, and the immobile field; she must incarnate not her own land, but that of her husband (p. 114). When the legitimate king acts appropriately, the earth and women are fertile (Hesiod *Works and Days* 232ff); Vernant suggests that sacred ploughing in the historical period may perpetuate the marriage of the king and his land (p. 115).

Vernant brilliantly delineates these crucial terms—the couple Hestia-Hermes, emblematic of male and female, opposed but inseparably linked—in one of their aspects. The description seems to cover the relationship between the sexes in its entirety, but of course there are other "couples": Pheidias linked Aphrodite and Eros, for example, as well as those deities that have other kinds of complementarity: husband and wife, brother and sister, mother and son, protectress and protégé.

There are women "outside" the hearth, outside the categories of virgin and chaste mother: Maenads, Amazons, *hetairai*. They too must be considered in light of the ideological complexity of the *polis*. As Zeitlin points out, Greek women worshipped not only Demeter, but Dionysos as well (Zeitlin, "Cultic Models," 133–38). As Maenads they are not fertile fields, not receptacles, but wandering Hermes-like creatures whose interiority is not fertile but hungry, empty, ready for the consumption of raw flesh, even for the cannibalism suggested in the grim fate, the *sparagmos*, of Pentheus.

Nonetheless, Vernant's essay is invaluable. It establishes the dialectical relationship between male and female; it considers the function of the woman at different stages of life, as daughter, wife, mother; it sees her as religious symbol, as belonging to the economy of the household and the state, as symbolizing house and city.

13. Jean-Pierre Vernant, "Ambiguity and Reversal: On the Enigmatic Structure of *Oedipus Rex*," trans. P. duBois, *New Literary History* 9, no. 3 (1978): 475–501.

14. Bernard Knox, *Oedipus at Thebes* (New Haven: Yale University Press, 1957).

15. John Fine points to the ultimate consequences of the wartime anxieties about the earth:

> In the years before the Peloponnesian War family land may have been alienable, but attachment to one's share of the native soil, with all its family and religious associations, rendered the thought of disposing of it almost sacrilegious. From the beginning of the fourth century, however, buying, selling, and mortgaging land were becoming common procedures. . . . the uprooting of the peasants in the war, the elimination of whole families by the plague, the long separation from the land, the constant plundering of the enemy, and the cynical attitudes acquired in the struggle to survive may have released many Athenians from the old traditional concept of the sacred obligation to preserve family land. A new idea was emerging that land was just another commodity.
>
> (Fine, *The Ancient Greeks*, 529–30)

Perhaps what we must do is reverse the analogy, see what an incestuous act against the earth would be. Is it failing to see agriculture as a religious act? Abandoning the farmland of Attica? Privatizing property? Perhaps it is to abandon the farmland to the Spartan invaders, to allow promiscuity of that sort, the inappropriate possession and ravaging, wounding, damaging of the earth by the enemy that is felt to be an impious act that brings on the pollution and the plague.

16. M. M. Bakhtin / P. N. Medvedev, *The Formal Method in Literary Scholarship,* trans. Albert J. Wehrle (Cambridge, Mass.: Harvard University Press, 1985), 17, 21–25.

17. On the *Ion,* see Loraux, *Les enfants d'Athéna,* especially "Créuse autochthone," 197–253.

18. Loraux, *Les enfants d'Athéna,* 225. "Surdetermination tragique, celle même du personnage de Créuse, stérile comme Persephone, déesse des Enfers, et cependant mère en quête d'un enfant perdu" (246). Apollo, by dissociating birth from death, that is, the dangerous proximity of the autochthon's birth to death, "ouvrait enfin à la lignée érechthéide le temps humain de la vie" (247). Loraux also points out the ambiguous nature of opening; it meant life for Ion, death for the Kekropids (248). The child enclosed in a basket recalls the *kistos* of the Arrephoroi (250), for some a "matrice chthonienne." Loraux proposes instead an allusion to the Delphic *omphalos* (250). Her reading is inconclusive, "l'énumeration méthodique de figures que la tragédie condense en inextricable lacis de significations" (252).

19. See Jean-Pierre Vernant, *La Mort dans les yeux* (Paris: Hachette, 1985).

20. See Froma Zeitlin, "The Closet of Masks: Role Playing and Myth Making in the *Orestes* of Euripides," *Ramus* 9, no. 1 (1980): 51–77. On the *Phoenissae,* see Marylin Arthur, "Euripides' *Phoenissae* and the Politics of Justice," Ph.D. diss., Yale University, 1975; idem, "The Curse of Civilization: The Choral Odes of the *Phoenissae,*" *Harvard Studies in Classical Philology* 81 (1977): 163–85; Foley, *Ritual Irony,* 106–46.

21. Fine, *The Ancient Greeks,* 72.

22. Ibid., 75.

23. Jean-Pierre Vernant, *Les Origines de la pensée grecque,* 2d rev. ed. (Paris: Presses Universitaires de France, 1969).

24. French, *Growth,* 169.

25. Thucydides, *The Peloponnesian War,* trans. Rex Warner (Harmondsworth: Penguin, 1972), 1.81.

26. Yvon Garlan, "La Défense du territoire à l'époque classique," in *Problèmes de la terre en Grèce ancienne,* ed. M. I. Finley (Paris: Mouton, 1973), 160.

27. de Sainte-Croix, *Origins,* passim.

Chapter 5. Stone

1. Woodhouse, *Solon the Liberator.*

2. See Françoise Frontisi-Ducrous, *Dédale: Mythologie de l'artisan en Grèce ancienne* (Paris: Maspero, 1975).

3. See Charles Segal, "Greek Tragedy: Writing, Truth, and the Representation of the Self," in Charles Segal, *Interpreting Greek Tragedy: Myth, Poetry, Text* (Ithaca: Cornell University Press, 1986), 75–109.

4. See Slater, *Glory of Hera.*

5. See Vincent Scully, *The Earth, the Temple, and the Gods: Greek Sacred Architecture,* rev. ed. (New Haven: Yale University Press, 1979).

6. See Ann L. T. Bergren, *The Etymology of Peirar* (State College, Pa.: American Philological Association, 1975).

7. On the scapegoat, see Vernant, "Ambiguity and Reversal"; René Girard, *La violence et le sacré* (Paris: Grasset, 1972); Jan Bremmer, "Scapegoat Rituals in Ancient Greece," *Harvard Studies in Classical Philology* 87 (1983): 299–320.

8. See K. B. Stark, *Niobe und die Niobiden* (Leipzig, 1863). There were tragedies written about Niobe by Aeschylus and Sophocles of which some fragments remain. Stark treats in detail the extant literary remains as well as representations of Niobe in art and mythology.

Tantalos speaks the following words in Aeschylus' lost *Niobe:* "I sow a field twelve days' journey wide, even the Berecynthian land, where Adrastea's seat and Ida resound with lowing oxen and bleating sheep, and the whole plain roars" (fragment 79 [158]). (There is also an extensive papyrus fragment in which Niobe herself speaks and does or does not speak of sitting and clucking over her children as a hen sits on her eggs.)

9. See Johannes T. Kakridis, *Homeric Researches* (Lund: C. W. K. Gleerup, 1949), 101; and M. M. Willcock, "Mythological Paradeigma in the *Iliad,*" *Classical Quarterly* 58, n.s. 14 (1964): 141–54.

10. Nagler, *Spontaneity and Tradition,* 194.

11. See also Nagy, *The Best of the Achaeans.*

12. Nagler, *Spontaneity and Tradition,* 194.

13. Ibid., 194 n.31, 195.

14. Kakridis, *Homeric Researches,* 135.

15. On petrifaction, see also the transformation of the Scherians' boat (*Odyssey* 13.163), and the serpent turned to stone (*Iliad* 2.319).

16. The rhetorical exemplum is broken after the middle by *hōs phatis andrōn,* "as men tell," and the rains and snow surround this parenthetical remark. The simile uses *hōs* not with Niobe but with the ivy that is like a rocky growth.

17. Charles Segal's discussion of this passage is particularly sensitive and illuminating. He speaks of the specifically feminine character of Antigone's journey into the unknown; she is like a Kore-Persephone who is not reborn, does not return to bring spring to the earth, but brings her husband down to her in death.

> No longer a principle of continued life, this Kore-figure appropriates a *mater dolorosa,* ever-weeping Niobe, image of her own crystallized grief. No new life after a sojourn in darkness awaits her, but perpetual sadness and loss. Haemon, plunging into the cave, claims his bride-of-death as an inaccessible Kore, whom he can embrace only in a grimly funereal version of a sexual union.
>
> (Segal, *Tragedy and Civilization,* 181)

Segal points out the most important feature of this analogy between Antigone and Niobe; both are childless, one a virgin, the other a mother. Antigone is like a mother to her brother, mourning over him so that she is turned to stone by Kreon.

Achilles is like Niobe because at the end of the *Iliad* he is like a king of the dead, the receiver of all, the mother of Patroklos mourning for his lost child, yet with pity for Hektor's father. Antigone uses the same myth to assimilate herself to legend; she is outside of history, as women are for Sophocles.

18. He says that a golden lamp for the goddess was made by Callimachus; the oil in the lamp lasts for an entire year, though it burns constantly. A bronze palm above draws off the smoke. "The Callimachus who made the lamp . . . was the first to drill holes through stones, and gave himself the title of Refiner of Art" (1.26.7). (Liddell, Scott, and Jones [see chap. 6, n.18] define the term translated here as "refiner" as "enfeebling his art"; *katakēkō* means "melt or thaw away, dissolve, waste.")

Pausanias also lists a boar hunt and Cycnus fighting with Herakles, goes on to recount the legends of Theseus, and then describes a statue of Cylon and other images, including a bronze Athena by Pheidias with Centaur-Lapith reliefs by

Mys, a prize (*agalma*) from the Persians. "The point of the spear of this Athena and the crest of her helmet are visible to those sailing to Athens, as soon as Sunium is passed" (1.28.2). See J. G. Frazer, trans. and commentary, *Pausanias' Descriptions of Greece,* 6 vols. (London, 1898).

19. But see Kristian Jeppesen, "Where Was the So-Called Erechtheion?" *American Journal of Archaeology* 83 (1979): 381–94; idem, "Further Inquiries in the Location of the Erechtheion and Its Relationship to the Temple of the Polias," *American Journal of Archaeology* 87 (1983): 325–33.

20. See Boedeker, *Descent,* 100–124; Zeitlin, "Cultic Models."

21. Vitruvius, *On Architecture,* trans. Frank Granger, 2 vols. (London: Loeb, Heinemann, 1931–34).

22. William Bell Dinsmoor suggests that the caryatids may represent the Arrēphoroi, but they seem too mature. Are the Athenian caryatids suffering? They seem rather to be proud and stately and content (*The Architecture of Ancient Greece* [London: Batsford, 1927], 193).

Virginia Woolf's Jacob encounters the caryatids:

> Jacob got up and strolled across to the Erechtheum. There are still several women standing there holding the roof on their heads. Jacob straightened himself slightly; for stability and balance affect the body first. These statues annulled things so!
>
> (V. Woolf, *Jacob's Room* [Harmondsworth: Penguin, 1965], 143)

23. Helene P. Foley, "'Reverse Similes' and Sex Roles in the *Odyssey,*" *Arethusa* 11, nos. 1, 2 (1978): 13. See also Pierre Vidal-Naquet, *Le Chasseur noir: Formes de pensée et formes de société dans le monde grec* (Paris: Maspero, 1981).

24. Foley, "Reverse Similes," 14.

25. Is the regular temple, with its rectangularity and clarity and its secret inner room—a second space—some attempt to rationalize and control the female body, to render it visible and accessible?

26. Vidal-Naquet, *Le chasseur noir;* "Valeurs religieuses et mythiques de la Terre et du sacrifice."

27. See Vernant, *Mythe et pensée,* 97–143.

28. Scully, *Earth, Temple,* passim.

29. Maria Gimbutas, *The Goddesses and Gods of Old Europe, 6500–3500 B.C.: Myths and Cult Images* (Berkeley: University of California Press, 1982).

Chapter 6. Oven

1. See A. M. Snodgrass, "Central Greece and Thessaly," in *Cambridge Ancient History,* vol. III, pt. 1, eds. J. Boardman, I. E. S. Edwards, N. G. L. Hammond, and E. Sollberger (Cambridge: Cambridge University Press, 1982), 667.

2. See Jean-Pierre Vernant, "From Oedipus to Periander: Lameness, Tyranny, Incest in Legend and History," trans. Page duBois, in *American Classical Studies in Honor of J.-P. Vernant,* special issue of *Arethusa* 15, nos. 1, 2 (1982): 19–38.

3. J. K. Lacey, *The Family in Ancient Greece* (London: Thames and Hudson, 1968).

4. In the *Epic of Gilgamesh,* loaves are used as markers of time in the underworld. Loaves unconsumed go stale and rot, proving to the hero Gilgamesh that he has been asleep for days.

5. See Charles Segal, "The Raw and the Cooked in Greek Literature: Structure, Values, Metaphor," *Classical Journal* (1973–74): 289–308. Pindar implies that the story of the gods' cannibalism is *apiston,* unworthy of belief. The traditional account is that "Pelops, after being slaughtered and boiled at the banquet of

the gods, was fairer than ever when he came to life again" (Apollodorus, *Epitome* 11.3). Demeter or Thetis had inadvertently eaten his shoulder, which was replaced with one of ivory. Pelops' father, Tantalos, for these and other crimes, was tormented in the land of the dead, unable to eat although fruits hung over his head, unable to drink although standing in a pool of water up to his chin (*Odyssey* 11.582–92).

6. See Apollodorus 3.193; Ovid *Metamorphoses* 6.424.

7. See Marcel Detienne and Jean-Pierre Vernant, eds., *La Cuisine du sacrifice en pays grec* (Paris: Gallimard, 1979); and Froma Zeitlin, "The Motif of the Corrupted Sacrifice in Aeschylus' *Orestes,*" *Transactions of the American Philological Association* 96 (1965): 463–508. I am grateful to an anonymous reader for calling to my attention the significance of the Arkesilaos narrative.

8. Giulia Sissa, "Il corpo della donna: Lineamenti di una ginecologia filosofica," in *Madre Materia: Sociologia e biologia della donna greca,* ed. Silvia Campese, Paola Manuli, and Giulia Sissa (Torino: Boringhieri, 1983), 83–145.

9. Aristophanes, *The Knights, Peace, The Birds, The Assemblywomen, Wealth,* trans. David Barrett and Alan H. Sommerstein (Harmondsworth: Penguin, 1978).

10. Jeffrey Henderson, *The Maculate Muse: Obscene Language in Attic Comedy* (New Haven: Yale University Press, 1975), 63.

11. Ibid., 177–78.

12. Ibid., 143.

13. Ibid., 167.

14. Hippocrates, trans. W. H. S. Jones, 4 vols. (London: Loeb-Heinemann, 1923). See also *Hippocratic Writings,* ed. G. E. R. Lloyd (Harmondsworth: Penguin, 1978). Democritus says that the uterus is a mold, able to give form to its contents, according to Aristotle (*Generation of Animals* 740a35).

15. G. E. R. Lloyd, *Science, Folklore and Ideology: Studies in the Life Sciences in Ancient Greece* (Cambridge: Cambridge University Press, 1983), 58–111; see also G. E. R. Lloyd, "Hot and Cold, Dry and Wet in Early Greek Thought," in *Studies in Presocratic Philosophy,* ed. R. E. Allen and David J. Furley (New York: Humanities Press, 1970), 255–80.

16. Aristotle, *Generation of Animals* 726b30.

> . . . a boy actually resembles a woman in physique (*morphēn*), and a woman is as it were an infertile male (*arrēn agonon*); the female, in fact, is female on account of inability of a sort, viz., it lacks the power to concoct semen out of the final state of its nourishment . . . because of the coldness of its nature.
>
> (*Generation of Animals* 728a)

The colder body of the woman, in Aristotle's description, cannot cook the blood sufficiently to produce semen; the menstrual flow is the unconcocted result.

17. As Sissa points out, it is not only the father who might be thought to consume the child, but also the mother:

> Nel lessico ippocratico la metafora alimentare funziona come una vera e propria omonimia: l'orifizio uterino è *to stoma,* la gravidanza è descritta come *en gastri lambanein, sullambanein, ekhēn* . . . Aristotele, nel construire [in contrast] la teoria della maternità come nutrizione, nel fare della madre un alimento passivo divorabile e non divorante, elide esplicitamente la possibile confusione di utero e stomaco.
>
> ("Il corpo," p. 103)

Sissa sees not so much a historical progression of ideas, but that Aristotle belongs in a certain tradition; that his "science" is as ideological, as interested, as poetic on the woman question, as is the poet Aeschylus and his representation of the god Apollo.

Aristotle confronts what Sissa calls the pre-Socratic theory of feminine sperm, or seed, found in the Hippocratic corpus in the seventh and tenth books of the *Historia animalium.* "La ginecologia prearistotelica . . . assegna alla madre un ruolo simmetrico e analogo a quello maschile" ("Il corpo," p. 117). Thus she sees Aristotle's work as a refutation of an earlier, less metaphysical and perhaps more empirical tradition.

18. *A Greek-English Lexicon,* compiled by Henry George Liddell and Robert Scott, revised and augmented by Sir Henry Stuart Jones et al., with a supplement (Oxford: Clarendon Press, 1968). Hereinafter referred to as LSJ.

19. The Boeotians learned of the oracle by following a swarm of bees, which flew into the ground; they sought relief from a drought and were sent to Lebadeia by the Pythia (Pausanias, *Description of Greece* 11.1–2).

20. The bones of the mother, in the Deukalion myth, are stones that are like seeds. In those periods in which cremation of the dead was practiced, the unburned remains were often buried after cremation in ceramic vases.

Chapter 7. Tablet

1. For an argument against this description of the *skutala,* see Thomas Kelly, "The Spartan Scytale," in *The Craft of the Ancient Historian: Essays in Honor of Chester B. Starr,* ed. J. W. Eadie and J. Ober (Lanham, Md.: University Press of America, 1984), 141–69.

In the seventh *Olympian,* Pindar compares his song to a *phiale,* a bowl that is given to a bridegroom by his father-in-law. Thus the poem and more importantly for me, the bowl are containers like the bride, who is the gift the occasion celebrates:

> Even as when one takes up in his wealthy hand a golden bowl, the prime of his possessions, a bowl that foameth with the dew of the vine, and giveth it to the youth, whom, when betrothed to his daughter he welcomes from one home to another . . .
>
> (*Olympian* 7.1ff)

Even so, Pindar says, he sends his nectar, the Muses' gift, his song.

2. The vase, the *deltos,* the woman, the tattooed slave—each can carry an inscription without being able to read it. It is as if they were merely vehicles, surfaces, carriers ignorant of their burden—like Aeneas with his shield, carrying the future. And messengers are afraid, often, of the reception at the end of their journey. The guard who brings the news of Polyneices' burial to Kreon is afraid of the tyrant's wrath (*Antigone* 223–40).

Lévi-Strauss, who like Freud seems often in danger of claiming universality of application for his pronouncements, has compared women to words in his monumental work on "the exchange of women"; see The *Elementary Structures of Kinship,* trans. James Harle Bell, J. Richard von Sturmer, and Rodney Needham (Boston: Beacon Press, 1969), 481. We might also see women as analogous to signs and coins, which were, according to tradition, first produced and inscribed in the seventh century B.C. in Lydia. Like clay, the metal from which coins were formed was drawn from the earth.

3. See the following works by Eric Havelock: *Preface to Plato* (Oxford: Oxford University Press, 1963); *The Origins of Western Literacy* (Toronto: Ontario Institute for Studies in Education, 1976); *The Greek Concept of Justice* (Cambridge,

Mass.: Harvard University Press, 1978); and *The Muse Learns to Write: Reflections on Orality and Literacy from Antiquity to the Present* (New Haven: Yale University Press, 1986).

4. Kurtz and Boardman, *Greek Burial Customs,* 53, 55.

5. See Gimbutas, *Goddesses and Gods:*

> The dot, representing seed, and the lozenge, symbolizing the sown field, appear on sculptures of an enthroned pregnant goddess and are also incised or painted on totally schematized figurines. A lozenge with a dot or dash in its centre or in the corners must have been the symbolic invocation to secure fertility. Less abstract are the Early Cucuteni figurines from the western Ukraine where the entire body, particularly the abdomen and buttocks, were impressed with real grain. During the subsequent Classical Cucuteni phase the idea of pregnancy was expressed by the insertion of clay balls into the belly of a fat figurine.
>
> (P. 205)

This feature of the figurines is particularly interesting in light of D. Schmandt-Besserat's theory about the origin of writing in enclosed packets for enumeration that were subsequently marked on the outside; see the following works by D. Schmandt-Besserat: "An Archaic Recording System and the Origin of Writing," *Syro-Mesopotamian Studies* 1 (1977): 31–70; "The Earliest Precursor of Writing," *Scientific American* 238, no. 6 (June 1978): 50–59; and "An Archaic Recording System in the Uruk-Jemdet Nasr Period," *American Journal of Archaeology* 83 (1979): 19–48.

"Hollow clay balls filled with tokens were in time replaced by full clay balls—i.e., tablets—marked with signs. The token system ushered in a new phase: writing" ("Archaic Recording . . . Uruk-Jemdet Nasr," p. 25). See also D. Schmandt-Besserat, "Reckoning before Writing," *Archaeology* 32, no. 3 (May-June 1979): 22–31. For a critical view of this theory, see Stephen J. Lieberman, "Of Clay Pebbles, Hollow Clay Balls, and Writing: A Sumerian View," *American Journal of Archaeology* 84 (1980): 339–58, who argues that the calculi were subsequent to writing.

6. In addition to the ominous *sēmata lugra* of the *Iliad* and the terrible fate of Prometheus, who gave the art of writing to humans, there is the legend of Palamedes who was also said to have invented letters. He was destroyed by his own invention when the wily Odysseus forged a letter from Priam to Palamedes. He was put to death by the Greek army. Words can lie, but writing can pretend to come from another body. Odysseus hated Palamedes because it was he who saw through Odysseus' scheme to avoid going to Troy (Hyginus, *Fabulae* 95.2).

7. R. M. Cook, *Greek Painted Pottery* (London: Methuen, 1960). The quoted material in the next two paragraphs is from this work, pp. 156–58. Cook says that "nearly all painted inscriptions other than merchants' marks were put on before firing and nearly all incised inscriptions after firing" (p. 253). He classes inscriptions as "captions, signatures, mottoes (for all of which nonsensical groups of letters sometimes serve), and pithy dedications" (p. 253).

About captions, Cook says that "names against figures first appear during the second quarter of the seventh century" (p. 255); on the François vase not just people but objects are named. Later, individual figurines are named, not scenes. "The captions are written against the figures to which they belong, forward or backward" (p. 255).

There are also "mottoes" that refer to the beauty of boys, naming someone in particular as beautiful, or saying the boy is *kalos,* beautiful, or simply bearing the inscription *kalos.* "The accepted interpretation of these phrases is that they celebrate the homosexual charms of the popular aristocratic youths of the day" (Cook, p. 258; see also K. J. Dover, *Greek Homosexuality* [Cambridge, Mass.: Harvard University Press, 1978]). "These inscriptions are an interesting commentary on fashion, since they . . . were put on pots for public sale, many of which were exported" (Cook, p. 258). "Occasionally a woman's beauty too is celebrated" (p. 258). The existence of these inscriptions might suggest that the theme of inscription and fertilization is displaced to the homosexual object, as it is most explicitly in Plato's *Phaedrus.*

There are inscriptions recording dedication, Cook continues, that say things like "Zoilos dedicated me to Aphrodite" (p. 259), while a few other vases carry fired inscriptions of private ownership. Some inscriptions were added after firing, most often incised or cut into the surface of the pot. They include dedications as well as the owner's name, sometimes again in the form of a first person statement, like "I am the cup of Euthumos."

8. Gregory Nagy, "*Sēma* and *Noēsis:* Some Illustrations," in *Semiotics and Classical Studies,* ed. Nancy Felson Rubin, special issue of *Arethusa* 16, no. 1, 2 (1983): 35–55.

9. This Potiphar's wife motif occurs also in Euripides' *Hippolytus.* See Froma Zeitlin, "The Power of Aphrodite: Eros and the Boundaries of the Self in *Hippolytus,*" in *Directions in Euripidean Criticism,* ed. P. Burian (Durham, N.C.: Duke University Press, 1985), 52–110.

Hanging from her hand, as Phaedra hangs, is a *deltos* marked with her golden seal:

> THESEUS:
> "What is this tablet fastened to her dear hand? . . .
> Look, the familiar signet ring,
> hers who was once my wife!
> Come, I will break the seals,
> and see what this letter (*deltos*) has to tell me.
>
> (*Hippolytus* 856–65)

This tablet, like so many others, gives a voice to the dead, speaks death, suggests the vulnerability, the dialectic between the closed and opened body, and, like other Euripidean tablets, exposes the lie inside the folded lips, the closed door of the *deltos.* Theseus then opens the gates of his mouth to curse his son (cf. line 1060), to bring him death from the sea.

10. See Ann L. T. Bergren, "Helen's 'Good Drug': *Odyssey* iv 1–305," in *Contemporary Literary Hermeneutics and Interpretation of Classical Texts,* ed. Stephanus Kresic (Ottawa: Ottawa University Press, 1981), 201–14.

11. On the transition from the female body to a metallic surface for the inscription of desire in the development of coinage, see Vincent Farenga, "La tirannide greca e la strategia numismatica," in *Mondo classico: percorsi possibili,* ed. F. Buratta and F. Mariani (Ravenna: Longo Editore, 1985), 46. See also G. F. Hill, *Ancient Greek and Roman Coins: A Handbook,* rev. ed. (Chicago: Argonaut, 1964). It is now believed that the traditional view that the Lydians invented coinage is probably correct, but the Greeks adopted the practice at an early date.

A wall painting from the house of the Vettii at Pompeii is important evidence for ancient methods of coining. It depicts, among other stages in the process, the heating of metals in a furnace. (Note, too, that the production of ceramic vases also involved a furnace or oven.) G. F. Hill offers the following description of the process of striking the coin after its heating:

> The lower die—that of the obverse of the coin—was let into the anvil; the blank was laid over it; the reverse die—consisting in the earliest times merely of the end of a bar, roughened so as to grip the blank—was placed over all; and the hammer being brought down caused an impression to be made on both sides.
>
> (pp. 148–49)

Another method was casting, which is also described by Hill (pp. 155 ff.). (In his discussion, Hill includes the "ham-shaped pieces of Nemausus"—coins with knees, calves, and feet—and explains: "The person who would have liked to make an offering in kind, was able to give its equivalent in a coin the shape of which suggests the animal offered to his deity" [pp. 3–4].)

Some coins bore images which were puns on their city's name. For example, the coins at Selinus in Sicily bore the wild celery, while the rose adorned the coins of Rhodes.

Coins were variously inscribed, that is, marked with letters as well as iconic signs. The Syracusans may have issued coins to mark their victory over the Athenians at the river Assinarus (Hill, p. 193). "The practice of signing coins is almost confined to Sicily and Southern Italy; of names certainly belonging to engravers, there are none from Greece proper" (p. 195). Inscriptions were often used to designate the issuers of coins, less often the coins' denominations. Hill mentions a dedicatory graffito punctured into a Sicyonian stater, which declares the coin is an offering to Aphrodite (pp. 196–97). "Others . . . recall the love-inscriptions in vases" (p. 197).

12. Hill, *Coins,* 160.

13. Charles Seltman, *Greek Coins* (London: Methuen, 1933), 49.

14. Ibid., 52.

15. Ibid., 91.

16. Aristophanes, *The Birds,* trans. W. Arrowsmith (New York: New American Library, 1961).

17. In *The Frogs,* Aristophanes compares true coinage to false, after the desertion of the slaves from the silver mines at Laurion had forced the Athenians to issue bronze coins washed with silver; in the parabasis, he says the city now uses base coinage and men whom the city would not even have used as *pharmakoi,* scapegoats.

18. He speaks of humankind's former dwelling places as "in the recesses of sunless caves" (*antron en mukhois aneliois, Prometheus Bound* 453). Interesting, in light of Aristophanes' view of the womb as "the unspeakable recesses of the thighs" (*meron . . . aporretous mukhous, Ecclesiazusae* 12). The recesses are prehistoric, prenatal, female, sacred spaces.

19. On triangles, see Plato's *Timaeus.* LSJ under the letter *delta* cites the Hebrew word *daleth,* "door."

20. On the *Oresteia* trilogy, see Froma Zeitlin, "The Dynamics of Misogyny: Myth and Mythmaking in the *Oresteia,*" *Arethusa* 11, nos. 1, 2 (1978): 149–84.

21. See Thomas G. Rosenmeyer, *The Art of Aeschylus* (Berkeley: University of California Press, 1982), 92, and 324–25. See also H. J. Rose, *A Commentary on the Surviving plays of Aeschylus* (Amsterdam: Noord-Hollandsche, 1957).

22. See also the *Eumenides'* hymn of blessing (lines 625–709).

23. On *The Suppliants'* inscription, see lines 944ff.; see also E. G. Turner, *Athenian Books in the Fifth and Fourth Centuries* B.C. (London: M. K. Lewis, 1952), 9–10. Turner distinguishes among the inscription nailed to a wall as a public record, the *pinakes* that contained the secretary's minutes, and a papyrus that was preserved, bearing the official version: *ptukhais biblon* means "a piece of papyrus which after being written on, was folded horizontally several times and sealed" (p. 9). Papyri were written on with a reed pen, *kalamos*. A rigid stylus was used for writing on wax. Turner believes papyrus to be the basic writing material.

The Suppliants is dated between 466 and 459; see Oliver Taplin, *The Stagecraft of Aeschylus* (Oxford: Clarendon Press, 1977), 198. Taplin says of the lyric dialogue of lines 825–902, "[T]he outlandish language, interjections, and bestial imagery create a scene of violent yet colorful, alarming yet almost lewd boldness" (p. 214). A. F. Garvie says that Aeschylus "favored the democratic foreign policy of friendship with Argos" (A. F. Garvie, *Aeschylus' "Supplices": Play and Trilogy* [Cambridge: Cambridge University Press, 1969], 145). Garvie presents a general discussion of the historical background of the play (pp. 141–62). Danaus and Aiguptos are brothers, so the Danaids and the Aiguptoi are cousins. It is Danaus who commands his daughters to murder their husbands, only Hypermestra spares her husband Lynceus. Aeschylus, however, makes the Danaids themselves unwilling to marry their cousins. Was incest already associated with Egypt? Garvie answers, "The Greeks had no scruples about marriage between first cousins, while in Egyptian ruling circles it was normal for brother to marry sister. Moreover, had there been any such question of incest it would have been impossible for Lynceus and Hypermestra to have their marriage confirmed at the end of the trilogy" (p. 216). The Danaids may have been resisting a transgression of the laws of exogamy. The Danaids are *epikleroi,* however. George Thomson says, "To Aeschylus, living in the heyday of ancient democracy, the subjection of women was not only just, but preferable to the liberty which they had formerly enjoyed"; see *Aeschylus and Athens* (New York: Grosset and Dunlap, 1972), 289.

Garvie writes: "The argument of Thomson, though in general unacceptable, is valuable in that it dispels the illusion that the Danaids are mere representatives of Hellenic culture against a barbarian one; for they reject a marriage that is in itself perfectly legitimate and conventional" (p. 223).

Herodotus says that the Danaids brought the Thesmophoria to Greece from Egypt (*Histories* 2.171). Anthony J. Podlecki sees the play as in part a move of Aeschylus to support the Argives, represented as democratic like the Athenians, and to remind the audience of the reception of the ostracized Themistokles in the past; see *The Political Background of Aeschylean Tragedy* (Ann Arbor: University of Michigan Press, 1966), 55.

24. See Marcel Detienne, "Violentes 'eugénies'," in *La Cuisine du sacrifice,* 183–214.

25. Arthur, "Politics and Pomegranates."

26. R. S. Caldwell, "The Psychology of Aeschylus' *Supplices,*" *Arethusa* 7 (1974): 45–70.

27. Ibid., 63.

28. Ibid.

29. In going on to discuss the trilogy, of which *The Suppliants* is a part, Caldwell says:

> For both Freud and Aeschylus, an essential and continuing task of man [*sic*] is the struggle to free himself from the past, in a way that is

> not self mutilating but liberating. In the Danaid's relationship with Io, their equation of the mother of fantasy with the ancestress of the race, we see a portrayal of the grip in which man [*sic*] is held by the past, whether the individual past which a man [*sic*] begins with his birth or the supra-individual past which includes everything which can still affect the present.
>
> (p. 62)

I would agree with this statement, although certainly Aeschylus is a tempered optimist about the possibility of achieving liberation (cf. *Oresteia*), while Freud is gloomier.

What I read here is the constant misogyny of Aeschylus, Freud, *and* Caldwell, who want to see "man's" liberation in the light of *women's* archaism. It is the Danaids, like Clytemnestra, who are fixed in the past, focused on their father, trapped in pre-endogamous incest, just as it is Freud's women who never develop a moral sense, just as Caldwell sees the neurotic woman's desire as the "reduction" of man to her castrated state. Caldwell reads the text naively, as if the Danaids were real people, neurotics to be analyzed, instead of representations by Aeschylus of women, of archaic creatures.

But he is not wrong to find support for his view of the world, his misogyny, in Aeschylus. Caldwell assumes, as do Freud and Aeschylus, that the proper destiny of women is marriage. Aeschylus, in his *Oresteia,* does not end the tragedy with the marriage of Orestes, but with the coercive burial and the suppression of the Furies, another violent and archaic band of women. They are the past that must be overcome. The mother, and women, are the past. There is, behind all this, the desire to see women safely married, "mastered," and weaponless, and to set men free from them. The Greek democracy, with all its institutions—assembly, juries, and theater—was, as Vidal-Naquet has said, "un club d'hommes." There is not, in Aeschylus, a sense that the proper destiny of "man" or "men" is to marry and procreate. But women are dangerous, especially in their untamed, archaic, violent, premarital state, and their proper integration into society requires that they must be firmly under the control of a man, the law of the father or the husband. Women who would refuse marriage, even the violent abduction of the Aiguptoi, are branded as dangerous, not just by Aeschylus and his culture, but by ours.

Here, however, is the point: the Danaids are *not* castrated. Men may have feared castration, but they did not see women as castrated, and I don't believe Caldwell proves the contrary. How, for example, is a *meadow* (*leimōn,* lines 538–42), as Caldwell says, "denoting specifically the female genitalia" (p. 59), emblematic of castration? It is an emblem of growth, solitary flowering, reproduction, but not of mutilation, wounding, loss, absence, and lack. Rather than suggesting castration, the meadow connotes untouchability. See Jebb's note on *Trachiniae* 200, on the meadow of Zeus at Oeta: "Deianeira: O Zeus, who rules the meadow of Oeta, sacred from the scythe . . . (*atomon*)." And see Euripides' *Hippolytus* 75 ff. Jebb says, "In a Cretan precinct of the Dictaean Zeus, it was forbidden to keep flocks or sheepfolds, to sow, or to cut timber." The meadow, rather than being an emblem of castration, signifies virginity, the unbroken soil, parthenogenesis, and autarky.

Caldwell begins, significantly, by citing a statement by Freud: "If you want to know more about femininity inquire from your experiences of life, or turn to the poets." Not, listen to a woman. Once again we have the tradition; Caldwell listens to Freud, then he listens to Aeschylus, to learn about femininity. He treats the Danaids as if they were real female people, instead of "text," literary representations written by a man to be acted on a stage by men. If he finds there confirmation of his own misogyny and fear of his own castration, what does that tell us about femininity? Only what he and Aeschylus think. I believe that he misreads Aeschylus as well. But the basic epistemological choices of Caldwell are these: (1) He confuses the textual representations of women with real people; (2) He completely ignores history; and (3) He equates Aeschylean misogyny with his own and confuses Greek male castration fear with evidence for the actual terms of sexual differentiation in ancient culture.

30. Henderson, *The Maculate Muse,* 145–46.

31. Fine, *The Ancient Greeks,* 100–103.

32. Vernant, "Ambiguity and Reversal," 87.

33. See Segal, *Tragedy and Civilization,* on the play.

34. DuBois, *Centaurs and Amazons.*

35. R. C. Jebb, *Sophocles, Part V, The Trachiniae* (Cambridge, 1892), ad loc.

36. Ibid.

37. The *lebes* is also, significantly, a kettle or cauldron used for cooking. The word is used by Cassandra to refer to the bath in which Agamemnon will be killed by Clytemnestra in Aeschylus' *Agamemnon* (line 1129). Sophocles' Electra speaks of the *lebes* as a funeral urn (*Electra* 1400–1401). Pandora was decorated by the gods; so the funerary urn in the *Trachiniae,* a container of bronze, holds a message that will once again let loose disaster. In Aeschylus' *Choephoroi,* a bronze *lebes* is again the container that supposedly holds the ashes of the dead Orestes. In the *Trachiniae,* Deianeira's message resides in a deathly container.

38. On an obscene use of *sphragis* for phallos, see Aristophanes, *Birds* 1213.

39. Jebb, ad loc.

40. See Derrida, "Plato's Pharmacy," in *Dissemination;* and Bergren, "Helen's 'Good drug.'"

41. According to LSJ, *khoiros* is *pudenda muliebria.* See *Lysistrata* 1073.

42. The son substitutes for the expected *korēs* (girl), *sorou* (line 1365), which means funerary urn, or coffin. (LSJ note that the word is a nickname for an old man or woman, i.e., that the "girl" is perhaps not a girl at all.) Further, the son compares the flute-girl "Dardanis" to a torch (*dais,* line 1372), which is tattooed or punctured (*estigmenen,* line 1373) with *pitta* (resin or pitch) oozing from her middle (line 1375). The son asks what her asshole (*prōktos*) is; he says it's a knot in the pine.

43. Henderson, *The Maculate Muse,* 146. Although castration seems to have concerned Hesiod, it does not figure prominently in Aristophanic comedy. Much more important is the celebration of the enormous, inflated phallus, or the regrets about the old man's "rotten rope." *Xulon* is discussed in relation to *Lysistrata* (680ff.), where Henderson says that "*xulon* becomes a double entendre for cunt and *auchen* a double entendre for phallus. Thus (1) we should get hold of all these women and put their *necks* into the *wooden stock;* and (2) we should get hold of this here *cock* and put it into the *cunts* of all these women" (*The Maculate Muse,* 114).

Of the sealed heiress, Henderson says:

> *Kogche,* the cavity, (pink or red) of a seashell, used in technical writers for many bodily cavities, is a double entendre meaning "vagina". . . . Bdelycleon rebukes his father . . . you are wrong (1) to uncap the seal on her will and (2) to unseal her virginity. *Kogche* is common in this obscene meaning.
>
> (*The Maculate Muse,* 142)

On *khoirokomeion,* Henderson remarks, "Hesychius notes that a certain feminine garment was known as *khoirokomeion*" (*The Maculate Muse,* 132). "Of several words used to indicate the cunt whose basic notion is that of an opening or passageway, *thura* is the most popular" (p. 137). Agricultural euphemisms include the myrtleberry, rose, and fig; "Many comic double entendres involve comparisons with fields, either smooth or bearing some sort of short foliage. Indeed, pubic hair is almost always conceived of in agricultural terms as a flowering growth" (p. 135).

As Charles Segal points out in *Tragedy and Civilization:* "This parallel between the begetting of legitimate children in the house and agriculture is even written into the ancient betrothal ceremony (the bride is bestowed 'for the sowing, *arotos,* of legitimate children')" (p. 63). Plain, *pedion,* is used in *Lysistrata* (line 89).

Henderson lists *pule,* gate, *isthmos,* rings and circles. "A comparison of the female member to pits or great caves appears several times" (*The Maculate Muse,* 139). For example, "In the paratragic prologue of *Ecclesiazusae,* a grandiose double entendre is used to describe depilation by lamp; the image is from scenes of the sudden illumination of cavernous underworld regions (lines 12 ff.)" (*The Maculate Muse,* 141). Sea animals are compared to cunts (p. 142). "Many double entendres are based on cooking implements" (p. 141). Aristophanes also employs "the notion of the cunt as a split or crack," although this usage is relatively rare (p. 147). "*Pitta,* pitch or resin, indicates the female secreta at *Wasps* 1375, where the flute-girl is visualized as a burning torch, that is, burning with sexual passion" (p. 145). This is interesting in relation to the cloak Deianeira smears with her potion in the *Trachiniae,* and the description in Euripides' *Medea* of Creusa's body, affected by Medea's poisons. The women's *pharmaka* are like bodily secretions. In addition, pitch was used to color the wax that filled the interior of the *pinax* or *deltos*—the writing tablet (Turner, *Athenian Books,* 12).

For the male organ, Aristophanes uses many euphemisms, including words for acorn, pole, point or goad (*kentron*), sword (*xiphos*), horse, dog, bull, foot, rope, and others (Henderson, *The Maculate Muse,* 108–30). Most interesting for my point of view is *pedakion,* oar. In *The Peace,* Trygaeus says he will use his oar (*eikhon pedalion,* line 142) if he lands in water when he returns to Earth from Olympus.

The Spartan herald in the *Lysistrata* makes the connection between the *skutala* and the uncircumcised phallus; all the men of Greece are tortured by enormous erections because of the women's sex-strike. The magistrate points to his erection, asking him first if it is a spear (*doru,* line 985). The Spartan says it is a *skutala Lakonika* (line 991), and then the magistrate holds up his own *skutala* (line 992).

44. Zeitlin, "Closet of Masks." On the *Thesmophoriazusae,* see Froma Zeitlin, "Travesties of Gender and Genre in Aristophanes' *Thesmophoriazousae,*" in *Reflections of Women in Antiquity,* ed. Helene P. Foley (New York: Gordon and Breach, 1981), 169–217.

Chapter 8. The Platonic Appropriation of Reproduction

1. See Harry Berger, "Plato's Flying Philosopher," *The Philosophical Forum* 13, no. 4 (1982): 385–407.
2. Derrida, *Of Grammatology,* 6–13.
3. Derrida, "Plato's Pharmacy," 168.
4. See Pucci, *Hesiod;* and Loraux, "Sur la race des femmes."
5. On utopianism in the fifth century, see F. Solmsen, *Intellectual Experiments of the Greek Enlightenment* (Princeton: Princeton University Press, 1975). See also Arthur, "Dream of a World without Women."
6. Julia Kristeva, *Powers of Horror: An Essay on Abjection,* trans. L. S. Rou-

diez (New York: Columbia University Press, 1982). See also Zeitlin, "Power of Aphrodite."

7. On the question of Plato's attitudes toward women, see, among many others, Dorothea Wender, "Plato: Misogynist, Paedophile, and Feminist," *Arethusa* 6, no. 1 (1973): 75–90; Julia Annas, "Plato's *Republic* and Feminism," *Philosophy* 51 (1976): 307–21; Mary O'Brien, *The Politics of Reproduction* (London: Routledge and Kegan Paul, 1981); and Nancy Hartsock, *Money, Sex and Power: Toward a Feminist Historical Materialism* (New York: Longman, 1983).

In the *Timaeus,* Plato's character Timaeus uses the metaphor of sexual difference to talk about the parts of the soul:

> Within the chest, they fastened the mortal kind of soul. And inasmuch as one part thereof is better, and one worse, they built a division within the cavity of the thorax—as if to fence off two separate chambers, for men and for women—by placing the midriff between them as a screen.
>
> (69e–70a)

The manly part is closer to the head, obedient to reason, while the heart must be cooled by the lungs in order that it "be subservient to the reason (*logōi*) in time of passion." Women are associated with the heart's blood, which like the womb moves throughout the body and threatens anarchy.

8. On the institution of pederasty in ancient Greece, see Dover, *Greek Homosexuality.*

9. On the *Symposium,* see John Brenkman, "The Other and the One: Psychoanalysis, Reading, *The Symposium,*" in *Literature and Psychoanalysis. The Question of Reading: Otherwise,* ed. Shoshana Felman (Baltimore: Johns Hopkins University Press, 1982), 396–456.

10. On transvestism, see Froma Zeitlin, "Travesties of Gender and Genre."

11. G. J. DeVries, *A Commentary on the "Phaedrus" of Plato* (Amsterdam: Adolf M. Hakkert, 1959).

12. Nagler, *Spontaneity and Tradition,* 59–60.

13. Parke, *Festivals,* 77–79; see also Angelo Brelich, *Paides e Parthenoi,* vol. 1 (Rome: Ateneo, 1969), 31, 72; and Jean-Pierre Vernant, "La guerre des cités," in *Mythe et société* (Paris: Maspero, 1974), 39.

14. See Segal, *Dionysiac Poetics,* 158–214.

15. On Sappho, see Jack Winkler, "Gardens of Nymphs: Public and Private in Sappho's Lyrics," *Women's Studies* 8, nos. 1, 2 (1981): 65–91; Anne Giacomelli, "The Justice of Aphrodite in Sappho Fr. 1," *Transactions of the American Philological Association* 110 (1980): 135–42; and W. W. Fortenbaugh, "Plato *Phaedrus* 253c3," *Classical Philology* 61 (1966): 108–9.

16. See H. D. Rankin, "On *ADIAPLASTA ZOIA,*" *Philologus* 107 (1963): 138–45; see also Miles Burnyeat, "Socratic Midwivery, Platonic Inspiration," *Bulletin of the Institute for Classical Studies* 24 (1977): 7–16; and Paul Plass, "Plato's Pregnant Lover," *Symbolae Osloenses* 53 (1978): 47–55.

Chapter 9. Conclusion

1. Lacan, *Ecrits,* trans. Sheridan, 292–325.
2. Ibid., 322.
3. Keuls, *Reign of the Phallus,* 402.
4. Mitchell and Rose, *Feminine Sexuality,* 26.
5. Gallop, *The Daughter's Seduction,* 96–97.
6. Ibid., 16

7. Ibid.

8. As much as I disagree with Gallop's mode of engagement with psychoanalysis, inhabiting it uneasily rather than historicizing it, I find her prose exhilarating and her work among the most exciting to read of all feminist works.

9. Gallop, *Reading Lacan,* 20.

SELECT BIBLIOGRAPHY

Anderson, Perry. *Passages from Antiquity to Feudalism.* London: New Left Books, 1974.

Arthur, Marylin. "Politics and Pomegranates: An Interpretation of the Homeric Hymn to Demeter." *Arethusa* 10, no. 1 (1977): 7–47.

———. "Cultural Strategies in Hesiod's *Theogony:* Law, Family, Society." *Arethusa* 15 (1982): 63–82.

———. "The Dream of a World without Women: Poetics and the Circles of Order in the *Theogony* Prooemium." *Arethusa* 16 (1983): 97–116.

Ashmole, B., and N. Yalouris. *Olympia: The Sculpture of the Temple of Zeus.* London: Phaidon, 1967.

Austin, C. "De nouveaux fragments de l'*Erechthée* d'Euripide." *Recherches de papyrologie* 4 (1967): 11–67.

Austin, Michael, and Pierre Vidal-Naquet. *Economies et sociétés en Grèce ancienne.* 2d ed. Paris: A. Colin, 1972.

Badiou, Alain. *Théorie du sujet.* Paris: Seuil, 1982.

Barlow, Shirley. *The Imagery of Euripides.* London: Methuen, 1971.

Barthes, Roland. *Image—Music—Text.* Trans. S. Heath. New York: Hill and Wang, 1977.

Baudrillard, Jean. *For a Critique of the Political Economy of the Sign.* Trans. Charles Levin. St. Louis: Telos, 1981.

Bell, Malcolm. "Stylobate and Roof in the Olympieion at Akragas." *American Journal of Archaeology* 84 (1980): 359–72.

Beltrametti, Anna Albertina. "Il mito greco dal discorso del metodo al discorso sul metodo negli Atti del Convegno di Urbino." *Quaderni Urbinati di Cultura Classica* n.s. 8 (1981): 51–63.

Bérard, Claude. *Anodoi: Recherches sur l'imaginaire des passages chthoniens.* Rome: Institut Suisse de Rome, 1974.

Bergren, Ann L. T. "Language and the Female in Early Greek Thought." *Arethusa* 16 (1983): 69–95.

Boedeker, Deborah. *Descent from Heaven: Images of Dew in Greek Poetry and Religion.* Chico, Cal.: Scholars Press, 1984.

Bowersock, G. W., W. Burkert, and M. C. J. Putnam, eds. *Arktouros: Hellenic Studies Presented to B. M. W. Knox.* Berlin and New York: W. de Gruyter, 1979.

Bremmer, Jan. "Scapegoat Rituals in Ancient Greece." *Harvard Studies in Classical Philology* 87 (1983): 299–320.

Brenkman, John. "The Other and the One: Psychoanalysis, Reading, *The Symposium.*" In *Literature and Psychoanalysis. The Question of Reading: Otherwise,* ed. Shoshana Felman, 396–456. Baltimore: Johns Hopkins University Press, 1982.

Brown, N. O. "Psychoanalysis and the Classics." *Classical Journal* 52 (1957): 241–45.

Burkert, Walter. *Greek Religion*. Trans. John Raffan. Cambridge, Mass.: Harvard University Press, 1985.

Burnett, A. P. *Catastrophe Survived: Euripides' Plays of Mixed Reversal*. Oxford: Clarendon, 1971.

Burton, R. W. B. *Pindar's Pythian Odes*. Oxford: Oxford University Press, 1962.

Calame, Claude. *Les Choeurs de jeunes filles en Grèce archaïque*. 2 vols. Rome: Ateneo e Bizzarri, 1977.

Caldwell, R. S. "The Pattern of Aeschylean Tragedy." *Transactions of the American Philological Association* 101 (1970): 77–94.

———. "The Misogyny of Eteocles." *Arethusa* 6 (1973): 197–231.

———. "The Psychology of Aeschylus' *Supplices*." *Arethusa* 7 (1974): 45–70.

———. "Selected Bibliography on Psychoanalytic and Classical Studies." *Arethusa* 7, no. 1 (1974): 115–34.

Campese, Silvia, Paola Manuli, and Giulia Sissa. *Madre materia: Sociologia e biologia della donna greca*. Torino: Boringhieri, 1983.

Carriere, Jean Claude. *Le Carnaval et la politique: Une Introduction a la comédie grecque suivie d'un choix de fragments*. Paris: Belles Lettres, 1979.

Chase, Cynthia. "Oedipal Textuality: Reading Freud's Reading of *Oedipus*." *Diacritics* 9, no. 1 (1979): 54–68.

Chirassi, Ileana. *Elementi di culture precereali nei miti e riti greci*. Rome: Ateneo, 1968.

Chirassi-Colombo, I. "I doni di Demeter: Mito e ideologia nella Grecia arcaica." In *Studi Triestini di antichita in onore di L. Stella*, 183–213. Trieste: Facoltà di lettere e filosophia, 1975.

———. "*Paides* e *gynaikes:* Note per una tassonomia del comportamento rituale nella cultura attica." *Quaderni Urbinati di Cultura Classica* n.s. 1 (1979): 25–58.

Cité des images, La. Religion et société en Grèce ancienne. Institut d'archéologie et d'histoire ancienne, Lausanne, Centre de recherches comparées sur les sociétés anciennes. Paris: F. Nathan, 1984.

Clark, R. J. "Trophonios: The Manner of His Revelation." *Transactions of the American Philological Association* 99 (1968): 63–75.

Clément, Catherine. *Vies et légendes de Jacques Lacan*. Paris: Grasset, 1981.

Conacher, D. J. *Euripidean Drama, Myth, Theme and Structure*. Toronto: University of Toronto Press, 1967.

Congdon, Lenore O. Keene. *Caryatid Mirrors of Ancient Greece: Technical, Stylistic and Historical Considerations of an Archaic and Early Classical Bronze Series*. Mainz: Philipp von Zabern, 1981.

Cook, R. M. *Greek Painted Pottery*. London: Methuen, 1960.

Crotty, Kevin. *Song and Action: The Victory Odes of Pindar*. Baltimore: Johns Hopkins University Press, 1982.

De Foucault, J.-A. "Histiée de Milet et l'esclave tatoué." *Revue des Etudes grecques* 80 (1967): 181–86.

Delebecque, Edouard. *Euripide et la guerre du Peloponnese*. Paris: Belles Lettres, 1951.

den Boer, W. "Aspects of Religion in Classical Greece." *Harvard Studies in Classical Philology* 77 (1973): 1–21.

Derrida, Jacques. "White Mythology: Metaphor in the Text of Philosophy." In *Margins of Philosophy*, trans. Alan Bass, 207–71. Chicago: University of Chicago Press, 1982.

———. *The Post Card: From Socrates to Freud and Beyond*. Trans. Alan Bass. Chicago: University of Chicago Press, 1987.

de Sainte-Croix, G. E. M. *The Class Struggle in the Ancient Greek World: From the Archaic Age to the Arab Conquests*. Ithaca: Cornell University Press, 1981.

Detienne, Marcel. *Crise agraire et attitude religieuse chez Hésiode*. Latomus Collection, no. 68. Brussels: Berchem, 1963.

———. *The Gardens of Adonis: Spices in Greek Mythology*. Trans. Janet Lloyd. Atlantic Highlands, N.J.: Humanities Press, 1977.

———. "Mythes grecs et analyse structurale." In *Il Mito Greco*, ed. B. Gentili and G. Paione, 69–90. Rome: Ateneo e Bizzarri, 1973.

Detienne, Marcel, and J.-P. Vernant, eds. *La cuisine du sacrifice en pays grec*. Paris: Gallimard, 1979.

Deubner, Ludovicus. *De Incubatione*. Lipsiae, 1900.

Dover, K. J. *Aristophanic Comedy*. Berkeley: University of California Press, 1972.

———. *Greek Popular Morality in the Time of Plato and Aristotle*. Oxford: Blackwell, 1974.

———. *Greek Homosexuality*. Cambridge, Mass.: Harvard University Press, 1978.

Dreyfus, Hubert, and Paul Rabinow. *Michel Foucault: Beyond Structuralism and Hermeneutics*. 2d ed. Chicago: University of Chicago Press, 1983.

duBois, Page. "Sappho and Helen." In *Women in the Ancient World: The Arethusa Papers*, ed. J. Peradotto and J. P. Sullivan, 95–105. Albany: State University of New York Press, 1984.

———. *Centaurs and Amazons: Women and the Prehistory of the Great Chain of Being*. Ann Arbor: University of Michigan Press, 1982.

———. *History, Rhetorical Description, and the Epic: From Homer to Spenser*. Cambridge: D. S. Brewer, 1982.

Dupont, F. "Se reproduire ou se métamorphoser." *Tropique* 9–10 (1972): 139–60.

Elderkin, G. S. "The Cults of the Erechtheion." *Hesperia* 10 (1941): 113–24.

Farnell, Lewis Richard. *The Cults of the Greek States*. Vol. 3, Oxford: Clarendon, 1906.

Féral, Josette. "*Antigone*, or *The Irony of the Tribe*." *Diacritics* 8, no. 3 (1978): 2–14.

Fine, John V. A. "Horoi." *Hesperia*, suppl. 9 (1951): 167–208.

———. *The Ancient Greeks: A Critical History*. Cambridge, Mass.: Harvard University Press, 1983.

Finley, M. I. *Economy and Society in Ancient Greece*. Ed. B. D. Shaw and R. P. Saller. London: Chatto and Windus, 1981.

Foley, Helene P. "'Reverse Similes' and Sex Roles in the *Odyssey*." *Arethusa* 11, nos. 1, 2 (1978): 7–26.

———. "Marriage and Sacrifice in Euripides' *Iphigeneia in Aulis*." *Arethusa* 15 (1982): 159–80.

———. *Ritual Irony: Poetry and Sacrifice in Euripides*. Ithaca: Cornell University Press, 1985.

Forehand, W. E. "Truth and Reality in Euripides' *Ion.*" *Ramus* 8, no. 2 (1979): 174–87.

Foucault, Michel. "What Is an Author?" In *Textual Strategies: Perspectives in Post-Structuralist Criticism,* ed. Josué V. Harari, 141–60. Ithaca: Cornell University Press, 1979.

———. *Histoire de la sexualité.* Vol. 2, *L'Usage des plaisirs.* Paris: Gallimard, 1984.

———. *Histoire de la sexualité.* Vol. 3, *Le Souci de soi.* Paris: Gallimard, 1984.

Fowler, M. "The Myth of Erichthonios." *Classical Philology* 38 (1943): 28–32.

French, A. *The Growth of the Athenian Economy.* London: Routledge and Kegan Paul, 1964.

Freud, Sigmund. *The Standard Edition of the Complete Psychological Works of Sigmund Freud.* Translated from the German under the general editorship of James Strachey, in collaboration with Anna Freud, assisted by Alex Strachey and Alan Tyson. 24 vols. London: Hogarth Press, 1953–74.

Frontisi-Ducroux, Françoise. *Dédale: Mythologie de l'artisan en Grèce ancienne.* Paris: Maspero, 1975.

Gallop, Jane. "Phallus/Penis: Same Difference." In *Men by Women,* ed. Janet Todd, special issue of *Women and Literature,* n.s. 2 (1981): 243–51.

———. *The Daughter's Seduction: Feminism and Psychoanalysis.* Ithaca: Cornell University Press, 1982.

———. *Reading Lacan.* Ithaca: Cornell University Press, 1985.

Garlan, Yvon. "La Défense du territoire à l'époque classique." In *Problèmes de la terre en Grèce ancienne,* ed. M. I. Finley, 149–60. Paris: Mouton, 1973.

Garvie, A. F. *Aeschylus' Supplices: Play and Trilogy.* Cambridge: Cambridge University Press, 1969.

Gentili, Bruno. *Poesia e pubblico nella Grecia antica: Da Omero al V secolo.* Rome: Laterza, 1983.

Gilligan, Carol. *In a Different Voice.* Cambridge, Mass.: Harvard University Press, 1982.

Goheen, Robert F. *The Imagery of Sophocles' "Antigone": A Study of Poetic Language and Structure.* Princeton: Princeton University Press, 1951.

Goodhart, Sandor. "*Lēstas Ephaske:* Oedipus and Laius' Many Murderers." *Diacritics* 8, no. 1 (1978): 55–71.

Goux, Jean-Joseph. *Economie et symbolique.* Paris: Seuil, 1973.

Griffith, Mark. *The Authenticity of "Prometheus Bound."* Cambridge: Cambridge University Press, 1977.

Guralnick, N. "The Proportions of Korai." *American Journal of Archaeology* 85 (1981): 269–80.

———. "Profiles of Korai." *American Journal of Archaeology* 86 (1982): 173–82.

Heath, Stephen. "Difference." *Screen* 19, no. 3 (1978).

Herington, C. J. *The Author of the "Prometheus Bound."* Austin: University of Texas Press, 1970.

Hill, G. F. *Ancient Greek and Roman Coins: A Handbook.* Rev. ed. Chicago: Argonaut, 1964.

Hodge, A. Trevor, "The Mystery of Apollo's E at Delphi." *American Journal of Archaeology* 85 (1981): 83–84.

Hopper, R. J. *Trade and Industry in Classical Greece.* London: Thames and Hudson, 1979.

Hurwit, Jeffrey. "Image and Frame in Greek Art." *American Journal of Archaeology* 81 (1977): 1–30.

Irigaray, Luce. *Speculum: Of the Other Woman.* Trans. G. Gill. Ithaca: Cornell University Press, 1985.

———. *This Sex Which Is Not One.* Trans. Catherine Porter with Carolyn Burke. Ithaca: Cornell University Press, 1985.

Jakobson, Roman. "Two Types of Language and Two Types of Aphasic Disturbances." In *Fundamentals of Language,* ed. R. Jakobson and M. Halle. The Hague: Mouton, 1956.

James, E. O. *The Cult of the Mother Goddess.* New York: Praeger, 1959.

Jameson, Fredric. "Imaginary and Symbolic in Lacan: Marxism, Psychoanalytic Criticism, and the Problem of the Subject." In *Literature and Psychoanalysis. The Question of Reading: Otherwise,* ed. Shoshana Felman, 338–95. Baltimore: Johns Hopkins University Press, 1982.

Jardine, Alice A. *Gynesis: Configurations of Women and Modernity.* Ithaca: Cornell University Press, 1985.

Jeppesen, Kristian. "Where Was the So-Called Erechtheion?" *American Journal of Archaeology* 83 (1979): 381–94.

———. "Further Inquiries in the Location of the Erechtheion and Its Relationship to the Temple of the Polias." *American Journal of Archaeology* 87 (1983): 325–33.

Johnson, Barbara. "The Frame of Reference." *Yale French Studies* 55–56 (1977): 457–505.

———. "The Critical Difference." *Diacritics* 8, no. 2 (1978): 2–9.

Joplin, Patricia. "The Voice of the Shuttle Is Ours." *Stanford Literature Review* 1, no. 1 (1984): 25–55.

Kakridis, Johannes T. *Homeric Researches.* Lund: C. W. K. Gleerup, 1949.

Keuls, Eva C. *The Reign of the Phallus: Sexual Politics in Ancient Athens.* New York: Harper and Row, 1985.

Knox, B. M. W. "Euripides' *Iphigeneia in Aulide* 1–163." *Yale Classical Studies* 22 (1972): 239–61.

Komornicka, Anna M. "Sur le langage érotique de l'ancienne comédie attique." *Quaderni Urbinati di Cultura Classica,* n.s. 9 (1981): 55–83.

Kristeva, Julia. *Powers of Horror: An Essay on Abjection.* Trans. L. S. Roudiez. New York: Columbia University Press, 1982.

Lacan, Jacques. *Ecrits.* Paris: Seuil, 1966.

———. *Ecrits: A Selection.* Trans. Alan Sheridan. London: Tavistock, 1977.

———. *Le Séminaire XX Encore.* Paris: Seuil, 1975.

Laplanche, Jean, and Jean-Baptiste Pontalis. *The Language of Psychoanalysis.* Trans. Donald Nicholson-Smith. London: Hogarth, 1973.

Léveque, P. "Structures imaginaires et fonctionnement des mystères grecs." *Studi Storico Religiosi* 6, nos. 1–2 (1982): 185–208.

Lévi-Strauss, Claude. *The Elementary Structures of Kinship.* Trans. James Harle Bell, J. Richard von Sturmer, and Rodney Needham. Boston: Beacon Press, 1969.

Levy, Gertrude Rachel. *The Gate of Horn: A Study of the Religious Conceptions of the*

Stone Age, and Their Influence upon European Thought. London: Faber and Faber, 1948.
Lieberman, Stephen J. "Of Clay Pebbles, Hollow Clay Balls, and Writing: A Sumerian View." *American Journal of Archaeology* 84 (1980): 339–58.
Lintott, Andrew. *Violence, Civil Strife and Revolution in the Classical City*. Baltimore: Johns Hopkins University Press, 1981.
Lloyd, G. E. R. "Hot and Cold, Dry and Wet in Early Greek Thought." In *Studies in Presocratic Philosophy*, ed. R. E. Allen and David J. Furley, 255–80. New York: Humanities Press, 1970.
———. *Magic, Reason and Experience: Studies in the Origin and Development of Greek Science*. Cambridge: Cambridge University Press, 1979.
———. *Science, Folklore and Ideology: Studies in the Life Sciences in Ancient Greece*. Cambridge: Cambridge University Press, 1983.
Loraux, Nicole. "Sur la race des femmes et quelques-unes de ses tribus." In *Women in the Ancient World*, ed. John Peradotto and J. P. Sullivan. Special issue of *Arethusa* 11, nos. 1, 2 (1978): 43–87.
———. *Les Enfants d'Athéna: Idées athéniennes sur la citoyenneté et la division des sexes*. Paris: Maspero, 1981.
———. "Le Lit, la guerre." *L'Homme* 21 (1981): 37–67.
Lorie, I. M. "On the Botanical Excursus in *De Natura Pueri* 22–27." *Hermes* 97 (1969): 391–411.
MacCary, W. Thomas. *Childlike Achilles. Ontogeny and Phylogeny in the Iliad*. New York: Columbia University Press, 1982.
MacDowell, Douglas M., ed. *Aristophanes' "Wasps."* Oxford: Clarendon, 1971.
———. *The Law in Classical Athens*. London: Thames and Hudson, 1978.
MacKendrick, Paul. *The Athenian Aristocracy: 399 to 31 B.C.* Cambridge, Mass.: Harvard University Press, 1969.
Marcus, George E., and Dick Cushman. "Ethnographies as Texts." *Annual Review of Anthropology* 11 (1982): 25–69.
Marry, John D. "Sappho and the Heroic Ideal: *erōtos aretē*." *Arethusa* 12, no. 1 (1979): 71–92.
Marx, Karl, and Friedrich Engels. *The German Ideology, Part One*. New York: International Press, 1970.
Mastronarde, D. J. "Iconography and Imagery in Euripides' *Ion*." *California Studies in Classical Antiquity* 8 (1975): 163–76.
Miller, Harold W. "'Dynamis' and the Seeds." *Transactions of the American Philological Association* 67 (1966): 281–90.
Mitchell, Juliet. *Psychoanalysis and Feminism*. New York: Random House, 1974.
Mitchell, Juliet, and Jacqueline Rose, eds. *Feminine Sexuality: Jacques Lacan and the école freudienne*. Trans. J. Rose. New York: Norton, 1982.
Mylonas, George E. *Eleusis and the Eleusinian Mysteries*. Princeton: Princeton University Press, 1961.
Nagler, Michael N. *Spontaneity and Tradition: A Study in the Oral Art of Homer*. Berkeley: University of California Press, 1974.
Nagy, Gregory. "Phaethon, Sappho's Phaon, and the White Rock of Leukas." *Harvard Studies in Classical Philology* 77 (1973): 137–78.

———. *The Best of the Achaeans: Concepts of the Hero in Archaic Greek Poetry.* Baltimore: Johns Hopkins University Press, 1979.
———. "Theognis of Megara: The Poet as Seer, Pilot and Revenant." *Arethusa* 15, nos. 1, 2 (1982): 109–28.
———. "*Sēma* and *Noēsis:* Some Illustrations." In *Semiotics and Classical Studies,* ed. Nancy Felson Rubin, special issue of *Arethusa* 16, nos. 1, 2 (1983): 35–55.
O'Brien, Mary. *The Politics of Reproduction.* London: Routledge and Kegan Paul, 1981.
O'Flaherty, Wendy Doniger. *Women, Androgynes, and Other Mythical Beasts.* Chicago: University of Chicago Press, 1980.
Ortigues, M. C., and Edmond Ortigues. *Oedipe africain.* Paris: Plon, 1973.
Otis, Brooks. *Cosmos and Tragedy.* Ed. E. C. Kopff. Chapel Hill: University of North Carolina Press, 1981.
Owen, A. S., ed. *Euripides' "Ion."* Oxford: Oxford University Press, 1939.
Page, Denys. *Sappho and Alcaeus.* Oxford: Oxford University Press, 1955.
Parke, H. W. *Festivals of the Athenians.* London: Thames and Hudson, 1977.
Parker, Robert. *Miasma: Pollution and Purification in Early Greek Religion.* Oxford: Clarendon Press, 1983.
Paton, J. M., and G. P. Stevens. *The Erechtheum.* Cambridge, Mass.: Harvard University Press, 1927.
Peradotto, John. "Oedipus and Erichthonius: Some Observations on Paradigmatic and Syntagmatic Order." *Arethusa* 10, no. 1 (1977): 85–101.
———. "Originality and Intentionality." In *Arktouros: Hellenic Studies Presented to B. M. W. Knox,* ed. G. W. Bowersock, W. Burkert, and M. C. J. Putnam, 3–11. Berlin and New York: W. de Gruyter, 1979.
———. "Texts and Unrefracted Facts: Philology, Hermeneutics, and Semiotics." In *Semiotics and Classical Studies,* ed. N. Rubin. Special issue of *Arethusa* 16, nos. 1, 2 (1983): 15–33.
Peradotto, John, and J. P. Sullivan, eds. *Women in the Ancient World: The Arethusa Papers.* Albany: State University of New York Press, 1984.
Pindar's Victory Songs. Trans. Frank J. Nisetich. Baltimore: Johns Hopkins University Press, 1980.
Plato. *The Collected Dialogues.* Ed. and trans. Edith Hamilton and Huntington Cairns. Princeton: Bollingen, and Princeton University Press, 1961.
Podlecki, Anthony J. *The Political Background of Aeschylean Tragedy.* Ann Arbor: University of Michigan Press, 1966.
———. "Creon and Herodotus." *Transactions of the American Philological Association* 97 (1966): 359–71.
Powell, B. *Erichthonius and the Three Daughters of Cecrops.* Ithaca: Cornell University Press, 1906.
Pucci, Pietro. *Hesiod and the Language of Poetry.* Baltimore: Johns Hopkins University Press, 1977.
———. "On the 'Eye' and 'Phallos' and Other Permutabilities in *Oedipus Rex.*" In *Arktouros: Hellenic Studies Presented to B. M. W. Knox,* ed. G. W. Bowersock, W. Burkert, and M. C. J. Putnam, 130–33. Berlin and New York: W. de Gruyter, 1979.

Richardson, N. J. *The Homeric Hymn to Demeter.* Oxford: Oxford University Press, 1974.

Robertson, Noel. "The Riddle of the Arrephoria at Athens." *Harvard Studies in Classical Philology* 87 (1983): 241–88.

Rose, H. J. "The Bride of Hades." *Classical Philology* 19 (1925): 238–43.

———. *A Commentary on the Surviving Plays of Aeschylus.* Vol. 1. Amsterdam: Noord-Hollandsche, 1957.

Rosenmeyer, Thomas G. *The Art of Aeschylus.* Berkeley: University of California Press, 1982.

Roussel, D. *Tribu et cité: Etude sur les groupes sociaux dans les cités grecques aux époques archaïque et classique.* Paris: Belles Lettres, 1976.

Rousselle, A. "Observation féminine et idéologie masculine: Le Corps de la femme d'après les médecins grecs." *Annales* 35 (1980): 1089–1115.

Rubin, Nancy, and H. M. Deal. "Some Functions of the Demophon Episode in the Homeric Hymn to Demeter." *Quaderni Urbinati di Cultura Classica* n.s. 5 (1980): 7–21.

Rudhart, J. *Notions fondamentales de la pensée et actes constitutifs du culte dans la Grèce antique.* Geneva: E. Droz, 1958.

Russian Formalist Criticism: Four Essays. Trans. and ed. Lee T. Lemon and Marion J. Reis. Lincoln, Neb.: University of Nebraska Press, 1965.

Rykwert, Joseph. *On Adam's House in Paradise: The Idea of the Primitive Hut in Architectural History.* New York: Museum of Modern Art, 1972.

Sainte-Croix. *See* de Sainte-Croix.

Sansone, David. *Aeschylean Metaphors for Intellectual Activities.* Wiesbaden: Steiner, 1975.

Scarpi, P. *L'inno omerico a Demeter.* Firenze: L. S. Olschki, 1976.

Schein, Seth. *The Mortal Hero: An Introduction to Homer's "Iliad."* Berkeley: University of California Press, 1985.

Schmandt-Besserat, D. "An Archaic Recording System and the Origin of Writing." *Syro-Mesopotamian Studies* 1 (1977): 31–70.

———. "The Earliest Precursor of Writing." *Scientific American* 238, no. 6 (June 1978): 50–59.

———. "Reckoning before Writing." *Archaeology* 32, no. 3 (May–June 1979): 22–31.

———. "An Archaic Recording System in the Uruk-Jemdet Nasr Period." *American Journal of Archaeology* 83 (1979): 19–48.

Scully, Vincent. *The Earth, the Temple, and the Gods: Greek Sacred Architecture.* Rev. ed. New Haven: Yale University Press, 1979.

Sebeok, Thomas A., et al. "The Two Sons of Croesus: A Myth about Communication in Herodotus." *Quaderni Urbinati di Cultura Classica* n.s. 1 (1979): 7–22.

Segal, Charles. "The Raw and the Cooked in Greek Literature: Structure, Values, Metaphor." *Classical Journal* 69 (1973–74): 289–308.

———. *Tragedy and Civilization: An Interpretation of Sophocles.* Cambridge, Mass.: Harvard University Press, 1981.

———. *Dionysiac Poetics and Euripides' "Bacchae."* Princeton: Princeton University Press, 1982.

———. *Interpreting Greek Tragedy: Myth, Poetry, Text.* Ithaca: Cornell University Press, 1986.

Seltman, Charles. *Greek Coins.* London: Methuen, 1933.

Shapiro, H. A. "Courtship Scenes in Attic Vase-Painting." *American Journal of Archaeology* 85 (1981): 133–43.

Shostak, Marjorie. *Nisa: The Life and Words of a !Kung Woman.* New York: Random House, 1981.

Showalter, Elaine, ed. *The New Feminist Criticism.* New York: Pantheon, 1985.

Simon, Bennett. *Mind and Madness in Ancient Greece: The Classical Roots of Modern Psychiatry.* Ithaca: Cornell University Press, 1978.

Sissa, Giulia. "La Pizia delfica: Immagini di una mantica amorosa e balsamica." *Aut Aut,* n.s. 184–85 (1981): 193–213.

———. "Il corpo della donna: Lineamenti di una ginecologia filosofica." In *Madre Materia: Sociologia e biologia della donna greca,* ed. Silvia Campese, Paola Manuli, and Giulia Sissa, 83–145. Torino: Boringhieri, 1983.

Skovgaard Hansen, M. "Athéna invisible: Iconologie de l'Acropole." In *Mélanges Charles Morazé,* 65–87. Toulouse: privately printed, 1979.

Stark, K. B. *Niobe und die Niobiden.* Leipzig, 1863.

Sullivan, J. P., ed. *Marxism and the Classics.* Special issue of *Arethusa* 8, no. 1 (1975).

Taillardat, Jean. *Les Images d'Aristophane.* 2d ed. Paris: Belles Lettres, 1965.

Taplin, Oliver. *The Stagecraft of Aeschylus.* Oxford: Clarendon, 1977.

Tarn, W. W. *Alexander the Great.* Boston: Beacon, 1956.

Thalmann, William G. *Dramatic Art in Aeschylus' "Seven against Thebes."* New Haven: Yale University Press, 1978.

Thomson, George. *Studies in Ancient Greek Society: The Prehistoric Aegean.* London: Lawrence and Wishart, 1949.

———. *Aeschylus and Athens.* New York: Grosset and Dunlap, 1972.

Thucydides. *The Peloponnesian War.* Trans. Rex Warner. Harmondsworth: Penguin, 1972.

Turner, E. G. *Athenian Books in the Fifth and Fourth Centuries B.C.* London: H. K. Lewis, 1952.

Vellacott, P. *Ironic Drama: A Study of Euripides' Method and Meaning.* Cambridge: Cambridge University Press, 1975.

Vermeule, Emily. *Aspects of Death in Early Greek Art and Poetry.* Berkeley: University of California Press, 1979.

Vernant, Jean-Pierre. *Mythe et pensée chez les Grecs.* 2d ed. Paris: Maspero, 1966.

———. *Les Origines de la pensée grecque.* Paris: Presses Universitaires de France, 1975.

———. "From Oedipus to Periander: Lameness, Tyranny, Incest in Legend and History." Trans. Page duBois. In *American Classical Studies in Honor of J.-P. Vernant,* special issue of *Arethusa* 15, nos. 1, 2 (1982): 19–38.

———. *La Mort dans les yeux.* Paris: Hachette, 1985.

Vernant, Jean-Pierre, and Pierre Vidal-Naquet. *Tragedy and Myth in Ancient Greece.* Trans. Janet Lloyd. Atlantic Highlands, N.J.: Humanities Press, 1981.

Vian, F. *Les Origines de Thèbes: Cadmos et les Spartes.* Paris: C. Klincksieck, 1963.

Vitruvius. *On Architecture*. Trans. Frank Granger. 2 vols. London: Loeb, Heinemann, 1931–34.
Vivante, Paolo. *The Epithets in Homer: A Study in Poetic Values*. New Haven: Yale University Press, 1982.
Wagner, Roy. *The Invention of Culture*. Rev. ed. Chicago: University of Chicago Press, 1981.
Wasserman, F. "Divine Violence and Providence in Euripides' *Ion*." *Transactions of the American Philological Association* 71 (1940): 587–604.
Watrous, Livingston Vance. "The Sculptural Program of the Siphnian Treasury at Delphi." *American Journal of Archaeology* 86 (1982): 159–72.
Weber, Samuel. *The Legend of Freud*. Minneapolis: University of Minnesota Press, 1982.
West, M. L. *Hesiod's "Theogony."* Oxford: Oxford University Press, 1966.
Whallon, William. *Problem and Spectacle: Studies in the "Oresteia."* Heidelberg: C. Winter, 1980.
White, Hayden. "Ethnological 'Lie' and Mythical 'Truth.'" *Diacritics* 8, no. 1 (1978): 2–9.
Whitman, Cedric H. *Euripides and the Full Circle of Myth*. Cambridge, Mass.: Harvard University Press, 1974.
Wolff, C. "The Design and Myth in Euripides' *Ion*." *Harvard Studies in Classical Philology* 69 (1965): 169–94.
Wood, Ellen Meiksins, and Neal Wood. *Class Ideology and Ancient Political Theory: Socrates, Plato, and Aristotle in Social Context*. Oxford: Blackwell, 1978.
Woodhouse, W. J. *Solon the Liberator: A Study of the Agrarian Problem in Attica in the Seventh Century*. London: Oxford University Press, 1938.
Zeitlin, Froma. "The Motif of the Corrupted Sacrifice in Aeschylus' *Orestes*." *Transactions of the American Philological Association* 96 (1965): 463–508.
———. "A Postscript to Sacrifical Imagery in the *Oresteia* (*Agamemnon* 1235–37)." *Transactions of the American Philological Association* 97 (1966): 645–53.
———. "The Closet of Masks: Role Playing and Myth Making in the *Oresteia* of Euripides." *Ramus* 9, no. 1 (1980): 51–77.
———. "Cultic Models of the Female: Rites of Dionysus and Demeter." *Arethusa* 15 (1982): 129–57.
———. *Under the Sign of the Shield: Semiotics and Aeschylus' "Seven against Thebes."* Rome: Ateneo, 1982.
———. "The Power of Aphrodite: Eros and the Boundaries of the Self in the *Hippolytus*." In *Directions in Euripidean Criticism*, ed. P. Burian, 52–110. Durham, N.C.: Duke University Press, 1985.

INDEX